LATITUDES

AN ANGELENO'S ATLAS

LATITUDES

AN ANGELENO'S ATLAS

Edited by Patricia Wakida
Foreword by Luis Alfaro
Introduction by Glen Creason
Cartography by David Deis
Illustrations by Leighton Kelly

Heyday • Berkeley, California

This book was made possible in part by generous funding from the Durfee Foundation.

Library of Congress Cataloging-in-Publication Data
LAtitudes : an Angeleno's atlas / edited by Patricia Wakida ; foreword by Luis Alfaro ; cartography by David Deis ; illustrations by Leighton Kelly.
pages cm
ISBN 978-1-59714-297-7 (pbk. : alk. paper)
1. Los Angeles (Calif.)--Civilization. 2. Los Angeles (Calif.)--Maps. I. Wakida, Patricia, editor of compilation. II. Deis, David, cartographer. III. Kelly, Leighton, illustrator.
F869.L85L37 2015
979.4'94--dc23
2014031139

Cover Art: David Deis
Cover and Interior Design/Typesetting: Ashley Ingram

Orders, inquiries, and correspondence should be addressed to:
Heyday
P.O. Box 9145, Berkeley, CA 94709
(510) 549-3564, Fax (510) 549-1889
www.heydaybooks.com

Printed in Hong Kong by Imago
10 9 8 7 6 5 4 3 2

CONTENTS

Foreword

Luis Alfaro

There is something to be said for first impressions.

I was born and raised in downtown Los Angeles. When I was a kid I would don a little grey suit with a clip-on tie (I was a dapper barrio kid) and escort my grandmother to Los Angeles from Delano in California's Central Valley on the Greyhound bus, where they used to play Buck Owens when you pulled up to the Bakersfield stop before the Grapevine. We would make our grand entrance to the city at the seedy and always littered terminal at Seventh and Los Angeles Street.

Why, even at ten years old, would I wince at the thought that this was the first image visitors to our great city were greeted by? I would shield my granny like a golden-age Lindsay Lohan as we'd fight the Skid Row throng and make our way curbside to the family station wagon for a quick getaway.

I was an innocent. I still believed that the proper first drive into the city was the Mildred Pierce way: off the Pacific Coast Highway from Santa Monica (never mind that it was in the middle of the night and after a murder...); or the Lucy and Ricky Ricardo route: the Hollywood Freeway through downtown coming off the Golden State Highway, convertible top down and singing a quartet with Fred and Ethel all the way to the Brown Derby.

Even now, the first thing I do when I pick someone up at LAX is to drive down La Cienega, straight up to the Sunset Strip, over to Vermont and all the way to the Griffith Park Observatory, where, on a clear day (and with the help of that dollar-per-minute public telescope) you can see the entire city—and beyond—teeming with all manner of bungalow, skyscraper, and freeway, filling in every available space between the mountain and the sea. Let my visitor's first discovery be an overview of the grand experiment of this sprawling metropolis; let her imagination people it with adventurers and dreamers.

As I got older, my own favorite way into the City of the Angels was off Washington Boulevard, east and over by the iconic Sears building on Soto. The industrial stretch running alongside the Union Pacific Railroad tracks is bordered by the chronically corrupt City of Vernon, and there is a concrete underpass right past the Mike's Hockey Burger stand covered in a sea of graffiti—colorful, urban and full of that feeling they used to call "blight." It's our unacknowledged mini-version of the Golden Gate Bridge and the Arc de Triomphe, a backdrop from *The Warriors,* the movie where all the urban New York gangs meet in one location to settle all civic differences. It is a portal of neglect, but I love it because everything beyond is street corner after street corner of possibility as one drives into the newly created arts district, with flower and produce marts, and straight into the embrace of the downtown skyline. The march of Progress unfolds cinematically; the music swells, and the screen flashes *The End.*

Except that doesn't quite capture it all, does it? After my father died, I was hit with a terrible case of insomnia. Deep in my grief, I would get in the car at two or three in the morning and drive all over Los Angeles, desperately trying to exhaust myself towards sleep. I would go south, down to the ports to watch the ships unload at the harbor. Or I would go north, driving through Silver Lake, and end up at Astro diner on Glendale and Fletcher where the recently recovered hold court and nervously drink their substitute coffee. Some dark mornings I would walk along the beach in Santa Monica, a surprisingly busy and populated place. I never knew how alive and full of character the city was at all hours, day and night. How to reconcile, much less narrate, these scenes?

In some ways this was my most eye-opening traversal of the city, characterized not by Hollywood or aerial abstraction or narratives of blight and renewal but by a deep restlessness that loosened me from the shackles of preconception. After all, there are *18 million* people who come from more than 140 countries and speak 224 different languages here, making LA the largest county in the United States. There is no such thing as one monolithic Los Angeles that everyone knows.

Chandler, Fante, Bukowski, even Eloise Klein Healy's "Artemis in Echo Park" resonated through me as I drove by Echo Park Lake's lotus flowers just before sunup. I could hear the grit that Lynell George and Ruben Martinez so eloquently covered in the *LA Weekly*. Marisela Norte's bus rides, Steve Abee's cosmic city adventures, Wanda Coleman's howl of injustice, and even the ghost of Gil Cuadros's *City of God* sat next to me in the car on many a night during that period.

These writers were the sound track to my wanderings, and moments of harmony and dissonance peppered the score. The book you hold in your hands creates something of this effect as these superb writers chart and rechart Los Angeles, as they celebrate and scold, explore and intellectualize. It may not seem fair or flattering to compare this book to a sleepwalk through the city—certainly there is no shortage of energy in this wildly creative endeavor—but when else are you so open to flashes of insight than when you are on the cusp of dreams?

....

One night I even came upon a couple of exhibitionists making love on a semi-darkened street next to a newly refurbished motel at Fountain and Vermont. I stopped for a while and tried to make sense of the scene. All I kept thinking about was the lack of housing in Los Angeles and how it was forcing everyone out on the street in their love-making. At the time I felt out of my mind, but it occurs to me now that there is something of this line of thinking at work in this book. Envision if you will a map of streetlights and rising rents and public trysts—what might it reveal? This book will have you similarly looking around, seeing things with a new perspective, alive to possibilities as the skyline wraps its arms around you, letting you know that you're home.

Introduction

Glen Creason

"A city no worse than others, a city rich and vigorous and full of pride, a city lost and beaten and full of emptiness. It all depends on where you sit and what your own private score is."

—Raymond Chandler, *The Long Goodbye*

I often dream about maps. My subconscious is full of topos, cadastrals, nautical charts, bird's-eyes, tract sheets, subdivision lines, strip maps, street guides, fire-insurance atlases, eight-folders, and chamber-of-commerce one sheets—all crying out for interpretation, haunting me in my sleep just as they delight and challenge me in my waking life. When I was promoted to map librarian of the Los Angeles Public Library back in 1989, I was a total greenhorn, but drawer upon drawer of the century-old collection and thousands of questions from my dear patrons (the people of LA) took me to map school. In the past twenty-five years I have curated three map exhibits, filled many boxes with notes from cartographic studies, lectured about the lessons they teach, and written about a quarter of a million words on the maps of Los Angeles.

The maps of Los Angeles have been capturing the landscape and hinting at the stories of its people as far back as Jose Arguello, who drew up a plan of the Pueblo in 1786 for the Spanish colonial governor Felipe de Neve. That would-be perfect settlement at the fringes of European empire, on land long occupied by the native Tongva, was washed away by an uncooperative river in 1815 and rebuilt where it stands today. Spanish occupation gave way to Mexican governance, which in turn gave way to today's American era. In early maps we can watch as the lands of the Spanish missions were absorbed into the Mexican ranchos, until the rancheros were driven to bankruptcy by American capitalists flowing into town on the newly connected railroads. It was up to Lieutenant Edward O. C. Ord to survey the land and shape a Los Angeles that would befit a new world of American commerce. The Ord map guided the inexorable subdivision of the acres and acres of land that would be sold to the American settlers and carpetbaggers brought West by promises of a new Eden. See the maps of Henry Hancock, George Hansen, William Moore, A. J. Stahlberg, Frank LeCouvreur, and A. G. Ruxton for scenes of a city getting established.

The maps of LA show it all: dendritic watersheds were harnessed into manmade ditches, or zanjas, and reservoirs to nourish settlement and agriculture. Subdivision began almost immediately, as seen in maps by H. J. Stevenson and Valentine J. Rowan, and the city practically gave away donation lots to build a future tax base. Industries such as mills, breweries, and brickworks (and, later, refineries and automobile and airplane manufacturing centers) followed the water, and a nascent transportation system—a harbor, several railroads—fostered growth in all directions. Intricate drawings of sewers, gas lines, and a streetcar system round out our knowledge of the city's early infrastructure.

Almost from the beginning, Los Angeles was sold to the rest of the country as a dreamy Eden with open land, verdant hills, beautiful weather, plentiful jobs, and a promise of better things. There are numerous bird's-eye, pictorial, and real-estate-tract color lithographs of a rather enhanced view from the mountains to the sea. See the work of H. B. Eliot, B. W. Pierce, and Francis Lawrence's bird's-eye masterpiece for examples. Boosting LA's idealistic reputation accounts for much of the most compelling cartography, but there are other promises too: of oil, and ships loaded to the gunwales in the harbor, and mass-produced automobiles that quickly filled Southern California after World War I. Even as the Depression threw its wet blanket over America, LA kept fighting for the tourist buck. Business interests, wanting to lure rubes out West, inscribed the romantic beacon of Hollywood prominently on their maps, and optimists flooded the city by the thousands, suffering or succeeding mostly by luck.

Maps helped the city grow physically, spiritually, and intellectually. The cultural life highlighted on maps like "Greater Los Angeles, the Wonder City of America," "Hollywood, the Film Capital of the World," "The Travelure Map," and many of the creations of the All-Year Club of Southern California, a tourist organization that published booster maps in the 1940s, let the world know LA was a vital part of the American experience. These colorful panoramic maps of the thirties and forties feature LA's numerous cultural riches, including theater, music, and the haunts of great writers who reluctantly came, complained, and ultimately stayed. These maps proudly labeled the Planetarium, the Huntington Library, the Los Angeles Museum, and the Philharmonic Auditorium, not to mention Wrigley Field and Gilmore stadium. They showed Chicano murals, places of rhythm and blues, beaches where one could sunbathe nude, and the loci of literary culture. On such maps you can find Jim Morrison, Arnold Schoenberg, Charles Bukowski, Raymond Chandler, and Charlie Parker.

Alongside these colorful come-ons were street guides by the Gillespie Brothers, Jack Renie, and the ubiquitous Thomas Brothers, in addition to the always-fine Automobile Club packages. Maps of Los Angeles were handed out gratis almost everywhere. Humble street guides were the keys to life in the big city for the common man or confused visitors. As early as the 1890s, pocket maps not only showed the street grid but also enlightened newcomers to places like the magnificent Chutes Park or the Bimini Baths or the family-friendly ostrich farm over in South Pasadena. Like a cartographic switchboard they connected folks to the Orpheum, the Memorial Coliseum, the diorama of the Battle of Gettysburg, St. Vibiana's Cathedral, and eventually to more utilitarian localities like freeway on-ramps. In a very real way, the maps in the hands of the common folk evoked a love of the land. They inspired exploration and paved the way for the great streetcar routes that allowed subsequent generations to ramble across Southern California via public transportation.

This enlightenment and affection created by maps reverberates today. The City of Angels has reinvented itself numerous times, and maps continue to seduce, chronicle, and offer insight, even as the Internet, satellites, remote sensing, and crowdsourcing have changed their forms and the ways in which they are disseminated. Any map is a curated set of data with representational limitations—what insurance atlases call "out of coverage" areas—that inevitably inspires curiosity, the endless spiral of questions that haunt my dreams. *LAtitudes* explores some of the hitherto terra incognita of LA, and the results are thrilling for a map aficionado like myself. Here I can travel where I never could before. I am able to perambulate past the end of the grid, to fly-fish in the LA River, to walk in the steps of the undocumented, to accept the ugliness of the places I pass, to embrace the entire city of my birth. In these maps I can understand the uncertainty of the Valley homesteaders, the uneasiness of gay men sitting in a bar fearing a visit from the vice squad. I can feel the Cycleway beneath my wheels, sit beneath the old sycamore at El Aliso, join a herd of ornery longhorns straggling north, hear the many tongues of our people, and recall the joy of radio voices giving us hope again. I feel awakened to new places and faces, familiar-strange as though seen before in a dream. Having journeyed, via maps, all the way from the old Pueblo on the banks of the "Porciúncula" River, I find myself home again.

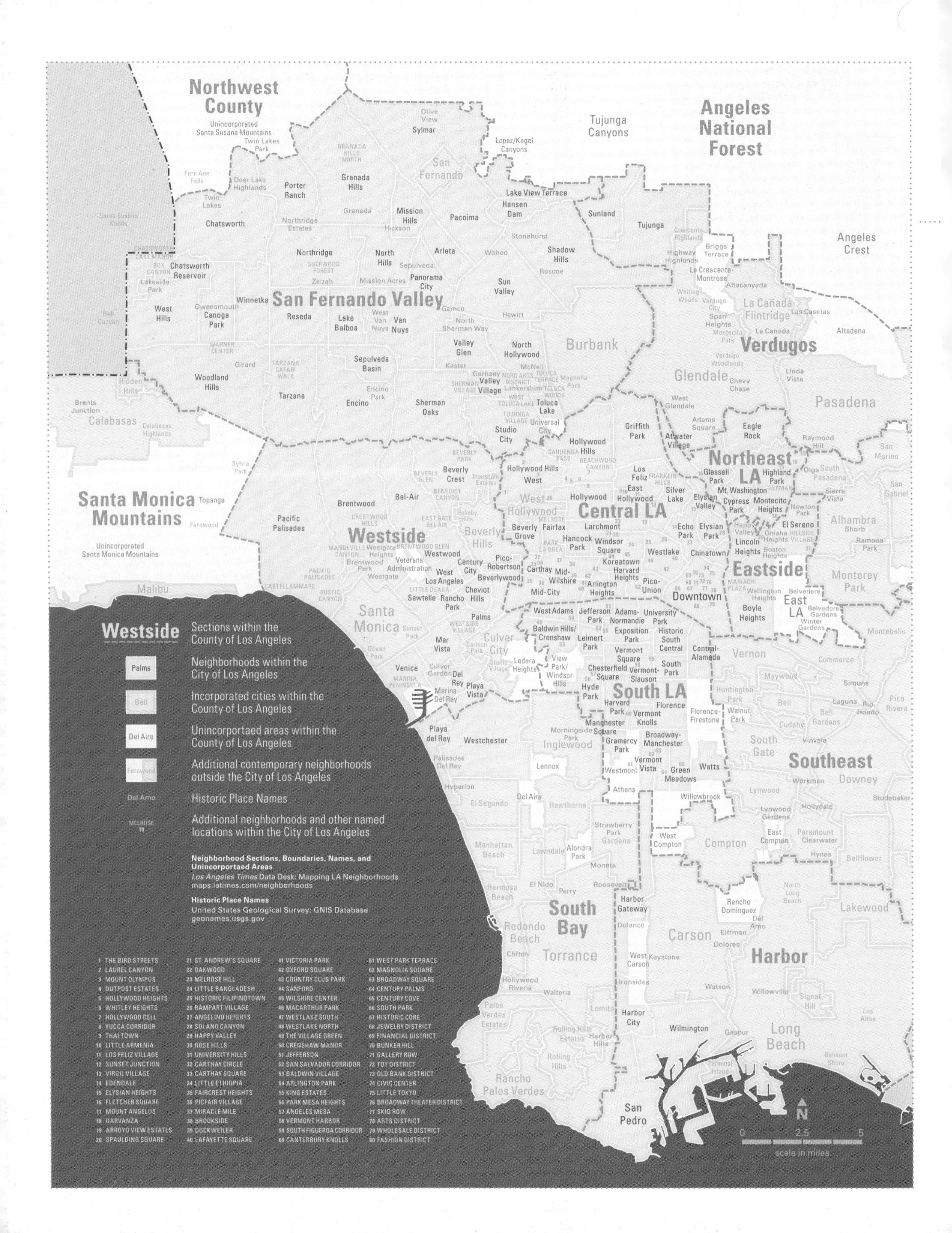

Westside Sections within the County of Los Angeles

Palms — Neighborhoods within the City of Los Angeles

Bell — Incorporated cities within the County of Los Angeles

Del Aire — Unincorportaed areas within the County of Los Angeles

Fernwood — Additional contemporary neighborhoods outside the City of Los Angeles

Del Amo — Historic Place Names

MELROSE 19 — Additional neighborhoods and other named locations within the City of Los Angeles

Neighborhood Sections, Boundaries, Names, and Unincorportaed Areas
Los Angeles Times Data Desk: Mapping LA Neighborhoods
maps.latimes.com/neighborhoods

Historic Place Names
United States Geological Survey: GNIS Database
geonames.usgs.gov

1 THE BIRD STREETS
2 LAUREL CANYON
3 MOUNT OLYMPUS
4 OUTPOST ESTATES
5 HOLLYWOOD HEIGHTS
6 WHITLEY HEIGHTS
7 HOLLYWOOD DELL
8 YUCCA CORRIDOR
9 THAI TOWN
10 LITTLE ARMENIA
11 LOS FELIZ VILLAGE
12 SUNSET JUNCTION
13 VIRGIL VILLAGE
14 EDENDALE
15 ELYSIAN HEIGHTS
16 FLETCHER SQUARE
17 MOUNT ANGELUS
18 GARVANZA
19 ARROYO VIEW ESTATES
20 SPAULDING SQUARE
21 ST. ANDREW'S SQUARE
22 OAKWOOD
23 MELROSE HILL
24 LITTLE BANGLADESH
25 HISTORIC FILIPINOTOWN
26 RAMPART VILLAGE
27 ANGELINO HEIGHTS
28 SOLANO CANYON
29 HAPPY VALLEY
30 ROSE HILLS
31 UNIVERSITY HILLS
32 CARTHAY CIRCLE
33 CARTHAY SQUARE
34 LITTLE ETHIOPIA
35 FAIRCREST HEIGHTS
36 PICFAIR VILLAGE
37 MIRACLE MILE
38 BROOKSIDE
39 DOCKWEILER
40 LAFAYETTE SQUARE
41 VICTORIA PARK
42 OXFORD SQUARE
43 COUNTRY CLUB PARK
44 SANFORD
45 WILSHIRE CENTER
46 MACARTHUR PARK
47 WESTLAKE SOUTH
48 WESTLAKE NORTH
49 THE VILLAGE GREEN
50 CRENSHAW MANOR
51 JEFFERSON
52 SAN SALVADOR CORRIDOR
53 BALDWIN VILLAGE
54 ARLINGTON PARK
55 KING ESTATES
56 PARK MESA HEIGHTS
57 ANGELES MESA
58 VERMONT HARBOR
59 SOUTH FIGUEROA CORRIDOR
60 CANTERBURY KNOLLS
61 WEST PARK TERRACE
62 MAGNOLIA SQUARE
63 BROADWAY SQUARE
64 CENTURY PALMS
65 CENTURY COVE
66 SOUTH PARK
67 HISTORIC CORE
68 JEWELRY DISTRICT
69 FINANCIAL DISTRICT
70 BUNKER HILL
71 GALLERY ROW
72 TOY DISTRICT
73 OLD BANK DISTRICT
74 CIVIC CENTER
75 LITTLE TOKYO
76 BROADWAY THEATER DISTRICT
77 SKID ROW
78 ARTS DISTRICT
79 WHOLESALE DISTRICT
80 FASHION DISTRICT

What's in a name? In Los Angeles, a city known for blurry boundaries and self-invention, neighborhood names are invaluable markers of identity in-the-now. This map offers a dense palimpsest of place names in Los Angeles County, each with stories—of politics, protests, and ethnic affiliations—behind them.

Naming Los Angeles

Rosten Woo

Imagine a point on the surface of the earth—far enough inland that it could not be approached by sea, near a source of water, and close enough to other people that you could employ them as laborers. Make a mark in the dirt. Face north and walk for an hour. Make another mark. Return to your first point and walk east for an hour. Mark again. Continue with this pattern of walking until you have marked a point in each of the cardinal directions. Mentally draw a line between these four markers. Everything inside this square is your settlement. You will call it El Pueblo de Nuestra Señora la Reina de los Ángeles de Porciúncula or The Town of Our Lady the Queen of Angels of the Little Portion, but officially it will be named El Pueblo de la Reina de Los Ángeles. You have marked this area out according to the Laws of the Indies, the rules of colonization and town planning issued by the Spanish crown in the sixteenth century. This square, barely five miles across, will grow to be nearly eighteen times as large, 469 square miles. To trace the perimeter of the city will one day consume sixteen days of continuous walking. But now, in 1781, your settlement is too big to truly inhabit or even imagine in much detail. In all likelihood you will never revisit those initial markers that you have laid. There are, after all, only forty-four people in your group of settlers.

The outer boundaries of your settlement will grow and shrink. In 1834, after Mexico has declared its independence from Spain, the Territorial Legislature will decide to expand the boundaries of your town. The corners of your square are moved an additional league in each direction. In 1850, your square is a possession of the United States. The California Legislature incorporates the city, but accidentally misquotes the boundary as four square miles instead of four square leagues, inadvertently shrinking the city from over one hundred square miles back to roughly its original size. It will take until 1896 for the city to begin growing again. The perimeter will be modified 208 more times and in some ways it will always remain a double boundary; sometimes Los Angeles will refer to the city, sometimes the county; the distinction between the two will be hazy to most of its residents, meaningless to visitors.

Imagine now that you live on a small tree-lined street in a spacious valley—almost fifteen miles northwest of that initial point. You would like to sell your home. When someone asks you where you live, you describe it as "basically Sherman Oaks" but you know that, honestly, it is more accurate to say "Van Nuys." You see homes across the street from yours selling for tens of thousands of dollars more than your own could. To the north there is a commercial strip, train tracks, and an industrial zone. By whose declaration are you in "Van Nuys" rather than "Sherman Oaks"? You feel like you have more in common with the south than the north. What would it take to be considered part of that other place? This is the testimony that you will eventually give to the city council. "Ours is the only Van Nuys neighborhood whose children are designated by the LAUSD to attend elementary school in Sherman Oaks. It is at these public schools in Sherman Oaks where our children meet and make their friends, and as parents so do we. Ours is the only Van Nuys neighborhood south of the Orange Line, Oxnard, and the industrial belt—THE ONLY ONE. All of our connections to our community—through our schools, our children, the closest hospital, grocery stores, post office, firehouse, parks and playgrounds, churches and synagogues, and everyday commerce, along with our [Community District 2] designation, are with Sherman Oaks. We respectfully ask that you recognize the community that we are already very much a part of."

Why do you give this testimony? You want the city to recognize, officially, that your street is part of Sherman Oaks. You start a campaign called "Part of Sherman Oaks" and you spend your nights and weekends walking door-to-door conscripting neighbors. You collect thousands of signatures. You need these signatures because the city has recently created an official process for neighborhood name changes, due to the volume of requests that are submitted. In the city's estimate, naming a place costs between $36,000 and $54,000 in staff time and materials. So now, in order to be considered for a change you must collect 5000 signatures; you need 500 to even begin the process. You collect these signatures over the course of three years.

The Van Nuys Neighborhood Council opposes your petition, as does the Sherman Oaks Neighborhood Council, and the Sherman Oaks Business Improvement District. Here is what Norma Jean Vescovo, the head of the Van Nuys Neighborhood Council, had to say about your group: "The name-change group says their demand is about self-determination and that annexation to Sherman Oaks hurts no one. This couldn't be further from the truth. This movement is about classism, prestige, and property values. This attempted amputation has already hurt Van Nuys. The Van Nuys community has been humiliated by the derogatory comments made publicly at the Sherman Oaks Neighborhood Council meetings and the arrogance displayed. The group has waged one of the ugliest battles I have ever witnessed, thrusting the hard edge of balkanization into our midst."

In the giant book of maps that every Angeleno carries in their car, *The Thomas Guide,* the neighborhood names are denoted by thin blue letters that float above the street grid. Sometimes they are capitalized; inexplicably, sometimes they are not. It is easy to imagine the map-maker at their desk in Irvine, California, moving these words around on a computer screen, fitting them between a highway and a park, up and down on the page—completely oblivious to the impact they are making on the ground.

Yours is just one in a long chain of renaming battles that have been fought in the Valley. In the Thomas Bros. guide from 1960, the San Fernando Valley contains seventeen neighborhoods. In 2013, there are between thirty-four (*Los Angeles Times*) and thirty-nine (Wikipedia). If you included every neighborhood that a resident of the San Fernando Valley imagines, you might end up with upwards of seventy.

You succeed. Only two council members vote against your motion. What will this success mean for you? The first thing that will happen is that the Los Angeles City Council will officially recognize your neighborhood. Surprisingly, even though you have just waged a three-year war to change your neighborhood's official designation, the decree will still only suggest that the borders of your neighborhood are "roughly" defined by a series of streets—"roughly" north of Burbank Boulevard, south of Oxnard, east of Sepulveda, and west of Hazeltine.... Still, the motion is passed. Your testimony will be stapled to the back of the motion,

1940 *Thomas Guide*
(17 neighborhoods)

Burbank
Canoga Park
Chatsworth
Encino
North Hollywood
Northridge
Pacoima
Reseda
San Fernando
Sherman Oaks
Studio City
Sun Valley
Sunland
Tarzana
Universal City
Van Nuys
Woodland Hills

1960 *Thomas Guide*
(23 neighborhoods)

Burbank
Canoga Park
Chatsworth
Encino
Granada
Montrose
North Hollywood
Northridge
Pacoima
Panorama City
Reseda
San Fernando
Sepulveda
Sherman Oaks
Studio City
Sun Valley
Sunland
Tarzana
Toluca Lake
Tujunga
Universal City
Van Nuys
Woodland Hills

1980 *Thomas Guide*
(34 neighborhoods)

Agoura
Brents Junction
Burbank
Canoga Park
Chatsworth
Encino
Glenview
Granada Hills
Hidden Hills
Highway Highlands
La Crescenta
Lakeview Terrace
Mission Hills
Montlake
Newhalt
North Hollywood
Northridge
Olive View
Panorama City
Reseda
San Fernando
Sepulveda
Sherman Oaks
Studio City
Sun Valley
Sunland
Sylmar
Tarzana
Tujunga
Universal City
Van Nuys
Verdugo City
Westlake Village
Woodland Hills

along with Norma's, tipped into a light green folder and placed in a cardboard box. That box will be filed away on the third floor of a concrete building behind the train station next to the LAPD's heliport and the hall of election records. The City Archive's single employee, Michael Holland, will pull this file should anyone need to see it.

Far more importantly, the Department of Transportation is instructed to install a series of powder-coated aluminum signs in your neighborhood. These signs hold the city seal and the words "Sherman Oaks." And then...nothing else will happen. Not officially. But the confidence in your voice will increase when someone asks you where you live. You will feel more connected to Sherman Oaks, where the median income (according to the way this neighborhood is defined by the *Los Angeles Times* in 2009) is $69,651, and less

2013 *LA Times*
(34 neighborhoods)

Arleta
Burbank
Canoga Park
Chatsworth
Chatsworth Reservoir
Encino
Granada Hills
Hansen Dam
Lake Balboa
Lake View Terrace
Mission Hills
North Hills
North Hollywood
Northridge
Pacoima
Panorama City
Porter Ranch
Reseda
Shadow Hills
San Fernando
Sepulveda Basin
Sherman Oaks
Studio City
Sun Valley
Sylmar
Tarzana
Toluca Lake
Universal City
Valley Glen
Valley Village
Van Nuys
West Hills
Winnetka
Woodland Hills

2013 *Wikipedia*
(39 neighborhoods)

Arleta
Cahuenga Pass
Canoga Park
Chatsworth
Colfax Meadows
Encino
Fallbrook
Granada Hills
Kagel Canyon
La Tuna Canyon
Lake View Terrace
Lake Balboa
Mission Hills
NoHo Arts District
North Hills
North Hollywood
Northridge
Pacoima
Panorama City
Porter Ranch
Reseda
Shadow Hills
Sherman Oaks
Studio City
Stonehurst
Sun Valley
Sunland-Tujunga
Sylmar
Tarzana
Toluca Lake
Toluca Woods
Valley Glen
Valley Village
Van Nuys
Warner Center
West Hills
West Toluca
Winnetka
Woodland Hills

connected to the neighborhood where it is $41,134. In 2012, someone looking for homes in your area will see an almost $500,000 difference between the asking prices north and south of Oxnard.

You are a Bangladeshi national. You moved to Los Angeles in 1996, to S Berendo Street, between Fourth and Fifth Avenues. You chose this neighborhood because your sister and your cousins already lived here. Since you've lived here you've seen signs go up around town to declare a Little Armenia, a Little Ethiopia, a Historic Filipinotown. You'd like your Bangladeshi community to be similarly recognized. You propose the name Little Bangladesh for "roughly" this area bounded by Wilshire Boulevard, Third Street, Western Avenue, and Vermont. Fifty thousand other Bangladeshis live in this area.

You collect your five hundred signatures. You submit the application. To your surprise there is a swift and forceful reaction from without. The Wilshire Center Koreatown Neighborhood Council strongly opposes your naming. "Irreparable harm would be caused by such a designation to its commercial and cultural growth since the area carved out as 'Little Bangladesh' constituted the heart of what is widely identified as Koreatown. Although Koreatown does not have an official neighborhood designation by the city it is widely recognized within different city administrative bodies, amongst the population, and within the international community as a whole. Some of the city bodies that have an internal designation of Koreatown include the WCKNC (Wilshire Center Koreatown Neighborhood Council), the CRA (Community Redevelopment Agency), LAPD, PAFD, and LAUSD, and it is recognized in the *LA Times*, the *NY Times*, and local TV news, and such popular online collections of human knowledge as Wikipedia and Google.com."

Interestingly, even though neighborhood signs have been placed by the city as early as 1963, you have never seen one in Koreatown. To your community, Koreatown does not describe where you live at all. The city council suggests that you meet with the WCKNC to figure out a compromise. In the end you get your designation, but it consists of less than one hundredth of the territory you proposed. Just a single stretch of W Third Street between South New Hampshire and S Alexandria Avenue, three blocks. Meanwhile, the area you originally designated as Little Bangladesh has become officially named Koreatown, to the chagrin of many Central American organizations in the neighborhood—which begin their own naming processes shortly thereafter.

You live in a house on Vermont across the street from a beautiful park. Your street has never been depicted in a major film and has rarely been seen on the news. And, for that matter, neither have any of the streets in a six-block radius. You live a mile from Central Avenue. Yet when asked where you live, you might tell someone South Central. And, when you say those words, that person might imagine people shooting at one another. In fact, the term South Central has long since ceased to relate to a geographic area. Instead, it indicates mostly "places where black people live." The local paper routinely describes anything that happens in the black community south of the 405 as happening in "South Central." Even if it is dozens of blocks west of Central Avenue. Even if it took place somewhere that already has a name: Crenshaw, or View Park, or Baldwin Hills, Leimert Park, or Vermont Square. South Central can refer to an area of nearly sixteen square miles.

You wish that South Central would cease to exist.

The idea comes to you one day in conversation with a friend. It is not the first time you've had an ambitious idea and more often than not, you've gotten your way. You're a retired school janitor with no special political connections. But you know how to make things happen. Three years ago, you cornered Mayor Riordan at a community meeting and he promised to replant the park outside your house. Two weeks later, $20,000 was spent making it over with new planters, playground equipment, and paint. A few years before that you got all of the potholes on your street filled. To City Hall you are a minor celebrity, a model community activist. Although your neighborhood has a name, Vermont Square (named after the park you worked so hard to restore), it is always overshadowed by the name "South Central." This is what you say to the city council: "I live in Los Angeles, but I live in 'South Los Angeles.' I live in a beautiful neighborhood just like anyone else." Councilman Nate Holden interrupts you: "Okay, so you're in South Los Angeles, and the same kinds of problems and crime are happening as what happened in South Central, but now it's defined as South Los Angeles. How does that really affect you?" "Well, when it happens, it happens, but at least it's the truth." "Changing the name doesn't change the circumstances." "There's so much in a name, Mr. Holden. So much."

The motion passes unanimously. But your motion is not a typical neighborhood name change. Your motion requests that the city discontinue the use of the term "South Central Los Angeles" on all City documents and replace this phrase with the term "South Los Angeles" as documents are updated and printed. Remarkably, this seems to work. In ten years, people will no longer have a convenient way to refer to Black Los Angeles. "South Los Angeles" covers such an enormous swath of territory (roughly fifty-one square miles, much larger than the area that was once called South Central) that it means almost nothing. It fails to describe, and therefore fails to label your community.

You eloped with your nineteen-year-old aide, whom you have known since she was four years old. Together, you have a child named Marisol. You are in love. As a show of your love and commitment to your daughter you suggest that the main street in a new planned development in your district, Huntington Terrace at Monterey Hills, be named Via Marisol. It has a nice ring to it, and since you are a red-haired Irishman in a mostly Latino district, anything you can do to show support for the Latino community seems like a great idea. Your wife studied Spanish at USC and has been invaluable in helping you connect with your district. Inconveniently, Via Marisol connects with another major street, named Hermon, and it seems confusing that Hermon should suddenly become "Via Marisol" at the edge of the development. You propose to change the name of Hermon as well, to match. This will require taking down the old street signs, putting up new ones, and getting Caltrans to change the name of the freeway exit. You figure that it is better, probably, if people don't focus on the fact that Marisol is your daughter's name—really, this is about consistency. A couple hundred petitioners oppose the street name change, because they believe that the street is critical to the integrity of the neighborhood, but mostly it passes without much controversy.

When they find out that it is your daughter's name, and not just an arbitrary Spanish name, the community is enraged. But it's too late; the signs have already been changed. Residents beg Caltrans to include Hermon on the 110 exit sign, but when they finally do, they misspell it "Herman." Decades after you are out of office, you are bitterly remembered by many of the 3,500 residents of the area that was once Hermon. A neighborhood organization forms, calling itself the Hermon Neighborhood Council. They work to perpetuate this name again. They install their own neighborhood marker, hold monthly meetings as the Hermon Neighborhood Council, and begin a campaign to secede from the Arroyo Seco Neighborhood Council.

Imagine that you've been given access to a database of every reported violent or property crime in the county to the nearest intersection. Let's say you've been asked to write a summary report for the residents of the county. How do you go about this task?

You could add up each kind of crime and divide by the total population. Then you'd have, for instance, a figure you could call murders per capita. But the county is 691 square miles, several million people. This is not a very useful or interesting number.

Alternately, you could list each intersection for each crime, maybe taking special note if the same exact intersection held more than one crime in a given month or six-month period. Somehow this too seems not that useful.

What you cannot do is to tell anyone their neighborhood crime rate. Why? Because neither the city, nor the county, have any official neighborhood boundaries.

If your data was for Chicago, your task would be simple. The city publishes a definitive map of all the neighborhoods, so you could tally the number of crimes that happened within the boundaries of a given neighborhood and list the number. Maybe even write a bit about whether this month was higher or lower than last month; if this week was higher or lower than last week. No one has to debate whether or not something happened in Irving Park or Avondale, it's there on the map.

But your data is for Los Angeles. So you're left with a mishmash of geographies that you might be able to organize the information into: zip codes, police precincts, community planning areas, census tracts—none of these mean much to most people. You might know your own zip code, but you probably don't have any idea of how big it is or where the next one begins.

If your data was for New York, you could say something definitive about a borough. But even the broadest regions of Los Angeles have trouble finding a firm definition. The Eastside? the Westside? Forget it.

Imagine this problem on a grander scale. Let's say you have information about asthma rates, potholes, income as organized by census tract. The next boundary terra firma that anyone has a chance of recognizing is the city limit.

You have been dreaming about making a neighborhood map for a decade—since you started working for the *Los Angeles Times*'s Valley Edition. Your dream map has a few rules: Every part of the city must be considered part of a neighborhood, and no one place can be considered part of more than one. The areas must be large enough that the statistical information is valid but small enough that actual people can relate to them. Your dream is not that the map will be definitive, only that it will be complete. Each neighborhood is built by adding together hundreds of census tracts.

The map takes two years to build and you revise it over five hundred times based on the sometimes gentle, sometimes irate, feedback of your newspaper's readers. But once you have it, you are able to tell entirely new stories about the city. You no longer have to explain a crime rate based on a two-mile radius from an intersection. You can tell someone that the median household income in Koreatown is $30,558, or that Brentwood is 84.2 percent white. In the future, you will be able to describe *changes* to these places. You can tell people that the wealthiest neighborhood has the slowest 911 times or that the poorest neighborhoods have the worst street conditions. Before this map, none of that was possible.

The year after you complete the map, the U.S. Census overhauls the way that they collect statistics. The new method means that data can be updated more regularly but in order to use the data you'll have to rebuild the neighborhood boundaries with different shapes. You begin thinking of how you'll draw the lines again.

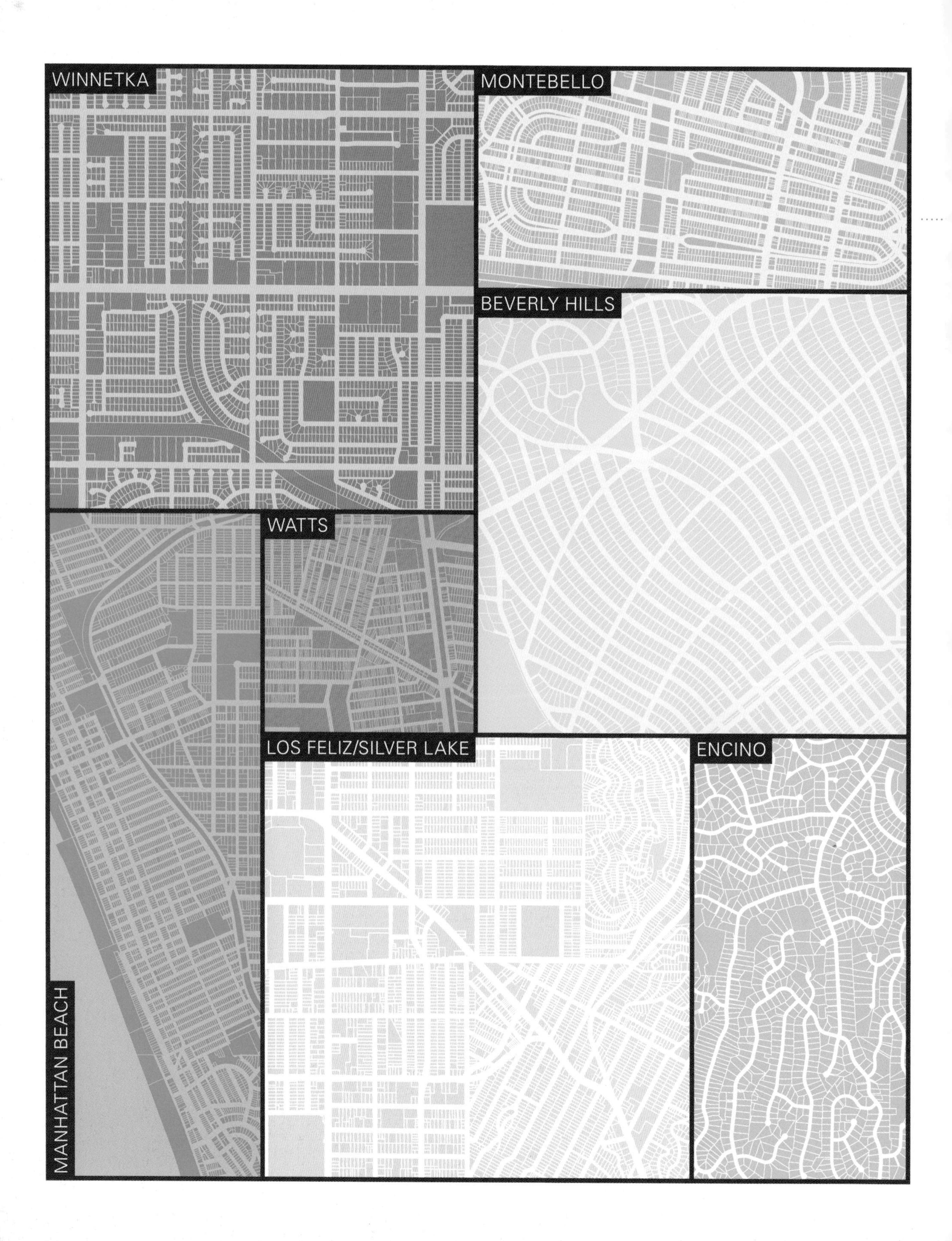

WINNETKA
MONTEBELLO
BEVERLY HILLS
WATTS
MANHATTAN BEACH
LOS FELIZ/SILVER LAKE
ENCINO

A kaleidoscope of abstract grid patterns illustrates LA's deepest bone structure of settlement. Different eras bequeathed different urban plans, from topography-obscuring grids to the telltale culs-de-sac of suburbia. Ancient mastodon trails and bygone streetcar paths became major thoroughfares, while coasts and hills demanded their own logic.

Gridding the City

Nathan Masters

Angelenos rarely think about street grids, though they encounter them on a daily basis. Grids govern the flow of traffic, the path of our commutes. Their dimensions—the width of streets and the distance between them—can make the difference between city blocks that swell with pedestrian activity and those that stifle it. How a city grid faces the points of the compass—directly north-south, or at an oblique angle—determines when or if sunlight pours through our windows. It breaks up prevailing winds or funnels them through our neighborhoods.

It also tells a story about the city's historical development.

Successive cultural and political regimes have passed through the Los Angeles Basin, and each has left an imprint on the landscape.[1] One after another, these regimes etched lines—footpaths, property boundaries, survey marks—that eventually determined the placement of streets and buildings. These lines are remarkably enduring. Compare the earliest known aerial photograph of Los Angeles—an 1887 image taken from a hot air balloon—to a satellite image today, and the similarity between the street patterns is striking. Buildings rise and fall, and redevelopment erases entire neighborhoods from the landscape, but street grids endure.

Grids are hardly a uniquely Los Angeles phenomenon. From the Aztec capital of Tenochtitlán to the American city of Philadelphia, societies have used the gridiron pattern to organize settlements and transportation routes. But in Los Angeles more than elsewhere, street grids are like a palimpsest, a document atop which succeeding authors have written their own stories, leaving faint traces of previous works.

Traveling through them, we can discern a story about the communities who have called this land home, from late Pleistocene hunters to the multicultural population of today. Though this approach to historical storytelling has real shortcomings—it's generally blind to communities who lacked political power—it connects us with the past through tangible if commonplace features of the landscape like an irregular intersection or a bend in the road.

Earliest Imprints

Unlike a medieval parchment palimpsest, the first authors of Los Angeles's street grids did not work from a blank page. The land that would become Los Angeles offered its earliest human visitors varied terrain—steep mountains, shoreline, rolling hills, wetlands, rivers, arroyos—that provided natural barriers to movement and settlement.

Even before the first humans arrived, transportation corridors spread across the coastal plain and the adjacent valleys. Pounded into the landscape by the feet of mammoths and other migratory grazers, these primitive highways descended from mountain passes toward watering holes on the coastal plain. One of these early highways led many a Pleistocene beast to its death in the asphalt pits near Wilshire and La Brea.

When the first known Southern Californians—possibly associated with the Clovis culture of big-game hunters—arrived roughly 13,000 years ago, they likely followed the existing game trails while also adding their own routes. The next cultural regime to establish dominance in the region, the more sedentary Millingstone people, did the same. So when the Gabrieleno (Tongva) people arrived between 3,000 and 1,500 years ago, they found a landscape primed for settlement. Many of their village sites and trading routes likely duplicated their predecessors'. These native Angelenos—most of their population and much of their culture obliterated in the eighteenth and nineteenth centuries by the Spanish scheme of colonization—thus bequeathed to their successors an irregular system of roads.

Succeeding generations have erased many of these ancient highways from the landscape, but some remain.

One ancient game trail—perhaps blazed by Pleistocene-era elephants—once led from the site of downtown Los Angeles through the San Gabriel Valley to present-day San Bernardino. From there, it turned north, becoming faint while crossing the Transverse Ranges at Cajon Pass. For the Tongva, this trail became a critical trade route linking them with the people of the Mojave Desert. When the Spanish arrived, they appropriated the trail and named it El Camino Real de San Gabriel y San Bernardino. (Here, the name "Camino Real" only signifies that the route was a state highway, not that it was the El Camino Real of romantic lore.) The highway linked the Los Angeles pueblo with the San Gabriel mission and marked the boundary between two ranchos, Azusa and La Puente. Later, Pacific Electric tracks followed the route, and today much of the ancient pathway survives as Mission Road and, further east, Ramona Boulevard.

Another trail with prehistoric origins extended west of present-day Los Angeles, connecting the large Tongva village of Yaangna with coastal settlements. Under the Spanish, the trail became a well-used highway, rutted with the tracks of wagons transporting asphalt pitch from the La Brea Tar Pits for the pueblos' adobe structures. And though the exact route is lost, Wilshire Boulevard today approximates the path of this ancient highway.

On its 15.8-mile trek from Grand Avenue in downtown to Santa Monica's Palisades Park, Los Angeles's grand boulevard traverses multiple street grids, each oriented toward a different point on the compass and only one pointing toward the cardinal directions. As a result, the boulevard bends and turns several times between downtown Los Angeles and the sea. Traveling down this iconic boulevard by car, bus, bike, or foot, we journey through space as well as time, observing in the urban geometry traces of the past.

The Beginnings of a Spanish Grid

We begin our journey at Wilshire's eastern terminus, rooted in Los Angeles's original street grid: a pattern conceived by the Spanish Empire, drafted by an American military officer, and realized by private property owners. Today at this intersection, drunken revelers stumble out of Casey's Irish Pub, while the thirty-story One Wilshire building—a telecommunications hub occupied by computer servers and network routers but few humans—

towers overhead. But when the Spanish began colonizing Alta California in 1769, neither Wilshire nor Grand existed. Wildflowers and grasses grew where the roads intersect today. Nearby, at the base of a ridge that would later become known as Bunker Hill, the ancient highway leading to the La Brea Tar Pits crossed a willow-lined arroyo.

When they arrived in what would become Los Angeles, the Spanish encountered a landscape already laced with foot trails and dotted with villages. But they brought their own set of cultural preferences about the shape of settlements and a detailed code of instructions related to their development. Those ideas and legal prescriptions ultimately resulted in the city's oldest street grid, centered on the heart of the Spanish pueblo and superimposed on the indigenous network of trails.

Since 1573, the Laws of the Indies—a body of laws that governed Spain's imperial holdings—had spelled out in 148 separate ordinances how authorities were to plan new towns. The city planning ordinances dictated everything from a settlement's site and position to the width of its streets. Most importantly for the eventual shape of Los Angeles, they mandated the creation of a central plaza—"the starting point for the town"—and specified its size, shape, and orientation. Streets would extend at right angles from the plaza's four corners, each of which would point toward the four principal points of the compass. The resulting 45-degree skew in the streets' orientation was meant to prevent the prevailing winds from surging through the streets.

Los Angeles's original town planner, Governor Felipe de Neve, and the *pobladores* who carried de Neve's plan to fruition hewed closely to the Laws' prescriptions. A 1786 map confirms that the settlers had oriented the plaza so that its corners edged toward the points of the compass. This first plaza no longer exists, but when residents established a new plaza in the 1820s, they preserved the tilt of the original.

Though bulldozers have claimed most of the pueblo's original streets and pathway, this newer plaza survives to this day across Alameda Street from Union Station, shaded by sprawling Moreton Bay figs and further overshadowed by the tourist promenade of Olvera Street, which empties into the plaza. Visitors here can see how the plaza—now a circle with a bandstand in the center—anchored the street system of Mexican Los Angeles. The road separating the plaza from La Iglesia de Nuestra Señora Reina de los Ángeles (the Plaza Church) began as Calle Principal, a street extending from the plaza's southwest corner, its direction parallel with the front of the Plaza Church.

The city, home to roughly 1,500 people in the 1840s, never achieved a sufficient size to realize an actual grid pattern of settlement. At the end of the American conquest in 1847, Los Angeles had only the rudimentary beginnings of a street grid. In fact, only a few well-defined streets existed, intersecting with various highways leading to the mission, the harbor in San Pedro, and the tar pits. And even the streets that did exist refused to conform to a regular grid pattern. "Its streets are laid out without any regard to regularity," an American observer, Edwin Bryant, noted in January 1847.[2]

Ord's Grids

Upon conquering the city, one of the newcomers' first tasks was to impose American cartographic standards on existing Hispanic settlement patterns—a prerequisite for converting city lands into private property. Under Spanish and then Mexican law, Los Angeles was entitled to four square leagues (about twenty-seven square miles), held by the pueblo in common trust. Most of that land sat unused when Robert Stockton's troops marched into the city; its limits, in fact, had never been mapped. But as part of the United States, Los Angeles would need to parcel out its corporate lands to real-estate speculators and new settlers—thus strengthening the American hold on the city and providing a source of public revenue.

Enter Edward Otho Cresap Ord.

Acting on orders from California's military governor, the Los Angeles ayuntamiento (city council) hired the thirty-year-old U.S. Army lieutenant as the city's first surveyor in the summer of 1849. The council tasked Ord with mapping the existing vineyards and pastures that cloaked the low-lying land on the floodplain of the Los Angeles River, as well as identifying natural features like hills and watercourses. But Ord's most important job was carving the higher ground into two new grids of parcels and streets.

Ord and his apprentice, William Rich Hutton, must have been a quizzical sight on the dry, uncultivated plains around the city, dragging their survey chains through fields of wild mustard and wandering cattle. A no-nonsense West Point graduate who later served as a Union general in the Civil War, Ord had strong feelings about command. During the survey, he insisted on using his own compass even after it showed signs of trouble. "In some cases I think mine would be better," Hutton confided in a private letter to his uncle.

Nevertheless, Ord, Hutton, and their three local assistants made short work of the survey, finishing their fieldwork in two weeks. When Hutton sketched the resulting map, filed with the city in September 1849, a pair of regularly patterned gridirons—one north of the plaza and one south—accompanied the city's existing footprint.

Neither grid aligned with the cardinal directors, nor did it exhibit the 45-degree skew envisioned by the Laws of the Indies. Rather, the orientation of the grids reflected a compromise between existing settlement patterns and topography. In both grids, Main Street extended out from the plaza, running parallel to a range of bluffs that divided the high ground, safe for settlement, from the low-lying floodplain of the river. North of the plaza, the grid was skewed 22 degrees off the cardinal directions. South of the plaza, the grid tilted 38 degrees. In both cases, Main Street approximated existing pathways.

North of the plaza, Ord and Hutton sketched a grid that still anchors Chinatown today. They gave many of the streets, projected onto what was then open countryside, colorful, bilingual names. Calle del Toro, or Bull Street, dead-ended at a bullfighting ring. Calle de Eternidad, or Eternity Street, led to the town cemetery. Most of these names are forgotten; Bull Street is today North Hill, and Eternity is North Broadway. Meanwhile, another of Ord's creations, High Street, now honors its creator as Ord Street.

Southwest of the plaza, the surveyors drew an even larger grid that today forms the core of downtown Los Angeles. A series of numbered streets, from First to Twelfth, extended far into the open countryside. Paralleling Main Street were Calle Primavera, or Spring Street; Fortín, or Fort (now Broadway); Loma, or Hill; Accytuna, or Olive; Caridad, or Charity (now Grand); Esperanzas, or Hope; Flores, or Flower; and Chapules, or Grasshopper (now Figueroa).

Though Ord's survey established the city's first true grids, his perpendicular lines were more a projection of future land use than a description of existing patterns in 1849. The intersection of First and Spring where City Hall towers over the city today was then the fringe of urban development. Beyond were fields of mustard and hills ablaze each spring with wildflowers, with nothing but wooden stakes and stone monuments marking the corners of Ord's blocks, 200 yards wide and 112 yards deep. It would be several decades before private property owners developed these blocks and the streets Ord mapped and named became fully realized.

Hansen's Grid

As we resume our journey west along Wilshire, our stay inside Ord's grid is brief. Soaring over the Harbor Freeway—usually a slow, frustrated stream of automobiles—Wilshire bends slightly to the left, and we depart Ord's original grid for one mapped by later surveyors.

In 1849, Ord's projected grid extended far into what was then open countryside. But it encompassed only a fraction of the city's four square leagues. Heavily in debt, the newly American city of Los Angeles by 1853 found itself needing to convert more of its public lands into private real estate that could be auctioned off and taxed. The city would sell some parcels outright; prices started at a dollar per acre. Others it would give away on the condition that the new owners make certain improvements, like building an irrigation ditch or planting crops; the city would reap increased tax revenue from these so-called donation lots.

With Ord back on the East Coast serving in the army, the job fell to a newcomer: George Hansen. A brilliant civil engineer who would later plan the German agricultural colony of Anaheim, Hansen had arrived in Los Angeles virtually penniless and lacking standard surveyors' equipment. Nevertheless, he borrowed one hundred dollars from merchant Juan Temple, purchased the needed compass and chains, and marched off into what was then distant wilderness.

Rather than extending Ord's grid beyond its original bounds—Twelfth Street to the south and Grasshopper (now Figueroa) to the west—Hansen, working under the supervision of a more experienced surveyor, Henry Hancock, created a new grid that diverged from Ord's in both scale and orientation. His lots were enormous; each of the thirty-five-acre parcels could swallow six of Ord's city blocks. To get a sense of the scale, pause at Wilshire's intersection with Alvarado Street and take in MacArthur Park. The entire park occupies one of Hansen's lots. Hansen's streets also deviated from Ord's in orientation. The reason is a historical mystery, but streets in Hansen's grid only skew off the cardinal compass points by 28 degrees—10 degrees less than the grid that now anchors downtown Los Angeles. That difference accounts for Figueroa's subtle jog at Pico Boulevard and Wilshire's slight bend as it crosses the Harbor Freeway, whose concrete footprint hides the seam between the two grids.

Whereas Ord named his streets after features of the landscape, Hansen and

Hancock tried to establish a pattern that honored the city's dual Anglo-Hispanic heritage. Beginning with Washington Boulevard, Hansen and Hancock named the major streets running east-west after US presidents, with Adams and Jefferson following the namesake of the American Cincinnatus. The north-south streets they reserved for the governors of Alta California: Micheltorena, Alvarado, Figueroa, and Echandia. Hansen's and Hancock's early maps envisioned the pattern extending all the way to a street honoring President Andrew Jackson, but their plan never caught on.

Hansen's and Hancock's rectangular grid might have satisfied the goals of city leaders by facilitating the sale of land, but it had its shortcomings. In some cases the surveyors sacrificed common sense in favor of the logic of the gridiron. Ord had confined his streets and blocks to flat lands, leaving steep terrain like Bunker Hill and Fort Moore Hill untouched. Hansen and his contemporaries, however, superimposed perfectly straight roads over impossibly steep terrain, rather than mapping roads and parcels that conformed to the contours of the land. Laughably steep roads like Baxter and Fargo Streets are a legacy of the surveyors' rigid adherence to the grid pattern. So are the public stairways that climb slopes even more extreme along old survey lines.

By 1871, Hansen, Hancock, and a third surveyor, A. F. Waldemar, had traced lines across most of Los Angeles's public lands. But the lines were mere etchings on paper until the regional land boom of the 1880s, when urban development finally spilled outside the original Ord grid and real-estate developers turned the surveyors' lines into streets. Among those developers was Gaylord Wilshire, an eccentric millionaire who dabbled in socialism, kept company with George Bernard Shaw, and marketed his I-On-A-Co electric belt as a cure for constipation. In 1895, Wilshire partnered with his brother William to carve one of Hansen's thirty-five-acre lots into a new residential tract. The line bounding the lot on the north became Sixth Street; the one on the south Seventh. And through the middle of the subdivision Wilshire cleared a 1,200-foot gravel path. He named the new boulevard after himself.

Jefferson's Grid

Gaylord Wilshire's original boulevard ends where it meets the Lafayette Park Recreation Center. In Wilshire's time this was Sunset Park, an outdoor retreat lushly landscaped with date palms and jacarandas, but it's long since been paved over with basketball courts and skateboard ramps and encircled with a chain-link fence. As we pass through the remnants of Sunset Park and cross Hoover Street, the road jogs sharply to the left—an indication that we've left behind Los Angeles's original pueblo lands and entered the national survey grid of the United States. Here, Los Angeles streets follow the same patterns etched onto the Great Plains and clearly visible from the window on a trans-continental flight. Streets align with the cardinal points of the compass, and as we head due west down Wilshire, intersecting streets meet the boulevard at right angles.

The architect of these perfectly perpendicular intersections? Thomas Jefferson.

In 1784 Jefferson chaired a special congressional committee that drafted a detailed set of plans—later enshrined into law as the Land Ordinance of 1785—for administering the nation's public lands in the Ohio Valley and beyond. Rejecting a proposal to plan settlements and farms along natural features, Jefferson and his committee recommended a vast, rectangular grid of townships, each thirty-six square miles and divided into thirty-six smaller sections. Survey lines rather than rivers and mountains would govern the shape of property parcels and placement of roads.

This system was a product of its time. It captured the Enlightenment Age fascination with Cartesian geometry, favoring abstract points and lines over physical features. Its neoclassical design—a fitting choice for a man who designed Monticello—traced its lineage back to the Roman practice of centuriation, which divided fields into grids of perfect squares. Most importantly, it reflected the expansionist ethos of the young nation. With minimal work, surveyors could extend the grid westward indefinitely. The grid system facilitated the sale of far-off, unknown territory and helped homesteaders and speculators establish clear title to their land. Owners of sections could easily subdivide their holdings using simple geometric division; one 640-acre section easily became four 160-acre quarter-sections, sixteen 40-acre sixteenth-sections, or sixty-four 10-acre lots.

The Public Land Survey System, as the national grid is known today, came to Southern California in the 1850s. Civil land grants like ranchos and Los Angeles's four square leagues of pueblo lands were excluded, but government surveyors gridded all the unclaimed land in between into townships and sections, which then promptly passed into private hands. On our trek down Wilshire, the busy transit hubs at Vermont and Western avenues, spaced one mile apart, mark our entry and departure from one such section. Both streets trace lines first drawn more than 150 years ago by U.S. Army surveyor Henry Washington.

Grids of the Wild Westside

Continuing our journey toward the sea, Wilshire soon enters the wild western part of the city, where sharp corners and odd angles replace perpendicular intersections. This is a realm of dueling principalities, a series of newer, clashing street grids representing a variety of historical characters, from Mexican-era rancho owners to turn-of-the-century traction magnates.

As the land boom of the 1880s transformed survey lines into actual streets, growing Los Angeles from its urban core outward, in the hinterlands it ushered in the arrival of new suburbs with their own street plans. Already, satellite towns like Santa Monica and Pasadena had sprung up on former rancho lands in the 1870s. With land prices and the region's population booming, more landowners liquidated their holdings, subdividing the agricultural plains surrounding Los Angeles into communities like Hollywood, Colegrove, Beverly Hills, and Sawtelle. Like other planners before them, these developers did not work from a blank page. Instead, they superimposed their plans atop existing boundaries, transportation corridors, and surveys. Often, the subdividers used these older lines as anchors for their street and property plans.

The Ranchos' Grids

A few blocks past Western, streets begin approaching Wilshire from the south at oblique angles—an indication that we have entered the patchwork of Mexican-era ranchos. Between here and the Pacific Ocean, Wilshire will pass through five separate ranchos.

The borders of these land grants, usually made by territorial governors to influential private citizens, exert an outsize influence on street grids in Los Angeles's Mid-City and Westside districts. For several miles between San Vicente and Larchmont Boulevards, Wilshire traces the southern border of the former Rancho La Brea, even bending toward the north near the Los Angeles County Museum of Art to follow a land grant boundary that dates to 1828. Inside the lands that once comprised Rancho Las Cienegas (granted 1823), north–south streets skew slightly toward the northwest, following property lines drawn in 1866 when the rancho's owners partitioned the land into thirteen long, slanted tracts. East–west streets, meanwhile, tend to follow true courses toward the points of the compass, creating parallelogram-shaped city blocks.

Errant Boulevards

Across Los Angeles, an occasional errant street like San Vicente or Venice injects even more chaos into the city's street plan. These boulevards, soaring across the city at odd angles, represent the imprint of the late-nineteenth and early-twentieth-century growth machine made possible by interurban rail lines. Tracks once ran down the middle of Culver, Exposition, San Vicente, Santa Monica, and Venice boulevards—and in many cases, the tracks preceded paved road.[3]

Some of these transportation corridors, often older than the surrounding urban development, anchor their own grids. Wilshire encounters one such grid when it passes Beverly Hills' ritzy Golden Triangle retail district. Here, tourists clutching luxury shopping bags stroll down streets like Rodeo Drive, which run perpendicular to a now-defunct streetcar line that once angled through town along present-day Santa Monica Boulevard. When Beverly Hills' town planners laid out the blocks here in 1906, the railway—later part of the vast Pacific Electric network—was the area's primary connection with the outside world and a logical choice to anchor the street grid.

The Pacific's Grid

Finally, when Wilshire reaches the city of Santa Monica, the road corrects its course to enter a grid that town founders Robert S. Baker and John P. Jones patterned after the Pacific shore. Santa Monica's numbered streets reflect the southeastern direction of the shoreline. Wilshire Boulevard and other intersecting streets, meanwhile, proceed toward the ocean, their bearings directly perpendicular to the cliffs of Palisades Park.

Unlikely Companions

Many people experience Los Angeles's street patterns through the windshield of a car. Fewer see them through bus windows or from the seat of a bicycle. But perhaps the best way to appreciate the quirks of the city's street plan is on foot. Walk north up Hoover Street and see Hansen's grid collide with Jefferson's; cross-streets approach at right angles on the left but meet Hoover diagonally on the right. Stand at Sunset and Santa Monica and watch the traffic make wide-arcing turns from one boulevard to the other; the intersection's odd configuration is a legacy of its origin as a streetcar junction.

Or perhaps lace up a pair of comfortable shoes and walk Wilshire's 15.8-mile trek to the sea. The journey may be tiring, but it's an opportunity to walk through many layers of Los Angeles history with some unlikely companions: a no-nonsense army surveyor, a sixteenth-century Spanish bureaucrat, a nine-ton Pleistocene-era mammoth.

1. For example, see Phil Ethington's essay "Ab urbe condita: The Regional Regimes of Los Angeles Since 13,000 Before Present" in *A Companion to Los Angeles,* edited by William Deverell and Greg Hise. This essay also owes much to Doug Suisman's study of LA boulevards and their relation to the city's street grid in *Los Angeles Boulevard: Eight X-Rays of the Body Public,* and to Neal *Harlow's Maps and Surveys of the Pueblo Lands of Los Angeles.*

2. Mexican authorities had already moved to introduce more regularity to the city's street patterns by the time American troops arrived. As early as 1836, a commission studied the arrangement of Los Angeles pathways. Its report bemoaned the disorderly patterns that prevailed at the time and recommended that the city draw up a map of existing streets, alleys, plazas, and property lots. Another commission appointed on the dawn of the American conquest in 1846 echoed the earlier group's findings.

3. Superhighways like the Hollywood (101) Freeway also seem to defy the city's grids, but others confirm the persistence of historic street patterns. Motorists on the Harbor (110) Freeway, for instance, head directly north while traveling through Jefferson's grid, but they make an abrupt course correction toward the northeast soon after entering Hansen's grid near USC. The freeway's builders followed the survey lines drawn more than a hundred years before their road's construction.

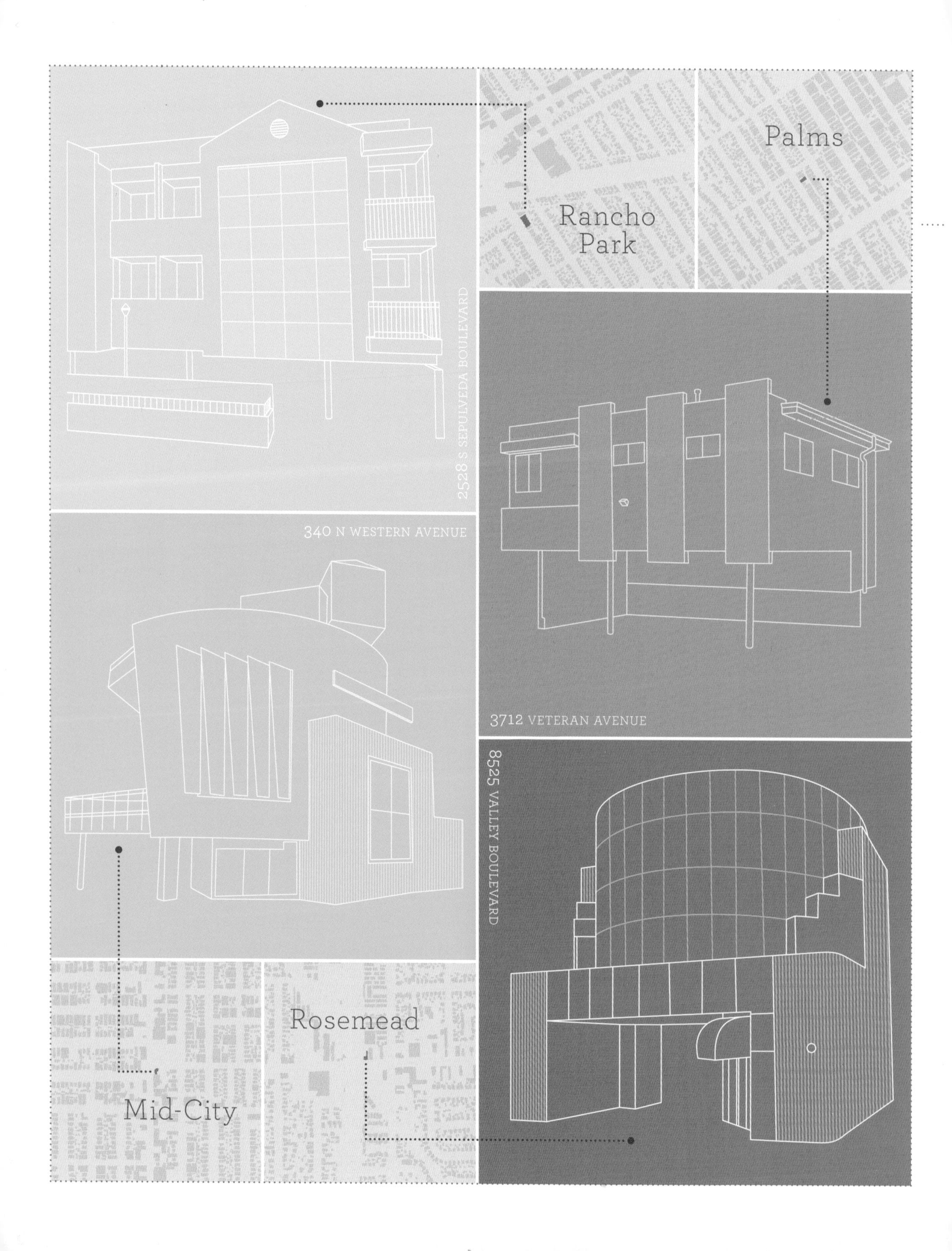
Palms
Rancho
Park
2528 S SEPULVEDA BOULEVARD
340 N WESTERN AVENUE
3712 VETERAN AVENUE
8525 VALLEY BOULEVARD
Rosemead
Mid-City

No single neighborhood, architectural style or period, or developer has a monopoly on ugly buildings in Los Angeles: from kitschy to physics-defying, they appear throughout the cityscape. This graphic is an homage to four of them, each described in the accompanying essay, that speaks to stylistic and functional diversity, as well as a strange power to charm and to fascinate.

Ugly Buildings

Wendy Gilmartin

340 N Western Avenue, Mid-City. Conceived at the tail end of the radical eighties by architect Jeffrey Daniels and completed in 1990, this KFC franchise epitomizes the blocky, colorful, asymmetrical, and never subtle building-as-symbol style that typified postmodernist architecture twenty years ago. With fin-like windows for wings, and a red roof for the rooster's comb, the chicken's "head" sports the weirdly mounted face of the Colonel, with his kindly smirk. Get it? It looks like a chicken *and* a chicken bucket. The jaggedly shaped ceilings inside and corrugated metal siding out front remind us that Daniels apprenticed under Frank Gehry (back when Gehry was doing innovative things with mass-produced, everyday construction materials like asphalt roofing shingles as wall coverings and leaving the 2x4 framing lumber exposed behind windows). Architects adore this building for its playful use of materials and its vaulted skylight next to the leaking Coke machine inside. They think it's fun that the Colonel's likeness is stuck where the "chicken head" should be. They stand up for it in casual conversations and feel nostalgia for it. Everybody else thinks it's really ugly.

Travelers from all the world's burgs, barrios, and banlieues touch down daily at LAX with Kodachrome visions of salty mists falling along Malibu's beaches, newly waxed and gleaming immaculate cars, spray-tanned celebrities and mellow, purple-ish sunsets, only to emerge from the terminal and head up the 405, towards ever more slowly moving traffic. When they finally stop at a standstill between freeway exits and begin to look around, they're met with the bare back walls of parking structures, identical grey condos peeking up from behind highway embankments, and black-windowed, soulless office towers. This relentless landscape of blah is what most visitors and many residents find visually unappealing about Los Angeles. "Why is LA so…ugly?" they ask.

"The mountains," we implore our visiting friends and family, "the beach, the hills, the bougainvillaea bushes, Chavez Ravine…! Those aren't ugly!" It gets an Angeleno hot and itchingly defensive. But a proud Angeleno needs to simmer down because a hater's gonna hate. Even the *Los Angeles Times*'s own architecture critic recently relented, "Much of what we lay our eyes on as we move through the city every day can be remarkably, even punishingly unattractive." Those who dismiss ugly Los Angeles will snark at our traffic, overpriced restaurants, and attitude too. And they'll never uncover the meaning and reward to be revealed in the city's messy stew of urban elements.

Los Angeles does have beautiful buildings. These are conceived by philanthropic boards of directors, and get reviewed by smart critics. They're associated with high art and protected and preserved by conservancies. Beautiful buildings have had all their bugs worked out by historical trial and error, or by teams of specialists who meet frequently to discuss any functional or formal issues through the course of construction. They're often situated in Edenic natural landscapes, standing massively in solid stone and rustic timbers. They have glorious culture and music and taste pouring from them, and they charge entrance fees. Folks tend to

agree the historic houses of Hancock Park and Crenshaw are beautiful, as are mid-century desert ranch-style homes and the Bradbury Building on Broadway downtown. Other local crowd-pleasers include Lloyd Wright's Hollywood Bowl, Los Angeles City Hall, Pann's diner on La Tijera Boulevard—the quintessential sixties incarnation of forward-thinking "Googie" design—and the Greene brothers' arts-and-crafts-era Gamble estate in Pasadena. These structures are exquisitely crafted, carefully kept, and honored.

Coasting through downtown, one takes in a visual index of a certain development type—the city core—where skyscrapers built in the 1970s and '80s soar at towering heights. Their glassy, steely architecture symbolizes financial stability, capitalism, investment, permanence. Older towers from the 1920s and '30s offer meticulous motifs etched in stone, arching entrances to ornate lobbies, and detailing in a style of elegant grandeur long lost in building craft today. Combined, these two types of downtown buildings provide Los Angeles its skyline and visual locus. But as one moves out from the city core in any direction—on Third Street, Mission, Central—the environment changes. The buildings out here symbolize something else entirely. This is the vast, horizontal mass of Los Angeles's built ecology—a landscape of tacked-on siding and black glass, McMansions, yawn-worthy stucco apartments on tiny stilts, dumpy offices, monotonous parking structures, and sad strip malls. Out here amongst the lords of bad taste also lies the potential for a drastically different urban situation. Let the critics concern themselves with the architectural beacons of our contemporary times; ugly buildings are really where it's at.

Ugly buildings are the stock of the people, and they are products of their culture and history. They're kind of like us, in a way. They may suffer from financial hardship, or they are growing older and not dealing with wear and tear well. Some flaunt their ugliness. Some doll themselves up in gaudy, mismatched architectural accents like columns and spires and overly decorated copper drainpipes. Some are cloaked in gallons of plain beige paint so as not to stand out, or to just go away. Some are outfitted with intimidating spikes for fear of criminals or bird poop. These ugly buildings are contaminated with problems: they may be tragically out of the realm of the human scale, have weird materials stuck all over, are messy, are unkempt, are a mishmash of ideas and colors. But they have something else going for them that the architectural gems do not—they are a stealthy, prolific army that no one ever notices or talks about. We drive past, walk by, work in, and take the dog to the vet in ugly buildings. They are the background noise of the city. Ugly buildings don't alienate potential participants in their assessment or mocking.

....

8525 Valley Boulevard, San Gabriel. This small retail complex is built atop a one-story, textured brown-block base that steps down to the street like an inverted, pixelated pyramid. From within the center of the pyramid, a mirrored teal glass cylinder emerges to form the two-story volume of office space above. The effect is that of a disco ball being hatched from a brown-block egg. Tacked-on red and yellow tiles make no sense near the front door. The utility lines are left hanging out in front, and the fire-alarm bell looks like a crowning pimple on the dowdy facade. The dirty teal windows really accentuate the way the valley's stagnant air stains mirrored and hard, craggy surfaces. This bad egg manages to turn a lovely blue sky into a sickly, greenish reflection. It's like wearing brown-tinted sunglasses on a perfectly gorgeous day when the lenses unintentionally make everything look smoggier.

....

Much of the ugliness in Los Angeles stems from an attitude of disposability towards buildings. Build it quick and then flip it, tear down, rebuild, gentrify, repeat. Just as the abbreviated name of the city—"LA"—is tossed around because it is easy, swift and colloquial, Los Angeles's urban situation mirrors a suffering of formalism. Invisible circumstances and the substructure of the twisted and nuanced political, historical, and economic landscape directly inform the city's physical one, and behind each ugly building lies an ever unfolding storyline about political leaders, land speculators, handymen, and cottage industries written in dirty beige stucco and mirrored teal glass.

Angelenos have always been proud homesteaders, liberal in their front-lawn-watering and conservative in their tax-giving. Unlike other cities that enjoy grand civic spaces, Los Angeles prefers the open space of its backyards, and when Proposition 13 passed in 1978, it allowed California homeowners to maintain a steady property tax rate on their homes (and yards), even when inflated housing prices soared and continued to peak through the eighties. For local governments, however, Prop 13 was a death knell. The reductions in tax revenues spelled insolvency for some communities, and local governments quickly took aim at new construction for additional tax sources. (New construction was counted as a reassessed property—and therefore could take on an initial property-tax hike. New shopping malls and retail centers also became appealing to local governments for their guaranteed return in local sales tax.) Cities also increased fees on their own city services, which usually didn't require voter approval. Real-estate developers, consequently, were skewered with dueling attempts at collected revenue and were forced to skim as much "fat" off their respective projects so as to ensure the biggest payback on their investment. This meant constructing as many units as possible, as cheaply as possible, to the very maximum of the lots' lines. In general, land-use planning and development continues to encourage revenue production as a first-order goal. Condos, office buildings, and shopping centers exist as instruments to this monetary exchange, disassociated from their surroundings and never unprofitable.

A century before Proposition 13, men the likes of civil engineer and water baron William Mulholland, land mogul Henry Huntington, and *Los Angeles Times* publisher Harry Chandler, dedicated themselves to fueling a land-grabbing, money-making development machine in the city. This involved constructing many things cheaply and quickly, the extraction of resources to make these built things run efficiently, and then the luring of new residents to live and work in said built things. The repeated cycle of speculative booms and busts over decades rendered the region's buildings less as containers for people and more as real-estate investments, to be completed as fast as possible. By the 1950s, these mini-cycles grew into a monstrous juggernaut, and in an already ingrained system of land speculation where investors ruled, fast and cheap ugly spread like wildfire. Consequently, Los Angeles's famous and seemingly unplanned "sprawl" (we're actually more dense than New York's five boroughs combined) is a contrived, if not routine, feedback loop of disposable building stock construction, unfurling into the desert's deepest reaches. Stop in any neighborhood and consider the corner convenience store or an apartment complex built after the postwar period. The building's ugliness is merely a gateway to discovering this history.

Whether residents wanted it or not, Los Angeles never suffered or benefited from a dictatorial planner's iron fist—think New York's Robert Moses or Mayor Richard Daley in Chicago. Without the benefit of much master planning or hand-holding by powerful centralized bureaucratic agencies, building owners in Los Angeles are free to become mad doctors to a Frankenstein's monster of a building. On a broader scale, this frontier-like freedom spawns a region of misfit Quasimodos driven by quick renovations for a resale, a handyman's bad hunch, a developer's notion of status and wealth, or a bland corporate branding strategy—all consequences of the city's persistent defiance against rules and good taste. Ours is a historically individualistic and corruption-fearing city. Los Angeles deliberately established a progressive political system in the 1920s (under the 1925 charter), and continues to be run by handfuls of councils and boards under the auspices of which many large-scale, impactful development projects stall or become watered down. Add an intentionally weak mayor (per the city's subsequent charters) and it's easy to see why a master-builder figure never emerged in Los Angeles.

3712 Veteran Avenue, Palms. Here's the thing—rent is high, jobs are difficult to get or keep right now, and on top of that, some struggling folks even have unlucky relatives or friends living on their couches. In general, living is hard, but it doesn't have to be this hard. This sad, grey stucco box recalls the hideous public housing projects of Stalinist Russia or an experiment in minimalism gone awfully wrong. But hundreds of apartments like this one dot the streets for a reason. In the sixties the city needed cheap, multi-family apartments that could be constructed quickly. Folks were moving to Los Angeles in hordes. Low-cost, freeway-adjacent housing was a must, and developers complied. Today, these same structures are home to immigrants, actors, and college students—the demographics of transience.

ParexLaHabra is Los Angeles's largest stucco provider, known locally as LaHabra stucco and established in Anaheim in 1926, the company today is a subsidiary to a group of international companies specializing in residential and commercial cement and acrylic-based finishing systems like EIFS—a product that most people refer to as stucco plaster. LaHabra stucco provides the thick and bumpy white or pastel-colored coating found encasing the majority of apartments, office buildings, homes, and strip malls in Southern California and the world. The easy, unremarkable depthlessness and forgetful, uniform nature of the material makes it ubiquitous, as it can essentially appear to be anything or nothing at all.

For an endlessly patched-up and tinkered-with home-improvement project or for a Franken-building, stucco is also the easiest, cheapest finish to be found. It's simple to apply, inexpensive, and its texture covers up any surface cracking over time. It weathers poorly when dirt collects in all that bumpiness and crevices, leaving a mangy look, and it covers almost every apartment building built since 1950 in Los Angeles.

The prolific "dingbat" apartment building (named in the early sixties by a visiting professor at UCLA named Francis Ventre) format is as follows: skinny steel columns hold up a rectangular-shaped box that fills out most of the lot's property. This makes space for cars underneath. The sides, back, and front are smooth and vast canvases of stucco (usually), but each is (always) distinguished by a small decorative flourish at the street-facing side—something to set itself apart from the others. A sprinkle of glittery tile (389 Palos Verdes Boulevard, Torrance), a terrifying towering wooden eagle (321 Pasadena Avenue, South Pasadena), occasionally even a fancy name in cursive font (at Adams Arms, 4316 Alla Road, Marina del Rey). But it was architectural historian Reyner Banham who anointed the phrase "dingbat," when making the connection between the car, postwar development, and the building type. "Wherever a freeway crosses one of the more desirable residential areas of the plains," he wrote, "it seems to produce a shift in land values that almost always leads to the production of dingbats." Primitively modern, streamlined, cheap, and calibrated to be the interlocking residential component of the highway and its technology—the car—dingbats, in all their manifold variations, became Los Angeles's vernacular. They were also the best thing to ever happen to LaHabra stucco's fledgling Anaheim storefront.

Best Western Royal Palace, 2528 S Sepulveda Boulevard, West Los Angeles. Most people drive past this snooze-fest unaware, but if you live in the neighborhood or are lodging here on vacation, you're sure to notice all the little things that make this Best Western just blah. The deeply inset, chocolate-tinted front windows help the rooms avoid the worst of the glaring afternoon sun, but that good intention leaves the remaining expanse of the facade flat and spare, cloaking it in over 5,000 square feet of pimply tan and faded peach paint. But just as mid-century highway motels re-created themselves by offering updated amenities to a new kind of cross-country traveler, this Royal Palace (and others like it) could evolve as a new type of urban, transit-hub hotel. A little bit of brainstorming could reveal new amenities for a light-rail-riding tourist and hotel visitor that also outwardly serves the public waiting at the adjacent Expo/Sepulveda light-rail stop. The giant, flat nothingness of this Best Western's facade is the ideal place to project movies, videos, or graphics for anyone whizzing by on their way eastward to downtown or going west towards the beach.

Locally based artist John Baldessari has said he lives in Los Angeles *because* it is ugly, adding that if he "lived in a great beautiful city, why would [he] do art?" In a 2010 interview, Baldessari elaborated, "I always have to be slightly angry to do art and LA provides that." Early in his career, Baldessari found inspiration by accident in fragments of discarded urban trash—specifically torn scraps of derelict billboards and rundown buildings. His goal was not to find the beauty in ugliness, nor to remedy it. Mining a nugget of potential from within the mechanics of ugly—that was Baldessari's angle. He looked for something to make a painting out of, an accidental manipulation of form, a new association, an intensification of an object's bold unattractiveness. He found ugliness to be a handy tool with which to dismantle the status quo. In this spirit, the visceral reaction to the city's failures—its chicken-bucket KFCs, corporate blahs, and Frankenstein hodgepodge of a San Gabriel retail center—can be a creative impetus too.

Buildings are made of lumber, bricks, nostalgic associations, historical references, personal style, and what was available on the shelf at Home Depot that one day back in 1994. Like a sunset, which can be interpreted (visually) as an orange glow, (scientifically) as light refracting through molecules of smog , and (poetically) as an ending, longing, or love—a building too is a knotted-up mess of meanings and reality which one can't pick apart to decipher between representation and physics, symbols and feelings. The assertion of ugly is an assertion of complete subjectivity with specifics per each individual. Take Spanish architect Rafael Moneo's Our Lady of the Angels cathedral downtown, for example. Haters think the hulking building that straddles the elevated slice of terrain between the 101 freeway and Temple Street looks like a windowless pile of baked terra-cotta blocks, or a prison. Boosters claim the cathedral's impressive interior heights reproduce the religious, architectural iconography of Rome and the Renaissance but with a modern simplicity and refinement that is achieved effectively, precisely because of the contrasting heavy and somber shell of its concrete walls. Both opinions are correct. Both are valid. Beauty is easy, but ugly is messy, confounding, fantastic, contradictory, complex, shifts with fashion, and anyone is free to name it.

Just as the dingbat or the developer's maxed-out condo complex evolved at the intersection of larger economies and infrastructures like a homegrown cottage industry and the highway system, ugly buildings will continue to evolve at similar crossroads. Seldom do we consider what infrastructures could potentially coalesce to create new housing systems or public places. Or, conversely, what disruptions or redistributions in the white noise of building stock could spark a new economic/infrastructure mash-up? How would the city be reimagined, using ugly buildings as fodder? This is a

conversation that's gone on exclusively in the academic realm of urban planners, architects, and critics. But on the sidewalk, rarely is it debated how the less-desirables of the urban fabric might be modified to help or hinder privacy, participation, or recreation. Consciously or not, this path of inquiry already occurs throughout Los Angeles on a daily basis, during daily routines. The scale of a Walmart's facade and its vast, flat parking lot on a hot August day obviously falls under the "doesn't work" category, as does searching for an apartment on Craigslist only to find overpriced crap—this points to a dearth of affordable, desirable housing. Scrutinizing what "works" in the buildings folks enjoy and what doesn't work in the ones collectively abhorred can only happen effectively in the place where residents and the city meet face-to-face—in buildings.

Indignation will only get so far with ugly buildings. Toiling a bit longer with our disgust of a pungent hue, a dated style, an aversion to something misshapen, or, on the other hand, a positive sense of nostalgia the building inspires, the acceptance of something less than beautiful because it has character and soul (the thirty-two-foot-tall Randy's donut at the intersection of Manchester and La Cienega Boulevards isn't a beautiful building, but is achingly loved in this regard), this exercise in reading the city is a gutsy move towards provocation. What arouses insecurity or superficiality? What makes us satisfied or uncomfortable? What prods the sense of territorial ownership and the desire to defend it? Go on Angeleno, take an unabashedly judgmental look at the city. Practice description. Offend someone. It's a good debate to have, and it lends to a broadened collective sentiment about our shared city. More importantly, it changes the way that "ugly" operates.

Eighty percent of Southern California's buildings are more than fifty years old; hence the need for renovations is coming quickly to Los Angeles. An inspired transformation that usurps the potential of ugly buildings will only be initiated by looking with an interested eye rather than with a disdainful one. The freewheeling methodology of urbanism set in motion by developers and archaic power players still makes for an atmosphere where the private sector can build whatever we want. Ugly buildings are now poised to enable the next incarnation of LA's slow-motion makeover: one with mixed-up boundaries, or a yet unnamable hybrid, a shortcut, a parking structure that's lived in or shopped in, an office park that's a gathering area *and* a public landmark, or a manipulated street facade that changes traffic patterns. Rethinking the psychological and physical space in the city through a reimagining of its most typical buildings is easy to conjure—just step out on the street and start looking.

It is well known that Los Angeles hosts a vast network of freeways. This graphic, constructed from a series of twenty-five freeway interchanges aligned on top of one another, each drawn at the same scale and compass orientation, is a meditation on navigating the tangle.

Freeway Jam

David L. Ulin

Sandro said highways primed us for a separation from place, from actual life. The autostrada replaced life with road signs and place names. A white background and black lettering. MILANO. A reduction, Sandro said, to nothing by names.

"No different than here," I said. "You might as well deplore all highways."

He conceded it was true, but said America was *supposed* to be a place ruined and homogenized by highways, that that *was* its unique character, crass and vulgar sameness.

"It's your destiny," he said, smiling, his eyes filling with cold light.

—Rachel Kushner, *The Flamethrowers*

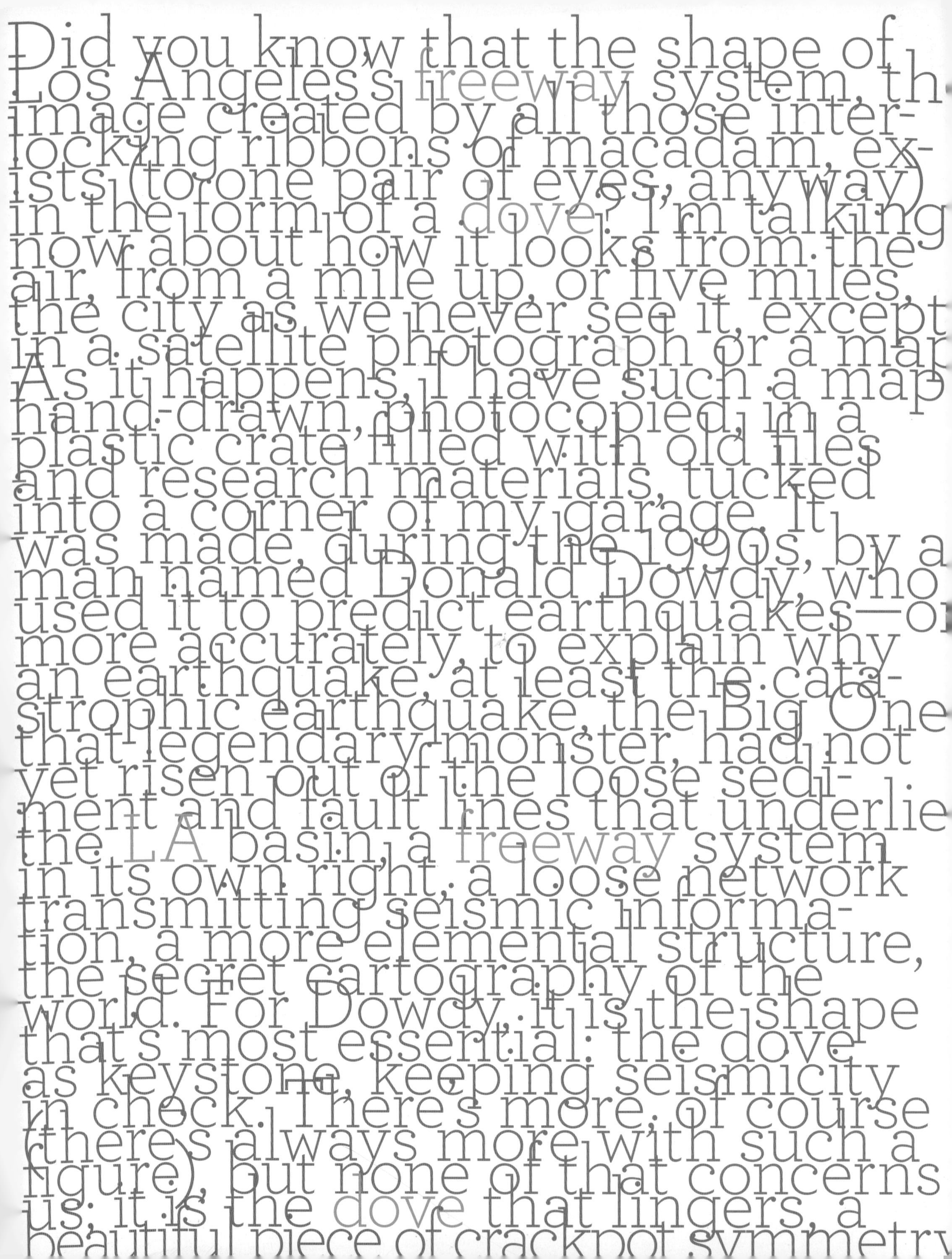

Did you know that the shape of Los Angeles's freeway system, the image created by all those interlocking ribbons of macadam, exists (to one pair of eyes, anyway) in the form of a dove? I'm talking now about how it looks from the air, from a mile up, or five miles, the city as we never see it, except in a satellite photograph or a map. As it happens, I have such a map, hand-drawn, photocopied, in a plastic crate filled with old files and research materials, tucked into a corner of my garage. It was made, during the 1990s, by a man named Donald Dowdy, who used it to predict earthquakes—or, more accurately, to explain why an earthquake, at least the catastrophic earthquake, the Big One, that legendary monster, had not yet risen out of the loose sediment and fault lines that underlie the LA basin, a freeway system in its own right, a loose network transmitting seismic information, a more elemental structure, the secret cartography of the world. For Dowdy, it is the shape that's most essential: the dove as keystone, keeping seismicity in check. There's more, of course (there's always more with such a figure), but none of that concerns us; it is the dove that lingers, a beautiful piece of crackpot symmetry

Did you know that the shape of Los Angeles's freeway system, the image created by all those interlocking ribbons of macadam, exists (to one pair of eyes, anyway) in the form of a dove? I'm talking now about how it looks from the air, from a mile up, or five miles, the city as we never see it, except in a satellite photograph or a map. As it happens, I have such a map, hand-drawn, photocopied, in a plastic crate filled with old files and research materials, tucked into a corner of my garage. It was made, during the 1990s, by a man named Donald Dowdy, who used it to predict earthquakes—or more accurately, to explain why an earthquake, at least the catastrophic earthquake, the Big One, that legendary monster, had not yet risen out of the loose sediment and fault lines that underlie the LA basin, a freeway system in its own right, a loose network transmitting seismic information, a more elemental structure, the secret cartography of the world. For Dowdy, it is the shape that's most essential: the dove as keystone, keeping seismicity in check. There's more, of course (there's always more with such a figure), but none of that concerns us; it is the dove that lingers, a beautiful piece of crackpot symmetry.

Dowdy is (or was) a crank in the grand tradition of Los Angeles cranks, a spiritual descendant of William Money, who in the 1870s predicted the destruction of San Francisco by fire and earthquake, a forecast that, in the words of California historian Philip Fradkin, "was bound to be realized sooner or later, given the two Bay Area earthquakes in the 1860s and the fact that most of San Francisco had burned to the ground six times between 1849 and 1851." Money lived in what Carey McWilliams once described as "a weird oval structure in San Gabriel, the approaches to which were guarded by two octagonal edifices built of wood and adobe"; he was, McWilliams continues, "the leading Los Angeles eccentric from 1841 until his death in 1880." We can't say the same about Dowdy who, had he not insisted on sending his map and other documents (many written in his own invented language and, thus, as indecipherable to the rest of us as a map with no known geographic reference points) to the Pasadena field office of the Unites States Geological Survey, would have remained wholly unrecognized, his particular pathology a private state of mind. And yet, like Money, Dowdy, or at least his paper trail, tells us something about LA's psychic space, the terrain in which reality and imagination meet. How fitting is it that in a city publicly defined by sprawl, by freeways, we might find a private counternarrative in which the most common of tropes (speed, diffusion, a sense not only that the center is not holding but that there is, indeed, no center to hold) becomes a metaphor for what is keeping us together, rather than what is shaking us apart.

I discovered Dowdy when I was writing a book about earthquakes; he offered a strategy for framing seismology through the lens of psychology or emotion, to see reflected in Southern California's unstable geology an instability of another kind. A decade later, though, I've come to think of him a little differently, as the harbinger of a city that is consistently misread. Such a sensibility was at the center of his map, with its hidden symmetries, hidden affinities, just below the surface of the earth. And they are at the center of Los Angeles's freeway system also, which remains, as it has ever been, not just a transportation matrix but also a metaphor. Forty-two years ago, in his book *Los Angeles: The Architecture of Four Ecologies,* Reyner Banham coined the word "Autopia," arguing that, "[a]s you acquire the special skills involved, the Los Angeles freeways become a special way of being alive." In Banham's view, this meant they were primarily public territory, LA's equivalent of the commons, an ecology (a word he used to indicate a structure or a set of structures, a way the city had of organizing itself) that allowed us to peer into the very essence of the place itself. "The first time I saw it happen," he writes, describing a common piece of freeway etiquette, "nothing registered on my conscious mind, because it all seemed so natural—as the car in front turned down the off-ramp of the San Diego freeway, the girl beside the driver pulled down the sun-visor and used the mirror on the back of it to tidy her hair. Only when I had seen a couple more incidents of the kind did I catch their import: that coming off the freeway is coming in from outdoors.... In part, this is a comment on the sheer vastness of the movement pattern of Los Angeles, but more than that it is an acknowledgment that the freeway system in its totality is now a single comprehensible place, a coherent state of mind, a complete way of life."

Banham, of course, was an outsider, a British architectural historian who, in the most literal sense imaginable, "went native" when he arrived in Southern California during the late 1960s. I admire him, not least because he was able to embrace LA on its own terms from the outset, a process that took much longer for me. I hated the city when I got here in the spring of 1991, refused, in some essential sense, even to see it as a city, refused to understand (or to accept) that it could cohere. I have a friend who learned Los Angeles by its freeways; throughout her first few years here, she would take long drives, out the 134, the 57, the 91, the 22, getting off at random exits, making her way home by local streets. This was before GPS was as common as air-conditioning, before navigation systems came standard and all you had to do to find a place was speak its name. My friend had to conjure up the city for herself, working her way back to where she started, always attuned to where was north, or west, the mountains or the sea. This reminds me of writer D. J. Waldie, riding every bus route, terminus to terminus, as a way of (re-)learning the city, an external map that becomes internalized...or the other way around. It reminds me of the project I undertook with my son on his birthday a number of years ago, to ride the Metro in its entirety: Red Line, Purple Line, Blue Line, Gold Line, Green Line (this was before the building of the Expo Line), Sierra Madre to Long Beach to North Hollywood to downtown LA. That we could do it in a single day was part of both the charm and the challenge, a way to bind the city, to make it comprehensible, to step inside (or *occupy*) it at a level we could comprehend. That we chose to enact this via light-rail says something about my son and me and how we think about, or interact with, Los Angeles, the kind of city we wish for it to be. Not all that different, then, from Donald Dowdy, with his fantasy of the freeways as a stabilizing influence, a vast mirror through which Southern California might reflect its deepest and most elemental self.

As for me, I avoided the freeways for as long as I could, trying to imagine a city in which they did not exist. The Los Angeles to which I was drawn (if, in fact, I was drawn to Los Angeles, which remains, even now, an open question) was the Los Angeles of Raymond Chandler: large sedans and Spanish-style bungalows, and those odd, archaic double lampposts, like the ones that span the First Street Bridge. I took any opportunity to walk, and when I had to drive, I kept to surface streets, telling myself I liked to watch the neighborhoods unfurl. That this was not untrue did not make it any less wishful, for what I was saying was that I wanted LA to be different, to be another city, to attend to the traditional hierarchies, to be an urban territory I understood. Born and raised in Manhattan, I thought of freeways through a single filter: as a way out of the city, which was not a place I had any desire to leave. I didn't live in the suburbs and I didn't want to; not for me, my friend's aimless freeway meanderings, since there was nothing, I thought, to discover there. The

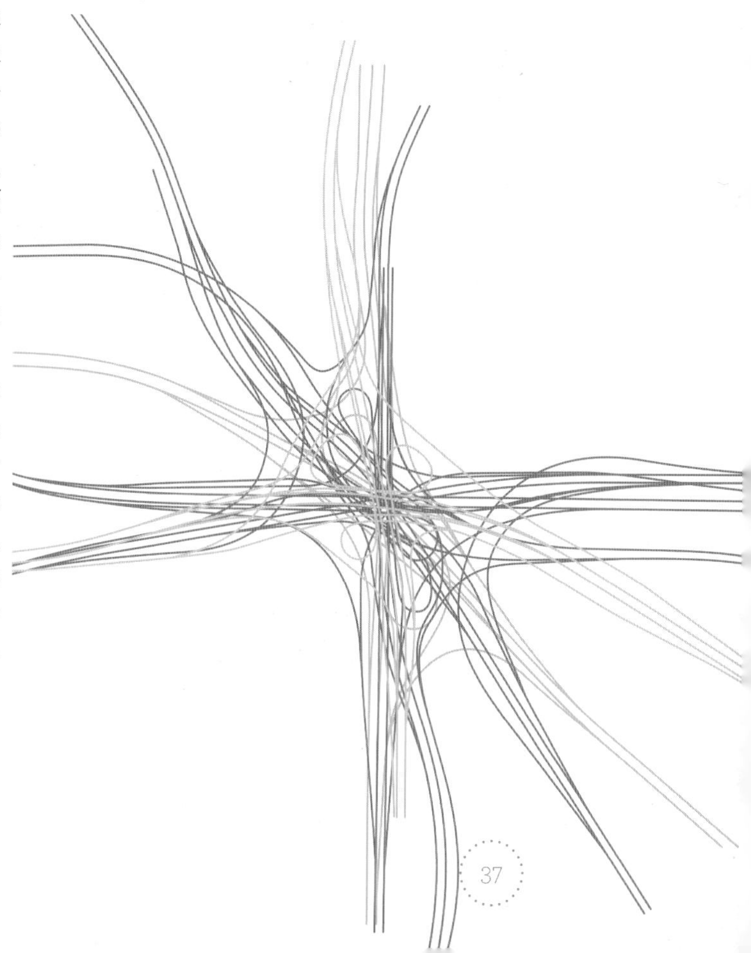

sprawl of Los Angeles did not excite me—rather, I was desperate to make it smaller, more immediate, the kind of city I had always known. "They say LA is large, but they lie," Carolyn See insists in her 1987 novel *Golden Days*, one of the first books I read on arrival. "It's true there are a zillion places no one in his right mind would live: Lakewood, Torrance, Brea, Compton, Carson, no one real lived there, any more than real people lived in those grey asphalt boxes that line the roads between New York's airport and its island. 'Real' L.A. had its thick, coiled root downtown, and on the east, little underground rootlets; obscure Mexican restaurants. Then a thin stem, the Santa Monica freeway, heading due west and putting out greenery, places in this western desert where you'd love to live—if things went right." Still, whatever small solace I might find in See's description, I also knew that LA was a complex system, that it could not be so easily contained. Free-floating, anxious, diffuse, it was evoked with particular acuity by Joan Didion, whose essay "Pacific Distances"—"A good part of any day in Los Angeles," she writes, "is spent driving, alone, through streets devoid of meaning to the driver, which is one reason the place exhilarates some people, and floods others with an amorphous unease"—gets very close to what it is about the place.

Didion's observation was embodied by the freeways, which were themselves essentially disembodied, or so it seemed to me. They floated above Los Angeles like a matrix, not so much bisecting neighborhoods as disregarding them, a superstructure erected on top of the existing city, both a part of it and apart. It didn't help that most were elevated, that on the 10, say, driving east out of downtown, what one saw were treetops, steeples, roofs, second and third stories, that the entire vista began at a height of thirty feet. Where were the streets in all of this, I wondered, where were the communities? How could we possibly know where we were when where we were was, in the most literal sense, imaginable, nowhere, a ribbon of road devoid of landmarks, reducing the cityscape to a succession of exits and on-ramps and the occasional cloverleaf? I was reminded of T. S. Eliot's caustic lines from "Choruses from 'The Rock'": "And the wind shall say: 'Here were decent godless people: / Their only monument the asphalt road / And a thousand lost golf balls.'" For Banham, this was a source of LA's peculiar charm, this vast and enduring mundanity, the idea that our grandest totems could be utilitarian, infrastructural, celebrating the beauty of the practical, the day-to-day. In *The Architecture of Four Ecologies,* he described the intersection of the 10 and the 405 as "a work of art, both as a pattern on the map, as a monument against the sky, and as a kinetic experience as one sweeps through it," and the entire freeway system as among "the greater works of Man."

And yet, as overstated as that sounds, as (let's be frank) ridiculous, Banham was, it turned out, onto something, although it took me a long time to figure out what. The tip-off came from the most mundane of freeway moments, albeit one quite different from the urban interactions Banham described. I was at the northern edge of Los Angeles, not far from Valencia, where the Antelope Valley Freeway sweeps into the 5. The interchange is named for Clarence Wayne Dean, the motorcycle cop who died there when his bike plunged through a gap in the collapsed roadway during the Northridge earthquake. What I'm referring to is no informal roadside memorial—no wooden crosses, no kachinas, no faded flowers bleached and waxy in the sun. No, this was official business, in much the same way as another city might name a street for a local hero, or a public square. My first reaction was, of course, judgmental: *Only in Los Angeles.* The more I thought about it, however, the more I came to realize this was the point precisely, that a man who'd spent his professional life on this stretch of freeway, like a beat (or even a kind of office) should be commemorated in the place where he had worked.

In *The Architecture of Four Ecologies,* Banham includes a telling map: a two-page spread delineating LA's freeways and airports, the rest of the city an empty blank. It's not unlike Dowdy's, in the sense that it eschews the details for a broader representation (Banham's intent is to frame an image of sprawl, of Los Angeles as quintessentially postmodern), although the real information is in what gets left out. Some of these omissions—the streets, the neighborhoods—are obvious, the standard elements LA is often said to lack. Yet others, let's call them the Clarence Wayne Dean Memorial Interchanges of the world, are even more important—not because they support the stereotype of a city defined less by its center than its lack of center, by transportation rather than by place, but because they contradict it, offering a tantalizing glimpse of the freeways as not imposed but integrated: a bit of three-dimensional, psychic space. Los Angeles is a metropolis built on the promise of fast movement over large distances. This is its peculiar manifest destiny, the victory of infrastructure over human scale. At the same time, it is equally a city of neighborhoods, which I had understood the first few months I'd lived here, had seen in the way one community segued into the next, a set of transition points only visible at foot speed. What if, then, we were to think about sprawl, about freeways, as neighborhoods in their own right? Or better yet, as a framework keeping all the other neighborhoods contained?

Such questions seem essential to me now, in a Los Angeles that no longer can fulfill the promises that so enthralled Banham half a century ago. The freeways don't work anymore, even as monuments: They are crowded, crumbling, under a constant siege of (re-)construction, despite overwhelming evidence that, as Nick Summers wrote recently in *Newsweek*, "demand from drivers tends to quickly overwhelm the new supply; today engineers acknowledge that building new roads usually makes traffic worse." Rush hour in LA has become a twenty-four-hour phenomenon, as the city draws ever closer to a state of terminal gridlock. Not long ago, I put on the live version of Jeff Beck's instrumental "Freeway Jam," recorded in 1976 during a concert tour I attended as a teenager, long before I ever came to Los Angeles. The first few seconds of the music left me stunned by recognition, not of the melody, per se, but of the sound effects: Beck on his guitar "talking" with keyboardist Jan Hammer, both of them creating sounds of honking cars.

Los Angeles is a metropolis built on the promise of fast movement over large distances.

Given that I've never liked the freeways, it would be easy to present this as an excuse to avoid them, to dream instead about a new LA. That's the impetus behind bike lanes and light-rail, which we now discuss with a Banham-esque edge of self-assurance, as if they represent the future of the city come to life. Still, while I'm as susceptible as anyone else to such ideas, they also make for an unlikely irony, which is that the more unusable freeways become, the more I find myself (at long last) using them—and in precisely the manner that was originally intended, as a mechanism for expanding the city, *my* city, a way of broadening my range. I work and teach downtown, in Riverside, Pasadena; I visit friends in Glendale and Eagle Rock. I wouldn't know how to find some of these places by surface streets if you held a gun to my head, and yet here I am. If Los Angeles is, first and foremost, an individualized landscape, one we come to understand and interpret initially by virtue of our own subjective movements through it, then I have, reluctantly, without quite ever having been aware of the transition, become an Angeleno, for whom the freeways are no longer imposition, exactly, nor anomaly, but rather a fundamental expression of the city we have built, both practical and metaphorical, a lens through which to see and not to see LA at once.

Here we find ourselves back in Donald Dowdy territory, in which the built environment takes on a set of meanings that we may not always recognize. A couple of years ago, I got involved in a project by the landscape photographer Michael Light: a book of Los Angeles images shot from the air, half by day and half by night. The idea was to destabilize our preconceptions of the city, to blur the line between the utilitarian and (let's say) the environmental, to read the structures—freeways, flood channels, overpasses, office towers—that we've come to take for granted not as assertions of our independence but rather as the opposite: expressions of just how much we rely on technology, on infrastructure and public projects, to survive. The photographs are stunning, at the same time intimate and distanced, depopulated but utterly human, if only in the sense of showing, in stark relief, what we've built in this place and how little any of it ultimately means. The implication of Light's work is that all of this will disappear, that it will return to the desert or to the ocean, that it will be swallowed up, inevitably, by the earth. It is a landscape so fantastic as to be unreal, if only we allow ourselves to visualize it on such terms. This, of course, has always been LA's driving tension, between what we can see and what we can never see, between the city that eludes us and the city that we know. How do we contain it? How do we make sense of such a place? We could do a lot worse, I'd suggest, than to believe that it is somehow held together by the network of the freeways, arranged into the image of a dove.

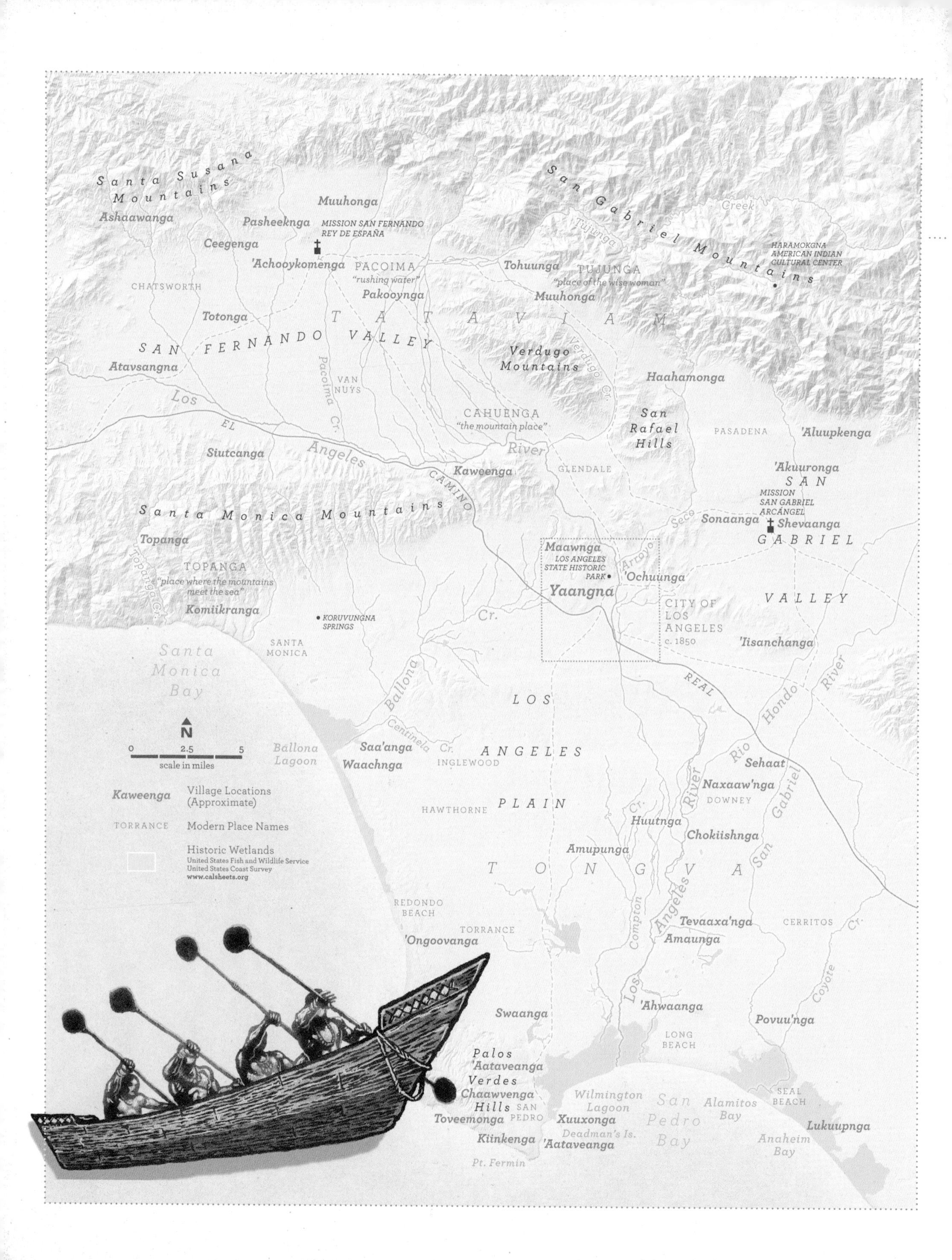

Santa Susana Mountains
San Gabriel Mountains
Muuhonga
Ashaawanga
Pasheeknga
MISSION SAN FERNANDO REY DE ESPAÑA
Ceegenga
'Achooykomenga
PACOIMA
"rushing water"
Tohuunga
TUJUNGA
"place of the wise woman"
Tujunga
Creek
HARAMOKGNA AMERICAN INDIAN CULTURAL CENTER
CHATSWORTH
Pakooynga
Muuhonga
Totonga
T A T A V I A M
SAN FERNANDO VALLEY
Verdugo Mountains
Verdugo Cr.
Atavsangna
Pacoima Cr.
VAN NUYS
Haahamonga
Los Angeles River
EL CAMINO REAL
CAHUENGA
"the mountain place"
San Rafael Hills
PASADENA
'Aluupkenga
Siutcanga
Kaweenga
GLENDALE
'Akuuronga
SAN GABRIEL VALLEY
MISSION SAN GABRIEL ARCÁNGEL
Santa Monica Mountains
Seco
Sonaanga
Shevaanga
Topanga
Maawnga
LOS ANGELES STATE HISTORIC PARK
Arroyo
'Ochuunga
TOPANGA
"place where the mountains meet the sea"
Topanga Cr.
Yaangna
Komiikranga
CITY OF LOS ANGELES c. 1850
KORUVUNGNA SPRINGS
Cr.
Santa Monica Bay
SANTA MONICA
'Iisanchanga
Ballona
LOS ANGELES PLAIN
Rio Hondo River
N
0 2.5 5
scale in miles
Ballona Lagoon
Saa'anga
Centinela Cr.
Waachnga
INGLEWOOD
Sehaat
Naxaaw'nga
DOWNEY
Kaweenga Village Locations (Approximate)
TORRANCE Modern Place Names
Historic Wetlands
United States Fish and Wildlife Service
United States Coast Survey
www.calsheets.org
HAWTHORNE
Cr.
Huutnga
River
Chokiishnga
San Gabriel
Amupunga
T O N G V A
REDONDO BEACH
Compton
Los Angeles
Tevaaxa'nga
CERRITOS
Cr.
TORRANCE
Amaunga
'Ongoovanga
Coyote
'Ahwaanga
Swaanga
Povuu'nga
LONG BEACH
Palos Verdes Hills
'Aataveanga
Chaawvenga
SAN PEDRO
Toveemonga
Wilmington Lagoon
Xuuxonga
San Pedro Bay
Alamitos Bay
SEAL BEACH
Lukuupnga
Kiinkenga
Deadman's Is.
'Aataveanga
Anaheim Bay
Pt. Fermin

Long before the arrival of Europeans in the late 1700s, a myriad of native Tongva tribal communities dotted the vast territory from Malibu to Orange County, east into Riverside County, and embracing the Southern Channel Islands. This map depicts only a fraction of the villages that once populated the area. Familiar place names like Tujunga and Cahuenga alert us to a deep, continuous history and connection with the land—a land once laced by a multitude of free-running surface streams, springs, and coastal wetlands before the flow of water was tamed and encased in concrete.

Coyote Tours

UNVEILING NATIVE LA

Cindi Moar Alvitre

The Coyote and the Water

A coyote, which, like all the rest of his kin, considered himself as the most austere animal on the face of the earth, not even excepting many himself, came one day to the margin of a small river. Looking over the bank, on seeing the water run so slow, he addressed it in a cunning manner, "What say you to a race?" "Agreed to," answered the water, very calmly. The coyote ran at full speed along the bank until he could hardly stand from fatigue, and on looking over the bank, saw the water running smoothly on.

He walked off with his tail between his legs and had something to reflect on for many a day afterwards.

—Gabrieleno story collected by Hugo Reid,
Los Angeles, 1852

To the cosmopolitan, Los Angeles is a city with no center and no history, or at least nothing one can visually connect to. The landscape is the work of a feeding frenzy of wily—"wile e"—urban planners, with scattered districts and neighborhoods, strewn-about high-rises, and an occasional green space, all resistant to the Athenian law of isonomy, or a unique center that defines a city. As one of the wealthiest cities on the planet, Los Angeles continues to lure the entrepreneurial coyote, always trying to outrun the river.

To the native—excuse me, native-native—the land is an ever-changing entity, sacred and alive, revealing herself to all those who speak her language. The indigenous people of the Los Angeles Basin have an intimate connection to the land, water, and creations—a silenced knowing of this city. These silenced knowings challenge perceptions of the present-day City of the Angels.

In the midst of the city of Los Angeles, and beyond, our roots are planted deep beneath the concrete of Beverly Hills mansions. Beneath the dreams of the Hollywood starlet lie the bones of our ancestors. In a city that maintains the largest Native American population in the nation, the Gabrieleno/Tongva remain the smallest tribal population amongst the diaspora of Native American tribes relocated to LA. As a "first contact tribe," we took the initial hits of European intrusion and our populations decreased almost to the point of extinction. And yet here we are, a multiplicity of Tongva communities throughout Los Angeles and Orange Counties, descendants of the survivors of an unspoken genocide that started with the arrival of Spanish missionaries in 1769.

The first nations people of the Los Angeles Basin covered a significant expanse of territory, reaching north to Malibu, traveling into the southern sectors of Orange County and east into Riverside County, including the four Southern Channel Islands. If you ask what we call ourselves, you will receive a number of responses that reflect geography and generational preferences, including Gabrieleno, Mission Indians, Shoshoneans, Tongva, Moompetem, and others. As confusing as it sounds, it actually illustrates that there was a confederation of tribal communities, not a single tribe. You identified yourself based on your village, so if you were from the community of Puvu, the sacred center that marks the emergence of human beings, you would be called a Puvu-vit, individually, or Puvu-vitem, collectively. Add your clan identity, your personal name, and your married name, and there you have it. Pretty simple, right?

Language is at the heart and soul of a worldview. With no fluent speakers, remembering a language relies heavily on the support of other tribes that have experienced similar challenges and linguists who documented the language. Efforts to connect and renew the Tongva language are very much alive, with at least two communities fully engaged in the language revitalization process. Will the Tongva community ever reach a level of complete fluency? As one language learner commented, "We may never reach a level of complete fluency, but to be able to pray and do ceremony in our language is most important."

Chumash of the north, and the Ajachemem of the south. Yet we are all connected by the navigable paths of the water that emerge from the mountain snows, overflow into the arroyos, feed into the Los Angeles River, merge with the San Gabriel River, and travel along the coastal communities and beyond to the Southern

Creating a cartography of coyote space is an act of resistance.

As unrecognized tribes, we are like ancient rivers prior to industrialization: elusive and without center. We exist in coyote space, an active, complex, and sometimes tragic domain. Controversy and curiosity abound on those rare occasions when we emerge as vessels of history and collide with the modern world!

Creating a cartography of coyote space is an act of resistance. Coyote space is about making visible what others cannot, or choose not, to see. Arbitrary political boundaries become meaningless. When they speak of the tribes who lived within what is now the region of Los Angeles, anthropologists separate the Gabrieleno/Tongva from the Tataviam in the east, the

Channel Islands. Water is the lifeblood of the people, and we cannot separate the people from each other, or from the nature, for we are all one and the same.

On the surface, a guided tour of a Tongva LA extends beyond the rigid boundaries of the romanticized California Missions and sheds light on towns like Tujunga, Cahuenga, Pacoima, Cucamonga, Topanga, Azusa, and other cities whose names end with "ngna" or "na," which indicate one of hundreds of pre-contact communities, each with their own creation narrative. Tujunga, for example, is a small community in the San Fernando Valley, nestled along the San Gabriel Mountains. Translated from Gabrieleno/Tongva, it is the place of tu'xuu, the old woman, where an immense grandmother monolith has guarded the canyons since time immemorial. Some say she represented a mother earth spirit. As a child, my family regularly took weekly drives and long walks along old trails to visit family. Peering into the deep, clear ponds along Tujunga Canyon was never a simple act when you'd been warned of water spirits that could lure you into the bubbling waters, drawing you into a cosmological abyss that was forever. What? I could never come back?

We can only begin to imagine the world of our ancestors. Theirs is a topography that challenges the perceptions of those educated within the Western paradigm. The Tongva see a dimensional space with an upper world, middle world, and under world, all occupied by beings that protect the precarious ecology of their realm. Humans, for example, occupy the middle world and are the last of the ancestral dreamtime, created not to control the hunukvitem, the pre-humans, but to take care of all that existed prior to us.

Even for the most recent generations, gathering acorns for weewish in expansive oak groves, harvesting acorns and berries in lush canyons, hunting deer in the thickets of the local mountains, and collecting medicine plants along the creeks and rivers are all perceived as the obligations of stewards of the land. This stewardship bands us together to protect the sacred urban landscape. Our elders define their very identities by environmental markers, and they become disgruntled and frustrated when villages and trails are replaced with streets and neighborhoods that have no resemblance to their memories of the land. My heart recalls the words of my father when he would see these changes. Heartbroken, he would say, "I want to go home."

Locating Yaangna

> Ultimately, it is about the land. As the original people of the land, we feel our mother earth. Her health reflects our health...if she is suffering, so are we.
>
> —Craig Torres,
> descendant of Yaangna

Where is home? An attempt to map Tongva LA is a futile act unless people are brave enough to listen to a tragic history.

Yaangna was the principal ancestral village that moved along the Los Angeles River for countless generations, before the water was confined and silenced within a concrete sarcophagus, separating the people from that which gives life. In pre-contact times people moved slowly, with the seasons, the food, and, ultimately, the water. Colonization and missionization accelerated the pace of relocation as native people tried to outrun the colonizers, always clinging to the river. After the secularization of the Missions, native people were cultural prisoners-of-war, released from generations of confinement into a permanently altered existence. Yaangna became a refugee camp for tribal families seeking some sense of tradition. Its inhabitants also took in relatives from the islands, the Pipimares, after they were forcibly relocated from Santa Catalina and other Channel Islands from 1816–1820.

The final blow to historic Yaangna took place in 1847, after it had been relocated multiple times from one side of the river to the other. On a cold fall evening in 1847, the last generation of Yavitem were turned out onto Calle de los Negros, the place of the dark ones, after their village was razed to the ground by the Los Angeles City Council. Since 1836, the Regidor of the Committee on Zanjas had received complaints like this one: "[residents] were compelled to drink water from the main zanja [where] Indians wash and bathe." Offended by the Indians' wildness and use of the water in the zanja, citizens of the Pueblo finally succeeded in extinguishing any displays of tradition…or sharing of common water.

Secularization of Mission San Gabriel had had dire consequences, and Yaangna had been the last traditional holdout of indigenous refugees, disenfranchised souls displaced by settler colonialism. The land was no longer the open expanse that had sustained the people. The abundance of steelhead shimmering in the river, the round hillsides dotted with oak trees and cottonwoods, the environment of subsistence—all were replaced by geometric layers of brick and mortar. Indian Mary was left to wander the streets.

The last documented location of Yaangna likely stood on a site that is now marked by nothing more than a center divider on the Hollywood Freeway at the intersection of North Alameda and Aliso Street. Yaangna may be buried beneath a gentrified LA, but somehow its soul continues to travel through the city. Craig Torres and I were leaving the city after a late-night Ancestor ceremony at the FarmLab. Unfamiliar with the city, we found ourselves driving down narrow, dimly lit side streets, where we saw hundreds of homeless people, refugees of economic and social disenfranchisement, darkened silhouettes seeking respite from the chill of winter cold along the greasy pavement. It was a haunting déjà-vu moment: our families experienced this 166 years ago. Time, unresolved intergenerational grief, and the present collided. These memories cling to the soul and are often triggered by the human tragedy and suffering that persists in Los Angeles. Los Angeles has an old soul, one that few will recognize and fewer will experience.

Fields of Hopi Corn: FarmLab

In the history of native Los Angeles, significant individuals have become iconic in their actions and their suffering. At the top of that list is Toypurina, a young woman and sabia, one with exceptional wisdom, from the village of Japchibit. In 1785, at the tender age of twenty-five, she, along with others (including a neophyte named Nicolas José), reacted to the colonial takeover of their homeland by planning to take over Mission San Gabriel. The revolt was intercepted after one of the guards was forewarned of the plot. Punishment was doled out: the men received lashes and Toypurina, the sole woman, was exiled to Monterey, removed from her homeland forever.

Toypurina has become an icon to many, including young Chicanas, who see her as a champion of historic brown feminism in the City of the Angels. Her imagined portrait has been incorporated into neighborhood murals and stenciled in sacred black, white, and red by clandestine guerrilla artists throughout the city.

Generations later, her few descendants have traveled south, seeking to reconnect to their ancestral homeland. Linda, a descendant granddaughter of Toypurina, journeyed from San Juan Bautista to meet members of the Tongva community and participate in a ceremony on the land at the FarmLab, acknowledged by many Tongva as a center of revitalization and the closest connection to the original Yaangna and the Los Angeles River.

Located just north of Chinatown, the FarmLab, or Anabolic Monument, is a ceremonial center and cultural phenomenon in the northern sector of the city. Now part of the Los Angeles State Historic Park, the thirty-two-acre site ("The Cornfield" in the local vernacular) was an industrial brownfield until artist Lauren Bon, along with generous community members, removed decades of industrial waste and toxic soils, replaced them with cleansed earth, and saturated the landscape with feathery tassels of hand-planted Hopi corn.

Those who had the honor of meeting Linda hung on her every word as she shared details and thoughts about her grandmother's traumatic experience and expulsion from her homeland by the Spanish courts. Linda's words were a recognition of shared experiences of the land.

If you sit on the land long enough, and quietly enough, you will hear her speak. And if you build a ceremonial lodge in the midst of downtown, in the middle of a cornfield...you will hear the water speak, a once fluid voice now permanently confined in a cement vault. Her voice moves through the hearts of the lodgepoles and the willows gathered along a clandestine creek in Eagle Rock. The sacred volcanic rocks crackle as the heat rises against the heavy canvas tarp, seeping into the lodgepoles, reviving the life of the wood, rehydrating an ancient memory absorbed from the river, where the water of Yaangna is confined. She wants to be free, she speaks to those who will listen.

Haramokngna: Retracing an Ancient Path out of the Industrial Wilderness

Ancient foot trails became roads, which became freeways, erasing the original footsteps of the ancestors as they traveled to gather, harvest, exchange, and visit with their relatives in the mountains. I envy the health of the ancestors, especially the runners, as they made their way up the mountainous trails sustained only by water and chia seed. I can see their deerskin pouches bouncing along, dropping seeds that will perhaps successfully propagate, marking the trail and providing sustenance to the people.

Runners travel in both directions, to the mountains and to the ocean. At the head of the Arroyo Seco is the site of Hahamongna. A winding trail welcomes the visitor, now earth citizen, to refocus and embrace the natural legacy of the land. Travel further and deeper into the mountain forest along the San Gabriel Trail, or the Angeles Crest Highway, and you will come upon Haramokngna, a living cultural center nestled atop Mount Wilson. It is a point of intersection for the five tribes of the San Gabriel Mountains—the Tongva, Tataviam, Serrano, Kitanemuk, and Chumash—where tribal communities come together to harvest pine nuts, teas, or medicine plants that grow at higher elevations. Deep, wintery snowdrifts and raging forest fires are reminders of the

delicate balance of life and destruction. We are reminded to both give life and take life.

At Haramokngna, traditions have been revived, demonstrating the resilience of the people. If you visit on a day when they are cooking, your Angeleno palate will be transformed. Thanks to the ethnobotanical wisdom of native educators such as Barbara Drake, Abe Sanchez, and Craig Torres, a Chia Café of sorts is at your service. The native food is a joyous choreography of yucca blossoms, chia seed, deer stew, and mesquite tortillas, and it proudly announces a return to healthful ways of living and the shedding of colonial byproducts that have contributed to First World diseases, such as the diabetes, hypertension, and heart disease that have devastated Native American people. Yucca blossoms, anyone?

Moomat Ahiko: Breath of the Ocean

> One day the fish were discussing ways to create more room for themselves as their number had become so great. Along came a large fish carrying the rock Toshaawt, which he broke open. In the center was a ball filled with gall, which emptied into the water. Soon the stream became salty and bitter and it overflowed the earth to become the present oceans.
>
> —Geronimo Boscana, *Chinichich,* 1933:31–32

Historically, the Los Angeles River converged with the San Gabriel and continued on to the sacred center of the Tongva world, Puvungna, and on to the Southern Channel Islands, said to the be land of the oldest and most powerful of all Southern California tribes. Coastal zones continue to be active cultural regions where Tongva communities have renegotiated urban space to create living cultural centers such as at Puvungna, a ceremonial center now located at California State University, Long Beach. And every once in a while, ancestors reveal themselves in dreams.

Moomat Ahiko is my story. On one of those hot summer nights when sleep is a rare commodity, my deepest longing for the ocean called an island warrior into my dreamtime. The shimmer of abalone beads caught my glance. His enormous brown shoulders were embedded in granite and soil, each a peak of the Santa Ana Mountains. His wet, black hair was pulled up on his deep burrowed forehead and his eyes were closed in meditation. Lava spewed out of his third eye, the sacred space between the eyebrows. My children were playfully tossing chunks of lava to each other. I watched in disbelief, well aware as a single mother of four that exhaustion plays tricks on the mind, even in dreamtime. Now there was a vast body of water filled with wooden planked canoes, and in each of the canoes were family and community members. We began to sing, counting each stroke as we paddled towards the warrior. And when we were all in unison, the warrior opened his eyes, the lava stopped, and the mountains opened like a magnificent door to reveal Catalina Island. We pulled the water, stroke by stroke, towards the island. I woke up, stunned and in disbelief, wondering what it all meant. Was it a dream or a vision?

I awakened not knowing how something so magnificent could be real. Weeks later, a gentleman who was knowledgeable about Southern California Indian maritime culture called with a generous offer to build a ti'at. Moomat Ahiko, Breath of the Ocean, was born, the first traditional Tongva plank canoe in over 150 years. She has become an icon and an inspiration to the Coastal and Island tribal communities; maritime tradition was considered to be extinct. As I write this, the Chumash are preparing to launch their tomols and journey to Limuw (Santa Cruz Island), their ancestral homeland off the Santa Barbara coast. It is a joyous time to inspire and be inspired. The revival of maritime culture has also renewed relationships with Pacific Island communities that share this vast expanse of sacredness.

The legacy of Yaangna and the silenced Los Angeles River have played out for well over two hundred years, through successive onslaughts of Spaniards, Catholic missionaries, Mexican rancheros, and Yankees. Seemingly all roads lead to Yaangna, like rivers to the ocean. Yaangna continues as a refugee space in the northern sectors of the city where immigrants, cosmopolitans, and guests seek acceptance and a place to call "home." As a historic site, she remains multiplicious and undefined. Yet there are those who come to know her inclusiveness in revived sectors such as the FarmLab. Her descendants work to restore her reputation, to make her visible and free of rusting colonial memory. This happens in increments, just as the native plant garden at the Anabolic Monument, perpetually in a state of transformation, becomes medicine for all. The FarmLab and Harakmongna have become ceremonial centers of contemporary Los Angeles, providing sustenance to refugees from many tribes. It is all we have as a landless people, but we share.

Coyote has found his way into the city once again, doing his magic and admitting to his own foolishness. How do the Tongva navigate through life? Look up at grandmother moon, look down at mother earth, and always thank the water.

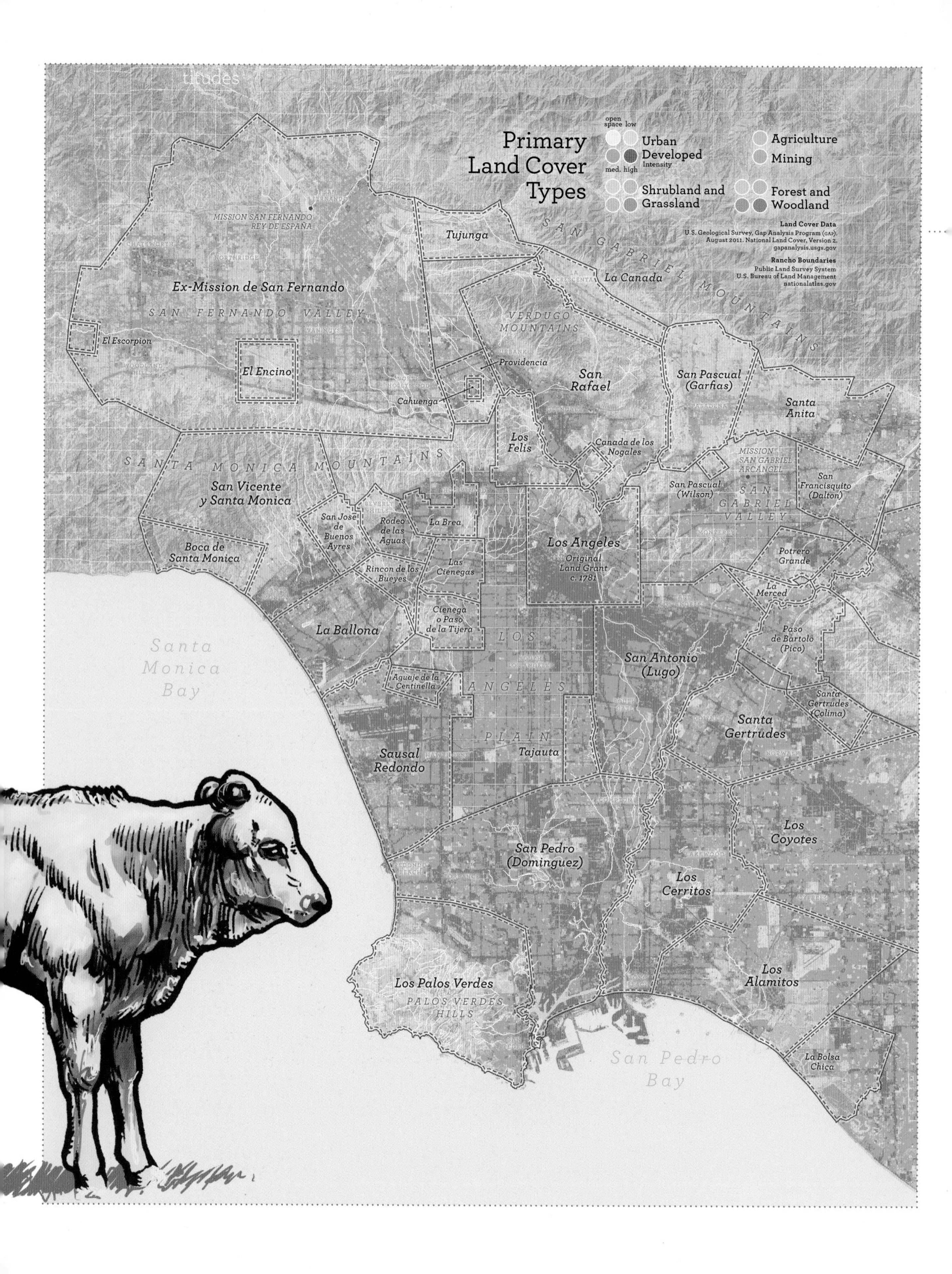

Primary Land Cover Types
open space
low
Urban
Developed
Intensity
med.
high
Agriculture
Mining
Shrubland and Grassland
Forest and Woodland
Land Cover Data
U.S. Geological Survey, Gap Analysis Program (GAP). August 2011. National Land Cover, Version 2. gapanalysis.usgs.gov
Rancho Boundaries
Public Land Survey System
U.S. Bureau of Land Management
nationalatlas.gov
MISSION SAN FERNANDO REY DE ESPAÑA
Tujunga
SAN GABRIEL MOUNTAINS
La Canada
Ex-Mission de San Fernando
SAN FERNANDO VALLEY
VERDUGO MOUNTAINS
El Escorpion
El Encino
Providencia
San Rafael
San Pascual (Garfias)
Cahuenga
Santa Anita
Los Felis
Canada de los Nogales
MISSION SAN GABRIEL ARCÁNGEL
SANTA MONICA MOUNTAINS
San Vicente y Santa Monica
San Pascual (Wilson)
SAN GABRIEL VALLEY
San Francisquito (Dalton)
San Jose de Buenos Ayres
Rodeo de las Aguas
La Brea
Los Angeles
Original Land Grant c. 1781
Boca de Santa Monica
Las Cienegas
Potrero Grande
Rincon de los Bueyes
La Merced
Cienega o Paso de la Tijera
La Ballona
LOS ANGELES PLAIN
Paso de Bartolo (Pico)
Santa Monica Bay
San Antonio (Lugo)
Aguaje de la Centinella
Santa Gertrudes (Colima)
Santa Gertrudes
Sausal Redondo
Tajauta
Los Coyotes
San Pedro (Dominguez)
Los Cerritos
Los Palos Verdes
PALOS VERDES HILLS
Los Alamitos
San Pedro Bay
La Bolsa Chica

In the spaces now occupied by strip malls, freeways and suburban housing tracts, a mere 150 years ago Los Angeles was roamed by vast herds of longhorn cattle. They were the primary business of Southern California's early Spanish and Mexican land grants—or "ranchos" as they were known—labeled on this map. Today, Angelenos could hardly be further removed from the rancho world of windswept prairies and lowing, grazing cattle. Envisioned as assorted cuts of meat, this map whets the historical imagination and allows us to contrast the natural and built environment of contemporary Los Angeles with its pastoral heritage.

The Bovid Metropolis

Teddy Varno

In January of 1776 two hundred-odd head of longhorn cattle reached the fledgling Mission San Gabriel Arcángel on the tree-scarce prairie that would in time become Los Angeles. They came unto this land as strangers, alien pilgrims driven by seven cowherds at the behest of the Spanish crown from the arid rangelands of southern Arizona across five hundred miles of cold desert to California. Down the trail they marched in rough columns, swaying in jerks left-to-right-to-left with their long necks craning forward and their heads bobbing up and down, strange stocky filthy blocks of muscle and sinew held aloft by wobbly thin peg legs, the bulls and the cows both sporting the sharp thin horns upon their heads that gave the breed its name. Beneath the California sun, warm even in mid-winter, the longhorns' hides of tan and roan and umber stood in stark contrast with the deep green of the rain-soaked hillsides. The silence of the open prairie was broken now at their arrival by the clumping and clomping of hundreds of hooves upon packed earth and the long drawn *moo* of a young nursing mother, a *vaca parida,* in search of her calf. As the herd moved toward its ultimate destination it stamped the ground flat and left behind a trail of fly-specked warm plops of cow shit.

Theirs had been no easy passage. The trail from Tubac, a small presidio outpost along the Santa Cruz River in frontier Arizona, had been long and harsh and the nights frigid; shivering young calves died from exposure when howling winds roared across the flat desert. As one punishing day followed another, the longhorns looked for opportunities to escape from the herd; they hid in the underbrush at the richer grazing spots and remained silent, hoping to be overlooked. At one lonesome bog by the side of the trail over fifty of the heavy animals became hopelessly mired in the mud, and there they were abandoned, lowing in desperation as they sank deeper and deeper into the muck. As arduous as the trek was, however, it was typical of the longhorns' experience of this New World. The first Iberian cattle had arrived with Columbus at Hispaniola in 1493, and their descendants followed in the wake of the conquistadores who landed on the Gulf Coast of Mexico two decades later. The cow and the bull became integral elements of the Spanish invasion of the Americas; they would be unleashed upon lush grassy landscapes where with minimal human guidance they would flourish and multiply, and then when the time was right they would be driven from these lands against their will across unrelenting barren terrains to reach the next prairie frontier ripe for colonization. Wherever they went they trampled the land and voraciously devoured the native flora, consuming too the croplands of indigenous peoples who were astonished by the immense herds that soon stalked the countryside. The longhorns thrived on the plains of the Mesa del Norte, the Mexican grasslands to the east of the Sierra Madre Occidental and to the west of the dry Chihuahuan Desert. By the eighteenth century, they had stalked the provinces of Sonora and Sinaloa in northern Mexico, and at the same moment that our intrepid herd was crossing into California its cousins to the east had begun to run feral across the plains of Texas. These were beasts built for motion, continent-crossers that had learned to adapt repeatedly to new environs and changing conditions. To them, Southern California would have been no final destination, but only a way station of their perpetual migration.

As the party arrived at the Mission San Gabriel Arcángel, the cowherds who accompanied the cattle could not help but be struck by the complete isolation of this new frontier from anything they would have known as civilization. To the east and to the north loomed imposing mountain ranges that cut the plains off from easy or regular access to the outside world. To the west and to the south the land ended at the cold waters of the Pacific Ocean; there was but one spot where ships might moor, at San Pedro Bay, and this bleak rocky coast was over thirty miles from the mission. There was as yet no pueblo of Los Angeles—that wouldn't be founded until 1781—and the native Tongva lived in numerous small villages scattered along the rivers and wide creeks of the region. Southern California was over 1,500 miles from the viceroy of New Spain in Mexico City, a remote territory on the furthest-flung fringes of empire.

To the longhorns, it was a veritable smorgasbord. Set free to roam and graze at leisure after their long journey, they discovered their El Dorado. All across the prairie were dense clumps of needlegrasses rising two to four feet from the earth, their green leaves and golden seed heads undulating in the pleasant breeze. Beneath them grew thick carpets of clover, wild onions, great bursts of deergrass plumes, and clusters of stems of California melic. Amidst this sea of green sprouted wildflowers of diverse color and hue: the fleshy lavender of the escobita, the brilliant yellow of goldfields and tidy tips, the light purple of the bluedick, and the pale moonglow of baby blue eyes. The heavy cattle had to step gingerly, for these verdant fields were pocked by the subterranean tunnels of gophers and ground squirrels, and with the exception of an occasional deer they found no herbivores with which they had to compete for the land's abundance; the herds of pronghorn antelope that had once roamed these plains fled skittishly upon seeing the newcomers. When they tired of what the prairie had to offer, the longhorns could climb into the foothills of the mountains, where they could graze on sagebrush, buckwheat, and chaparral, or they could lounge beneath sycamores and willows along the San Gabriel or Los Angeles Rivers.

The cattle took to this gentle new land. They became accustomed to its annual rhythm, to its rainy winters, when the grasses and flowers bloomed in one great efflorescence and the plants scattered their seeds across the landscape, and to its dry summers, through which those tough seeds lay dormant in the earthy clay and waited for the first rains of autumn to trigger their germination. Seasons passed and calves were birthed, and as the founding generation of longhorns shuffled off this mortal coil they took with them the memory of the arduous trail and of life beyond the Los Angeles prairie. Generation begat generation, the longhorns multiplied beyond the most hopeful expectations of the missionaries, and by 1820 there were hundreds of thousands of head of cattle roaming the open range of Southern California. The bulls, left uncastrated by ranch hands to encourage the rapid growth of the herds, aggressively staked their harems and threatened passersby who wandered too close with a goring. The bovid colonists of Southern California had claimed the land. They outnumbered the human colonists by several orders of magnitude; the pueblo of Los Angeles was a small island surrounded by a sea of cattle.

It was out of this new pastoral landscape that the rancho emerged. The first ranchos in Los Angeles were granted by the military governor of Alta California to three of his presidial soldiers in 1784. Beyond these, however, land concessions in California remained infrequent during Spanish rule. Settlers whom the crown felt it could trust were scarce, and beyond feeding the missionaries and their native converts there was little that could be done with the hordes of cattle in this province so remote from the center of empire. All this changed in 1822 when Mexico secured its independence from Spain and, freed from the mother country's mercantilist policies, opened California to international trade. The rancheros of Los Angeles could now skin the animals that filled their land and trade their hides and their tallow, their rendered fat, to the merchants of New England and of Peru, whose seaborne vessels began to appear with increasing frequency off the coast at San Pedro Bay. Eager to people its frontier province, the Mexican government divvied up the vast tracts of grazing land that had once belonged to the Catholic missions and liberally distributed them to a host of new petitioners.

Without reliable labor, however, the ranchero could not wrangle the stubborn, near-feral longhorns that wandered his grant. To tame these herds, he depended entirely on the vaquero, a mounted horseman—a master of the riata, the lasso—who with his equestrian virtuosity could win the trust of the cattle and could guide them en masse with the lightest of touches around the prairie. The vaquero tradition originated on the Iberian Peninsula and followed the longhorns across the Atlantic and into Mexico. In Southern California, where Hispanic settlers were few in number, it was the Tongva in the missions who learned to ride and to lasso, for skilled vaqueros could leave the rigid supervision of the priests and pursue more autonomous lives on the open range. This alarmed Spanish authorities, who had faced the fierce horse warriors of the Apache in Arizona, but given the limited options in Los Angeles they reluctantly consented to the arrangement. Horses were plentiful on the prairie; the region's first pioneers had introduced them like the longhorns to this land, and now bands of wild horses, so numerous that authorities sometimes hired exterminators to prevent them from depleting the grasslands, circulated among the cattle. Each rancho had its own caballada, its stable of broken and trained mounts, without which the work of the vaquero would have been impossible.

The boundaries that legally separated the ranchos were generally indistinct, but this did not concern the rancheros because those boundaries existed in reality only on paper. The longhorns grazed as one mass commune, and so marks of property were not etched in ink on paper but rather were burned into the very flesh of the animals. To maintain this property regime, each summer, at the close of the rainy season, the ranchos held rodeos to inventory their stock. Year after year, these roundups were held at the same locations, always some prominent spot on the landscape such as a lone oak or a towering boulder, and in time the older longhorns gained a memory of what these spots meant, so that all the vaqueros had to do to initiate the rodeo was to steer the elders to the gathering place and wait for the young to follow behind. The vaqueros would pass among the animals there to inspect their *fierros,* the rancho brands burned into their hips to designate ownership, and with tally sticks they would make a count of the size of their herd. Neighboring rancheros sent their agents as well to collect errant stock that had wandered off during the year. Those maverick animals that lacked a brand, the *orejanos,* could be legally claimed by the rancho holding the rodeo, their hips soon seared by a white-hot branding iron, while young calves birthed during the previous year, still too delicate to endure the painful procedure, had *señals,* distinctive shapes, carved out of the pinnas of their ears.

With the count complete, the ranchero would now reap his annual harvest. Some of the cattle, especially those aged beyond breeding, would be lead away from the others and marched a considerable distance from the rodeo gathering place, for longhorns were spooked by the scent of fresh blood and the sight of the *matanza,* the slaughter, and it would not do for those slated to live to witness what was about to unfold for the others. Those others would soon enough find themselves before an unfamiliar corral and here they might meet any of a number of fates. The lucky would quickly have their skulls bashed in by heavy clubs. Others would have their vitals pierced by sharp lances. Some might be walked to an open field where they would meet their death by *desjarretadera:* while one vaquero distracted the animal, another vaquero on horseback would trot past from behind and swipe the beast's hamstring with a crescent-shaped hocking blade affixed to a long pole, sending it with a crash and a scream and spasms into the earth, where the first vaquero would swiftly leap upon its shoulders to deal a lethal strike with a knife to the spinal cord. Around the slaughtering pens of the large ranchos thousands of horned skulls bleached beneath the sun.

After the longhorn was dispatched, its carcass was hoisted upon the tall beams of the corral, where it dangled vulnerably in the air. Its hide was sliced and its skin was forcefully yanked from its musculature. The soft fat tissue that connected skin to muscle, the only fat in the carcass that could become lard edible to humans, was carefully collected. The hide was pegged to the ground hair-down and upon its moist side were piled its meat, innards, and offal, all now aswarm with flies. The longhorns were thin, rangy animals built for survival rather than for fattening; their beef was stringy and lacked flavor. The average steer would yield around fifty pounds of meat, and this would be cut into thin strips, submerged in brine, and hung out in the sun for almost a week to become *carne seca,* a dry, tough, salty black jerky that was omnipresent in early Los Angeles and that could last for weeks or months. The two hundred pounds or so of fat that dropped out of the average carcass would be collected into leather hampers and later processed into tallow, a necessary ingredient for the industrial production of soap and candles. Oxcarts laden with dried hides and skins bulging with tallow creaked slowly from the ranchos down to San Pedro, where the merchant firms collected the commodities in rugged warehouses before shipping them around Cape Horn to the factories of Boston.

By 1848, when the administration of California passed into the hands of the US government, almost the entire Los Angeles prairie had become open range grazing land. Nearly every patch of earth that could bear grass from the Santa Ana Mountains west to the Pacific Ocean, from the San Gabriel Mountains south to San Pedro Bay, belonged to the longhorn. Where today we find asphalt and strip malls we would then have found cattle silently foraging with steely determination, young cows nursing their calves in the shade, bulls locking horns to do battle over mates. At Santa Monica Bay the rows of cowhides pegged into the sand to dry in the cool Pacific breeze resembled beach blankets spread beneath the high noon sun.

Within two decades, this would all be gone. The annexation of California by the United States had no immediate and direct impact on the grazing practices of Southern California's ranchos, but the position of the region within the wider world changed immediately when, four hundred miles to the north, gold was discovered near Sutter's Mill. Overnight, Los Angeles shed its remoteness. The rancheros paid the discovery little mind at first—their association with the northern part of the state had always been weak—but the gold drew prospectors and the prospectors had to be fed and as ship after ship landed in San Francisco, as the camps mushroomed around the bonanza mines, the price of beef in Northern California soared, so that soon the more enterprising fellows among the Los Angeles rancheros began to ask themselves why they were still slaughtering cattle for their three-dollar hides when in the meat markets of Sacramento a good stocky steer might sell for seventy-five dollars and even a tiny calf might fetch as much as twenty-five dollars. In San Pedro, inquiries were made with the Yankee seamen, but packing a vessel with obstreperous longhorns and launching it up the coast would be expensive and dangerous, so, instead, when the rains of winter ceased and the whole countryside was green and verdant the vaqueros began rounding up their stock, as many as two thousand at a time, and driving them against their stubborn will north into the mountains and through the Tejon Pass into the San Joaquin Valley, where at a pace of ten to fifteen miles per day the cattle reluctantly returned to the trail, the old accustomed trail of the longhorn, and marched for a month through the valley and up to Northern California where they were given a final pasturing on leased land to recuperate from their travels and to fatten so that they might secure the highest price possible from a middleman before ending their lives in a slaughterhouse near San Francisco or in some rugged mining camp in Gold Country.

As thousands upon thousands of head of cattle left Los Angeles each year the vast southern herds began for the first time to thin. The prairie itself had not changed, but its place within the international economy had. Southern California was no longer a frontier on the distant fringe of empire, but now neighbored a region undergoing crash urbanization. The rancheros, for whom the familiar rhythm of wet and dry seasons had furnished a comforting routine, could find now no solid foundation on which to build their way of life. Beef remained in high demand in the Bay Area and in Sacramento, but this quickly attracted new suppliers, many of whom had a competitive advantage over the rancheros of Los Angeles. The price of meat stabilized as an annual migration from the Missouri frontier filled San Francisco with plump, juicy Midwestern steaks, as longhorns driven on the hoof from Texas met their California cousins in the stockyard, and as bleating hordes of sheep arrived from the New Mexico range. While the ranchos shifted their focus to providing beef, the neglected trade in hide and tallow shrank and never recovered. The locus of the cattle industry on the Pacific coast moved from Southern California to the San Joaquin Valley, a region better positioned by its proximity to the cities to fatten the herds and move them efficiently to market.

Then in December of 1861 the land itself conspired to drive the longhorns out of Los Angeles. For forty-five days and forty-five nights the prairie was drenched by the winter rains. The downpour was relentless. The arroyos of the hillsides became raging rivers, buildings crumpled beneath the weight of their waterlogged adobe walls, and long deep lakes of rainwater pooled in the flatlands. Los Angeles was cut off from the rest of the world, an island unto itself, and scattered reports from travelers filtered in of entire towns in the mountains washed away, of cattle by the score floating down the Los Angeles River to the sea.

It was as though three years' worth of rain had fallen in a single season, and yet what the survivors faced next was even more cataclysmic: a severe drought that would stretch for three full years, from 1862 to 1865, one long ceaseless summer. The soaked landscape became now dry and parched and the earth could no longer sustain the longhorn herds. As that first fall turned to winter with no sign of rain, the situation grew desperate. Along the rivers and streams of the prairie the cattle congregated, clinging wretchedly to the last trickles of water passing over the dusty cracked ground. They looked to the vaqueros for guidance, but even the horsemen had disappeared; alongside the drought had come an epidemic of smallpox, and the authorities had instituted a quarantine, so that the day-to-day operations of the ranchos had ceased and the pastoral system was paralyzed. Emaciated longhorns, walking skeletons covered in raggedy hides, crowded around the ciénagas—the bubbling groundwater springs that formed at the bases of hills and mountains—and here as a mass they bawled their sharp long cries of distress, abandoned by a society on the verge of collapse. Some climbed into the hills in search of vegetation, where they were stalked by the great predators of the San Gabriels, the mountain lions and grizzly bears, who sensed their distress and hovered around the periphery of the herd to drag away the weak and famished as their kin looked on helplessly. Further south, the Bavarian settlers at the agricultural colony of Anaheim were forced to post full-time sentinels to guard their croplands from the raging mass of screaming cattle that tried repeatedly to break through to the lush irrigated green they could see just beyond the willows, their last hope for survival. As the drought entered its second and its third year, clumps of carcasses dotted the desolate prairie; the longhorns died together in bands like the herd animals that they were. Vaqueros rode the open range one last time to chase off the scavenging ravens and condors who now ruled the land and to strip the dead longhorns of their sun-bleached hides, which might still be sold at San Pedro, if even for just a pittance.

The era of the ranchos of Los Angeles had come to an end. The dependable cycle of wet and dry seasons that the rancheros and the longhorns had come to trust seemed inexplicably broken. Land speculators and squatters, Anglos from the east, now covered the prairie like locusts. They had no interest in cattle or the life pastoral; they schemed to bring intensive agriculture, state-sponsored irrigation, ever rising land prices. These recent arrivals were appalled at the low profit per acre that the ranchos had tolerated; they dreamed of breaking the prairie and of cultivating orderly rows of orange trees, of lime trees, of olives and apricots, tobacco and cotton, of mulberry trees festooned with precious silkworms. Besieged by creditors, their operations decimated, their very claims to the land challenged in federal courtrooms, the rancheros liquidated their holdings on a mass scale and yielded to the newcomers. Those hearty head of cattle that had endured both flood and drought were sold to ranchers in more distant, more remote locales; the vaqueros rounded them up and drove them north along mountain trails out of Los Angeles to the San Joaquin Valley and to the land beyond the Sierras, to the sagebrush frontier of Nevada and Idaho. Like their forebears, for whom the Los Angeles prairie had been terra incognita, they became the peripatetic pioneers behind whom the agents of empire would soon follow.

Back in Los Angeles, the rain returned. The cycle of the seasons set in once again, for there was nothing in truth unusual about this dry spell and this great flood; the grand rhythm of the prairie was far, far longer than the year-to-year horizon that bracketed the lives of the humans and the cattle, and it included periodic droughts and periodic deluges. The plants of the plains were prepared; their seeds, which had been sculpted by the landscape for centuries, could remain dormant in the dry earth for a decade if need be. Those who witnessed that next winter would claim that it was among the greenest in the living memory of any Angeleno, though there were no longer longhorns there to appreciate it.

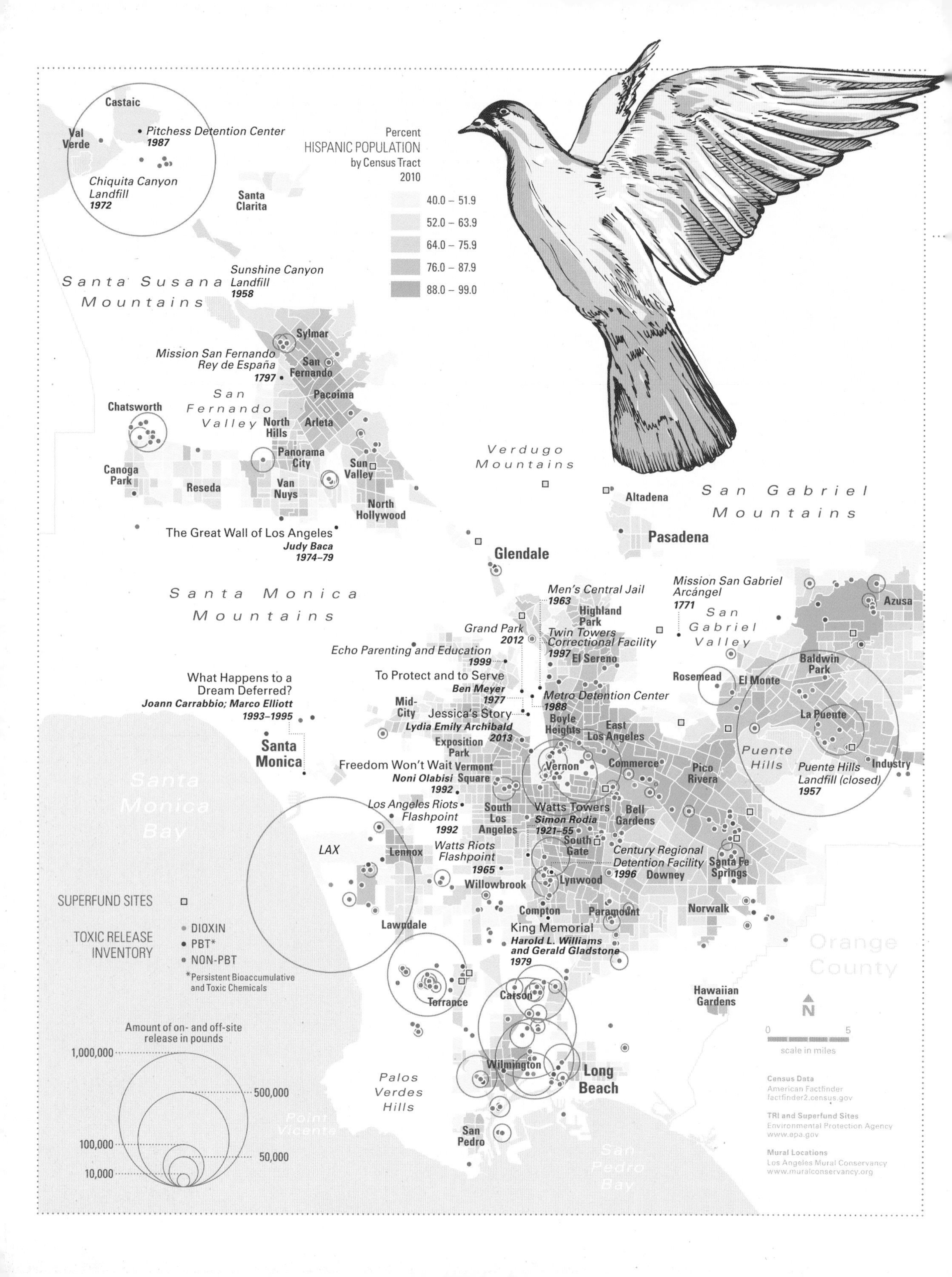

Percent
HISPANIC POPULATION
by Census Tract
2010
40.0 – 51.9
52.0 – 63.9
64.0 – 75.9
76.0 – 87.9
88.0 – 99.0
Castaic
Val Verde
Pitchess Detention Center
1987
Chiquita Canyon Landfill
1972
Santa Clarita
Santa Susana Mountains
Sunshine Canyon Landfill
1958
Sylmar
Mission San Fernando Rey de España
1797
San Fernando
Pacoima
San Fernando Valley
Chatsworth
North Hills
Arleta
Panorama City
Canoga Park
Reseda
Van Nuys
Sun Valley
North Hollywood
Verdugo Mountains
Altadena
San Gabriel Mountains
Pasadena
The Great Wall of Los Angeles
Judy Baca
1974–79
Glendale
Santa Monica Mountains
Men's Central Jail
1963
Highland Park
Mission San Gabriel Arcángel
1771
San Gabriel Valley
Azusa
Grand Park
2012
Twin Towers Correctional Facility
1997
El Sereno
Echo Parenting and Education
1999
To Protect and to Serve
Ben Meyer
1977
What Happens to a Dream Deferred?
Joann Carrabbio; Marco Elliott
1993–1995
Rosemead
El Monte
Baldwin Park
Metro Detention Center
1988
Mid-City
Jessica's Story
Lydia Emily Archibald
2013
Boyle Heights
East Los Angeles
La Puente
Santa Monica
Exposition Park
Vernon
Commerce
Pico Rivera
Puente Hills
Puente Hills Landfill (closed)
1957
Industry
Freedom Won't Wait
Noni Olabisi
1992
Vermont Square
Santa Monica Bay
Los Angeles Riots Flashpoint
1992
South Los Angeles
Watts Towers
Simon Rodia
1921–55
Bell Gardens
LAX
Lennox
Watts Riots Flashpoint
1965
South Gate
Century Regional Detention Facility
1996
Downey
Santa Fe Springs
Willowbrook
Lynwood
SUPERFUND SITES
TOXIC RELEASE INVENTORY
DIOXIN
PBT*
NON-PBT
*Persistent Bioaccumulative and Toxic Chemicals
Compton
Paramount
Norwalk
Lawndale
King Memorial
Harold L. Williams and Gerald Gladstone
1979
Orange County
Torrance
Carson
Hawaiian Gardens
N
0
5
scale in miles
Amount of on- and off-site release in pounds
1,000,000
500,000
100,000
50,000
10,000
Wilmington
Long Beach
Palos Verdes Hills
Point Vicente
San Pedro
San Pedro Bay
Census Data
American Factfinder
factfinder2.census.gov
TRI and Superfund Sites
Environmental Protection Agency
www.epa.gov
Mural Locations
Los Angeles Mural Conservancy
www.muralconservancy.org

Essayist Laura Pulido leads us through landscapes that are layered with generations of power struggles and painful memories. This map marks these sites, along with powerful community public murals and memorials, while revealing how state-sanctioned racial violence has altered the Los Angeles landscape. Particular ethnic communities continue to suffer persecution today from disproportionate exposure to toxic chemicals. The environmental justice movement seeks to distribute hazardous sites more equally among ethnic groups, but until such an outcome can be achieved, Los Angeles's landscape will continue to channel old patterns of racial prejudice into a more subtle form of violence against people of Mexican and Central American descent and other minorities.

Landscapes of Racial Violence

Laura Pulido

Violence begets violence, while nonviolence begets nonviolence.
—Echo Parenting & Education

In 2008 I moved to north Pasadena. Although a native Angeleno, I was unaware that such beautiful and relatively affordable residential areas existed in Los Angeles. I began taking regular walks, and, being a geographer, naturally studied the landscape. I spent the first couple of years figuring out the trees, the San Gabriel Mountains, the architecture, residential landscaping, and commercial land uses. Once I understood the landscape, I began to ponder its history. For example, my house was built in 1930, but when was the land parceled and sold as a housing tract? How did it transition from someone's estate to a neighborhood? What rancho was here? In the 1770s it became part of the San Gabriel Mission; before that, it was Tongva land. Was there a village nearby?

My curiosity opened a window onto larger issues of land, power, and conquest. After doing some reading, I realized that the western San Gabriel Valley is key to Los Angeles's history of conquest and dispossession. It turns out there were numerous Tongva villages in the area. Starting in the late 1700s the Spanish established missions, pueblos, and presidios as a way of claiming California and its population. After Mexico won independence from Spain and secularized the missions, the land that was intended for the natives was instead divided into large ranchos and granted primarily to Mexican men. How did a relatively small number of Spaniards manage to assume this land? How did Euro-Americans acquire it from the Mexicans in later years?

A close study of these questions will reveal that Los Angeles's soil is soaked with blood. Peoples' lands were forcibly taken from them—the Tongva's by the Spanish, the Californios' by the Americans. Conquerors asserted control by kidnapping, coercion, rape, assault, murder, cultural destruction, forced labor, and incarceration.

Conquest is a *process*, not an event. Taking land is not simply a matter of signing a treaty or conducting a massacre. Elaborate ideologies and attendant practices are required before, during, and after. Throughout the Americas white supremacy was the racial ideology that enabled conquest: The original occupants were considered distinct and inferior. Indeed, the language of conquest is infused with this thinking. For example, the Spanish term to distinguish Europeans from indigenous people, *gente de razón*, separates people of reson and those without. Those "without" must be subjugated to ensure that the will of the conquerors became manifest. In turn, indigenous people's inferior status was used to justify their domination.

There is ample evidence of violence in early Los Angeles. According to one nineteenth-century source, "[D]uring the year 1854 the average of violent deaths in Los Angeles City, was not less than one a day, for the most part Mexicans and Indians, but not infrequently persons in the higher walks of life." This violence is typically explained as "frontier justice," which suggests a degree of randomness, perhaps stemming from problematic individuals or a weak or nonexistent judicial system. However, Ken Gonzales-Day demonstrates in *Lynching in the West: 1850–1935*, that the violence was both racially motivated and largely *systemic*. "Frontier justice" as a narrative thus obscures the larger racial dynamics that actively shaped the region.

State-sanctioned racial violence refers to violence that embodies a racial logic and is at least partly systemic—in other words, the violence was executed by the state or the state knew about it and did not stop it. These actions form patterns and collectively illustrate the will of the state.

It was *through the state* (whether Spain, Mexico, or the US), that land was acquired and that people of color were killed, kidnapped, coerced into working, mutilated, and incarcerated—*not,* as we'd like to believe, through "bad" people operating in a supposedly aracial world.

In exploring the history of a place, artist Judy Baca considers the "spirit nature" of the land: All living things that pass through a landscape leave a trace—an energy, if you will—that inhabits the land. Just as individual trauma rests in the body, collective trauma rests in the land, even when it's rarely visible in the everyday landscape, due to our heavy investment in denial.

It is one thing to know the general history of a place, but visiting particular sites and becoming familiar with them offers a more visceral form of knowledge that connects us to our past. There are powerful resonances between the violence of the past and that of the present, and Los Angeles cannot break from its culture of racial violence or reconcile with its native people until we seriously engage with this history.

Mission San Gabriel and Sexual Violence

428 S Mission Drive, San Gabriel

If there is a ground zero for racial violence in Los Angeles, it is the San Gabriel Mission, established in 1771. Located twelve miles east of downtown, the Mission San Gabriel Arcángel was part of Spain's mission system in Alta California and was the primary vehicle through which Spain captured and converted Indians and coerced them into working. The mission system was a joint undertaking by state and church, involving soldiers as well as priests. Soldiers accompanied the priests to assist in the colonization process, but consistently undermined the church's efforts by engaging in sexual violence against the native women. Junípero Serra, overseer of the mission system, wrote, "this mission [San Gabriel] gives me the greatest cause for anxiety; the secular arm down there was guilty of the most heinous crimes, killing the men to take their wives." In October 1771, for example, a group of Indians attacked soldiers working on the mission. Father Francisco Palóu attributed the attack to "a soldier [who] had raped an Indian girl from the rancheria." In some villages women were hidden, but soldiers would beat the men to force them to reveal their whereabouts. The Tongva required the raped women to undergo a purification process and any resulting offspring were strangled and buried. Eventually the priests discovered the infanticide and added yet another layer of violence to this escalating cycle. The mission administrator, Padre Salvadea, did not distinguish between miscarriages and infanticide, and, according to Hugo Reid, an early Angeleno who researched the Tongva, he imposed the following punishment on all women with dead babies: "The penalty inflicted was, shaving the head, flogging for fifteen subsequent days, iron on the feet for three months, and having to appear every Sunday in church...with a hideous painted wooden child in her arms!"

Rape was not the official policy of either the Spanish crown or the Catholic Church. Mission priests understood that sexual violence was a major impediment to conversion; it made Indians abhor the soldiers and avoid the missions. Indeed, priests pressured government officials to control the behavior of the soldiers. According to Sherburne Cook, "[D]isciplinary measures were taken in 1777 [against]...'those who go by night to the nearby villages for the purpose of raping the native women.'" Laws were passed, policies adopted, but the sexual violence continued.

Feminist scholars such as Andrea Smith and Antonia Castañeda argue that rape is a fundamental part of the colonization process, as it powerfully subjugates entire communities. The Spanish believed that Indian women, particularly non-Christians, were racially inferior, which facilitated the justification of the assaults.

The original mission was relocated approximately five miles west in 1775. Portions of the mission complex still stand, as both a tourist destination and a functioning parish. Outside the church there is a sign inviting tourists to the gift shop. What exactly are we commemorating? In addition to the rapes, Indians were beaten, forced to work, and 6,000 are buried here (most died from disease). Such a casual approach to tourism is only possible by overlooking the past. We choose to remember this history by way of a bucolic landscape—eroding buildings, palm trees, a statue of Junípero Serra courtesy of the Daughters of the American Revolution—but where are the voices of the women and babies that haunt this place?

La Zanja Madre and Unfree Labor

125 Paseo de la Plaza, Los Angeles

As an undergraduate I learned that California Indians died out after conquest because they were not accustomed to regimented work. What such a narrative flagrantly overlooked, however, is the fact that Indians built Los Angeles's early infrastructure, including the missions, ranchos, and public spaces. One early writer explained their involvement in the building of the mission: "A sufficient number of neophytes having been secured[,] active work was commenced. Ground was cleared... adobes made; timber cut and hauled; and the mission buildings erected."

Although Indians toiled primarily in the fields, they did all manner of work, including domestic service, crafts, ranching, and message-running. Chattel slavery did not exist in Alta California, although the life of the Mission Indians has been described as a form of serfdom or de facto slavery. In 1834 the missions were secularized and church lands were transferred to individuals. Indian labor remained essential: "These same Indians built all the houses in the country, and planted all the fields and vineyards."

Why were the Indians willing to do such work? Some were eventually driven by hunger when their traditional hunting-gathering lifestyle was rendered impossible by the usurpation of their land by Spain and Mexico. Others were coerced into working—through physical force and even by law. Indeed, the Act for the Government and Protection of Indians (1850) codified the numerous ways in which Spanish, Mexicans, and Euro-Americans sought to produce an unwilling workforce in California, what is often called, "unfree labor." For instance, as historians Michael Magliari and Stacey Smith have shown, both Mexicans and Euro-Americans "adopted" Indian children and compelled them to work. They kidnapped adults and children. They took prisoners of war. They claimed the rights of debt-peonage. They "leased" convicts. Often, they simply did not pay their workers. In Hugo Reid's household, for example, "most of the servants assumed that they would stay with the Reids all their lives, working without wages."

The Zanja Madre in Olvera Street illustrates the practice of convict leasing. Zanjas, or water ditches, were a key part of Los Angeles's early infrastructure. The Zanja Madre, the main ditch, distributed water to smaller ditches, which then delivered it to individuals for irrigation and domestic use. Such water systems were a hallmark of Hispanic settlements throughout the southwestern US, and, requiring continuous labor, were communally maintained.

Over time, wealthy residents began sending Indians and poor workers to fulfill their maintenance obligations. In 1836, the ayuntamiento (city council) had the city constable "arrest all drunken Indians and compel them to work on [the] zanja." This practice illustrates how racialized violence works. The state actively produces criminals by rendering illegal certain behaviors, such as loitering, vagrancy, or drunkenness—of course, these behaviors are in part *responses* to the destruction of the Tongva way of life and homeland. Once these laws are established, local policies are adopted to produce an unpaid, powerless workforce.

Today, a remnant of the Zanja Madre is located in heavily touristed Olvera Street. It is paved with bricks and presented as charming and quaint, but one does not have to dig too deep to understand the purpose and significance of the zanja. Water is the lifeblood of a semi-arid environment and tremendous effort went into securing and dispersing it. The zanja system lasted late into the 1800s, and while many people contributed to it, we cannot overlook the fact that it was built and maintained in part by people who were forced to work often against their will and without fair compensation.

This scenario should not be unfamiliar to Angelenos. The most undesirable work in Los Angeles is still done by nonwhite people with limited legal rights.

Grand Park and Lynchings

Intersection of N Hill Street and northern boundary of Grand Park, Los Angeles

Los Angeles's racial hierarchy changed dramatically after the Mexican-American War (1846–48). There was a great deal of chaos in its aftermath, as one set of legal, economic, and cultural systems unevenly replaced another. As part of conquest, Euro-Americans racialized Mexicans as inferior, depicting them as dirty, lazy, racial mongrels. Indeed, the term "greaser" was introduced at this time. In keeping with Manifest Destiny, many whites saw the US takeover as inevitable and just: they reasoned that they were better equipped to make the land productive. Not surprisingly, Mexicans resented and resisted the new racial order, and tremendous violence ensued, including the lynching of Mexicans.

Gonzales-Day found that out of 352 lynchings in California from 1850–1935, 210 (59.6 percent) of the victims were people of color. Forty-five took place in Los Angeles, of which thirty-six were nonwhite (80 percent). Of these thirty-six lynchings, nineteen were Mexicans, fifteen were Chinese, and two were Indians. The Chinese lynchings all occurred during the Chinese Massacre of 1871. While anti-Chinese sentiment was intense, violence was not an ongoing pattern: it culminated in a single, horrific event. By contrast, the lynching of Mexicans was a more common feature of Los Angeles life.

Upon the conclusion of the war, banditry was widespread. Among Mexicans, this was partly a response to rapid impoverishment, but banditry also functioned as a form of resistance. Numerous Mexican lynchings involved cases where the public employed "popular justice" against Mexican bandits without a trial. That this happened overwhelmingly to Mexicans was not accidental, but represents general attitudes towards Mexicans and the state's inability/refusal to ensure due process for them.

This particular site was the city's first jail, established in 1853. In November 1858, Pancho Daniel was lynched on a beam in the jailyard. Daniel had been a leader, along with Juan Flores, of a group of bandits who killed a sheriff in San Juan Capistrano in 1857. The murder triggered a massive hunt for Flores and Daniel. Fifty-two Latino men were arrested, and numerous Mexicans, some with no connection to the crime, were lynched. Daniel eluded the authorities for some time but was eventually caught and imprisoned. A change of venue to Santa Barbara was granted, but a group of residents opposed due process. They demanded the keys from the jailer, took the prisoner out, and hanged him. The inquest concluded that the "deceased came to his death from strangulation, by a crowd of persons to the jury unknown."

While there is no trace of the jail today, the presence of the justice system can still be seen and felt. Decades ago the area was concretized and today it is surrounded by a metro stop, and numerous public buildings. In 2012 the city built Grand Park over the former site of the jail itself. Although urbanization powerfully erases previous land uses, it has not eliminated the past: Among the public buildings found in proximity to the site are the Los Angeles Superior Court and the Los Angeles County District Attorney's Office, contemporary embodiments of the justice system and prosecutorial power.

Men's Central Jail and Mass Incarceration

441 Bauchet Street, Los Angeles

Welcome to the largest jail on earth. Men's Central Jail is run by the Los Angeles County Sheriff's Department and detains men who have been arrested but not yet convicted. The jail is a key site in the geography of the prison-industrial complex (PIC), a constellation of institutions, policies, and relations that are committed to "solving" social problems via incarceration. Thousands of mostly poor Black and Brown men are placed in cages here, with devastating consequences for their communities.

The jail is known for its severe overcrowding, violence, and illnesses. It was constructed in 1963 and initially designed to house 3,323 inmates. Because of the massive criminalization of the late twentieth century, the facility was expanded and now houses close to 5,000 souls. In *Golden Gulag: Prisons, Surplus, Crisis and Opposition in Globalizing California,* Ruth Wilson Gilmore identifies four "surpluses" that emerged in the 1970s and led to the extraordinary growth of California's prison system: a surplus of capital that needed to generate a return; a surplus of rural land that need to be put to "productive" use; a surplus of labor due to economic restructuring; and surplus state capacity, which was generated by neoliberal ideology intent on shrinking the state. The problem of these surpluses was resolved by building a massive prison system. Repeating historic patterns, nonwhite poor people were targeted by a series of new laws accompanied by a cultural and policy shift from rehabilitation to revenge. Collectively, these shifts resulted in mass incarceration.

Mass incarceration is *not* an inevitable response to social transgressions. Many steps were required to get here: the public had to be convinced that it was not safe, that a certain class of people was preying on it, and that incarceration was our only hope. Because the criminal is not envisioned as white, racism plays a key role in the growth of the PIC. Criminalization is the process of making acts, ways of being, and relationships illegal that were not previously so (recall the drunken Indians). Examples include Proposition 184 (1994), the "three-strikes" law; Proposition 21 (2000), that treats youthful offenders as adults; enhanced sentences for certain offenses; and an entirely new body of law aimed at immigrants since 9/11.

This criminalization disproportionately targets people of color. African American men, who constitute approximately 3 percent of the state's population, comprise 44 percent of those convicted under "three strikes." Likewise, Latinas/os, through the criminalization of immigration, are now the single largest ethnic group in federal prisons, despite constituting only 15 percent of the national population. At the same time these new laws and propositions were being adopted, Proposition 209 (1996) was passed, ending affirmative action in California. As paths to the middle class were blocked on the outside, ever more people were locked up in the inside.

The work of abolitionists, the recession of 2008, and California's budget crisis have all illuminated how expensive—socially and economically—the PIC is. We desperately need to find new ways of addressing social transgressions.

Standing outside the building, you realize that there are thousands of people locked up on the inside; while on the outside, life goes on. All that separates us are thick walls—and race and class. How many of those who pass the building daily are aware of it and consider the lives of those on the other side of the wall?

Racial Violence Past, Present, and Future

The eugenics movement; the Japanese American internment; Repatriation; the Zoot-Suit Riots; the Sleepy Lagoon murder trial; Chief Parker; Watts 1965; Rodney King; MacArthur Park 2006; the Rampart scandal; mass deportations post 9/11—these are all examples of Los Angeles's history of state-sanctioned racial violence. The city is built on exceptional and everyday human rights violations.

History is essential to recovering this past, but geography provides crucial insights. We begin by conceiving of these sites as *landscapes*—not only in the sense of how a place looks, but also how it is produced. The geographer Don Mitchell has argued that part of landscape's power is its ability to obscure. Landscapes are deeply layered places encompassing generations of power relations. They are acts of creation, as it takes tremendous power to rearrange the earth. Consider what it took to build the San Gabriel Mission: Each structure and field required enormous will and capacity on the part of the church, state, and workers. Imagine Indians carting the materials needed for bricks *twelve miles* from a quarry in what is now West Covina.

Landscapes are expressions of power, but they are also personal and sensory. They invite us to reformulate our relationship to place and time in intimate ways. We must incorporate sites of state-sanctioned racial violence into a remapping of Los Angeles and consider how these landscapes have changed, remained the same, reverberate in the present, and how we may be connected to them. I am hopeful this intimacy will compel us to reflect on our status as "settlers" who have not only benefitted from racial violence but are also burdened by it in multiple ways, including the violence of today.

It is easy to condemn eighteenth-century Franciscans and believe that we have morally evolved. But a closer look at Men's Central Jail challenges this assumption: few of us actually pay attention to what happens in the jail and the way that life is parceled along racial and class lines there. How do we not *see* a building that occupies an entire block in downtown LA? Part of the answer is the architecture and landscaping, but equally important is the degree to which we distance ourselves ideologically and emotionally from the jail. Because criminalization is racialized and classed, most of us are oblivious to it unless we have an incarcerated loved one. The jail is as emotionally distant and physically invisible as the sites of nineteenth-century lynchings. The fact that we are able to overlook the racial violence that occurs in our front yard suggests that we have not evolved so far.

Where do we go from here? A starting point is becoming aware and intimate with these places. Equally important is to support local efforts seeking to break the cycle of violence in Los Angeles. One example is Echo Parenting & Education, located in Echo Park. Formerly known as the Center for Nonviolent Education and Parenting, Echo, as it is known, encourages people to parent consciously. Simply put, without consciousness we will replicate the parenting of previous generations, which has been all too quick to embrace violence. Echo defines violence broadly as "anything that hurts the heart, mind or body of a child and leads to disconnection and distrust." Echo's philosophy is to parent with respect—for oneself and for one's children. Echo changed its name to reflect its geographical location, but also to build on the metaphor of "echo": "[W]hen we are kind, that kindness echoes long after we are gone." And so it is with our children. By raising nonviolent children, we will hopefully provide them with the tools and awareness to address problems through nonviolent means and thus create a new Los Angeles and a new relationship to our history.

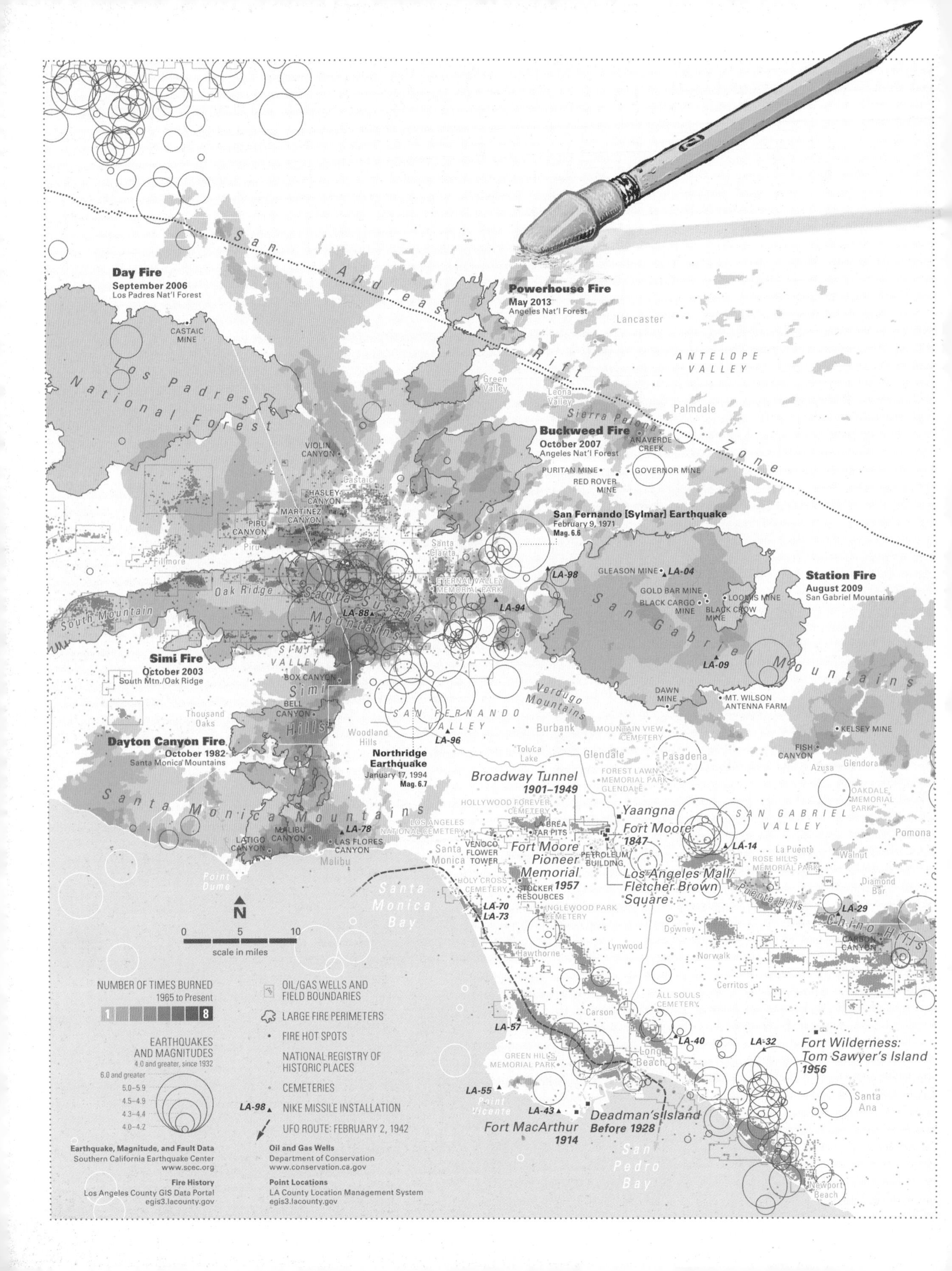

San Andreas Rift Zone
Day Fire
September 2006
Los Padres Nat'l Forest
Powerhouse Fire
May 2013
Angeles Nat'l Forest
Lancaster
ANTELOPE VALLEY
CASTAIC MINE
Los Padres National Forest
Green Valley
Leona Valley
Sierra Pelona
Palmdale
Buckweed Fire
October 2007
Angeles Nat'l Forest
ANAVERDE CREEK
PURITAN MINE
GOVERNOR MINE
RED ROVER MINE
VIOLIN CANYON
Castaic
HASLEY CANYON
MARTINEZ CANYON
PIRU CANYON
Piru
Fillmore
San Fernando [Sylmar] Earthquake
February 9, 1971
Mag. 6.6
Santa Clarita
LA-98
GLEASON MINE
LA-04
Station Fire
August 2009
San Gabriel Mountains
Oak Ridge
South Mountain
Santa Susana Mountains
ETERNAL VALLEY MEMORIAL PARK
LA-88
LA-94
GOLD BAR MINE
BLACK CARGO MINE
LOOMIS MINE
BLACK CROW MINE
San Gabriel Mountains
SIMI VALLEY
Simi Fire
October 2003
South Mtn./Oak Ridge
LA-09
BOX CANYON
Simi Hills
BELL CANYON
Thousand Oaks
Verdugo Mountains
DAWN MINE
MT. WILSON ANTENNA FARM
SAN FERNANDO VALLEY
LA-96
Woodland Hills
Burbank
MOUNTAIN VIEW CEMETERY
KELSEY MINE
Dayton Canyon Fire
October 1982
Santa Monica Mountains
Northridge Earthquake
January 17, 1994
Mag. 6.7
Toluca Lake
Glendale
Pasadena
FISH CANYON
Azusa
Glendora
Broadway Tunnel
1901–1949
FOREST LAWN MEMORIAL PARK GLENDALE
HOLLYWOOD FOREVER CEMETERY
OAKDALE MEMORIAL PARK
Santa Monica Mountains
LOS ANGELES NATIONAL CEMETERY
LA BREA TAR PITS
Yaangna
SAN GABRIEL VALLEY
Pomona
Fort Moore 1847
MALIBU CANYON
LA-78
LATIGO CANYON
LAS FLORES CANYON
Malibu
Santa Monica
VENOCO FLOWER TOWER
Fort Moore Pioneer Memorial 1957
PETROLEUM BUILDING
LA-14
La Puente
ROSE HILLS MEMORIAL PARK
Walnut
Point Dume
HOLY CROSS CEMETERY
STOCKER RESOURCES
Los Angeles Mall/ Fletcher Brown Square
Diamond Bar
Santa Monica Bay
Puente Hills
LA-70
LA-73
INGLEWOOD PARK CEMETERY
LA-29
Chino Hills
N
0 5 10
scale in miles
Downey
CARBON CANYON
Hawthorne
Lynwood
Norwalk
NUMBER OF TIMES BURNED
1965 to Present
1 8
OIL/GAS WELLS AND FIELD BOUNDARIES
LARGE FIRE PERIMETERS
FIRE HOT SPOTS
NATIONAL REGISTRY OF HISTORIC PLACES
CEMETERIES
NIKE MISSILE INSTALLATION
UFO ROUTE: FEBRUARY 2, 1942
EARTHQUAKES AND MAGNITUDES
4.0 and greater, since 1932
6.0 and greater
5.0–5.9
4.5–4.9
4.3–4.4
4.0–4.2
LA-98
Cerritos
ALL SOULS CEMETERY
Carson
LA-57
LA-40
LA-32
Fort Wilderness: Tom Sawyer's Island 1956
GREEN HILLS MEMORIAL PARK
Long Beach
LA-55
Point Vicente
LA-43
Deadman's Island Before 1928
Fort MacArthur 1914
Santa Ana
San Pedro Bay
Newport Beach
Earthquake, Magnitude, and Fault Data
Southern California Earthquake Center
www.scec.org
Fire History
Los Angeles County GIS Data Portal
egis3.lacounty.gov
Oil and Gas Wells
Department of Conservation
www.conservation.ca.gov
Point Locations
LA County Location Management System
egis3.lacounty.gov

Wildfires and earthquakes brutally reconfigure the natural and built landscapes. Abandoned mines and missile bases are vestiges of the consuming preoccupations of eras past. Counterpoints to our human cemeteries are the myriad oil and gas wells that bespeak vast caches of underground fossil fuels, the product of millions of years of organic decomposition. These wells are found even in the most densely populated areas, where they are kept out of sight behind fake building fronts. This turbulent, secretive landscape that creeps into our collective subconscious is the backdrop for Jason Brown's essay, which relates strange, covered-up, or barely memorialized episodes in our human history.

The Fortifications and Catacombs of the Conquests of Los Angeles

Jason Brown

Necropolis of the Lizard People

It started as an ordinary treasure hunt. Then it became a search for the catacomb city of a lost civilization. Then it became a quest for something far harder to grasp.

The treasure hunters asked the County for permission to dig up a forgotten box of gold, guided by a sheepskin map with "the romantic markings of old pirate maps," and a dowsing pendulum described by the *LA Times* as an X-ray doodlebug. The County Supervisors approved this proposed gold hunt with a quiet hiss, binding the seekers with the standard contracts. With that, the gold diggers of 1933 got down to work.

The visible architecture of their dig was a pyramid of timbers on top of Fort Moore Hill. But this modest steeple perched over shafts that extended hundreds of feet into the earth. The diggers burrowed ever further, seeking a gleam in the heavy yellow clay that sucked all light into its depths. After months of gold-less digging, the pirate-map treasure hunters eventually gave up.

But George, the miner with the doodlebug, was still looking for something.

When he'd pull his head free of the hole, the colors of the above world felt alien. Intoxicating. The sky was a blinding blue, cutting his earth-dimmed eyes with a clarity he had never felt before. Soon, this feeling would fade, and the world was merely the world again. But seeking that sense of wonder, he'd return to the darkness, trying to break through a final crumbling wall and gaze into a secret place where the wonder was hidden.

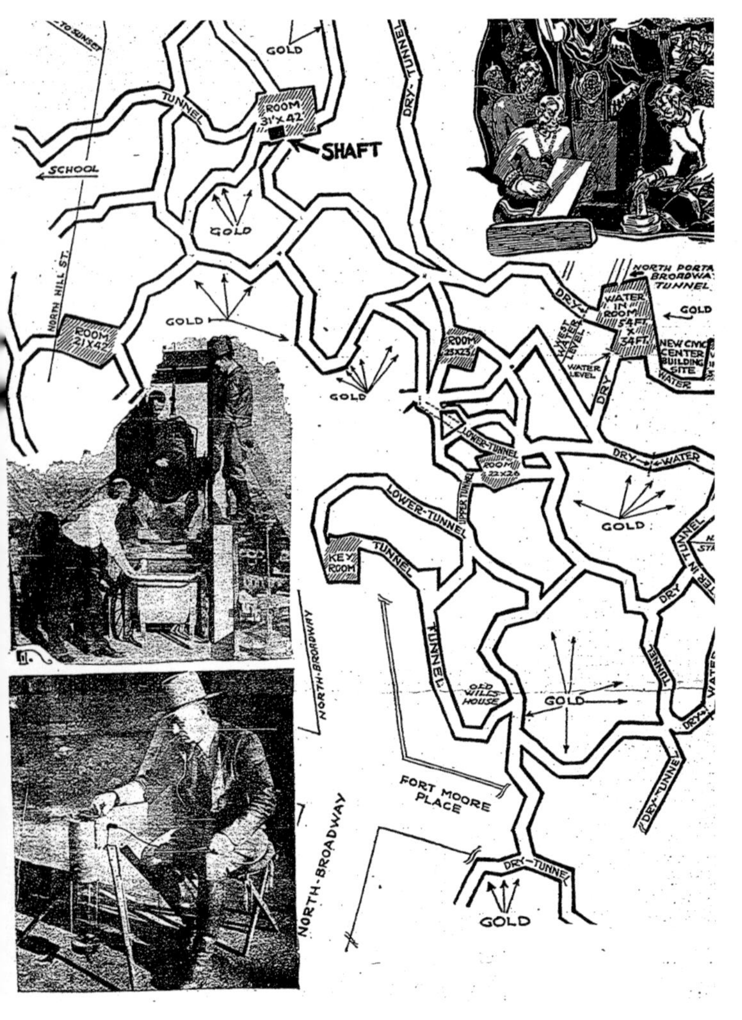

So George went back to the County Supervisors to explain what he was *really* looking for. In the guttering torchlight of their chambers, he told them of a forgotten race, thousands of years old, who used their advanced technology to dig an underground fortress beneath the hills of Los Angeles. This mighty lizard-shaped bunker was built to withstand a gathering cataclysm, a fire in the sky that threatened their entire civilization. But their fortress did not hold. They were wiped out. And all that remained of them were golden tablets, buried beneath Los Angeles, inscribed with memories they tried to save for a future they would never see.

Upon hearing this explanation, the Supervisors smiled grimly, and nodded their cowled heads with a sibilant affirmation. They sanctioned his quest for the fastness of forgotten truths and bound him with another contract. George returned to his mine on the hill, clawing his way ever deeper towards that great unknowable fortress below.

Scientists do not know exactly what George found down there, but they are pretty sure it was not the ancient lizard-shaped catacomb city of a forgotten civilization. Upon further analysis, scientists said that the Lizard People's apocalypse erased them with such total ferocity that they never actually existed. They said that this secret history may have been the dim memory of a future still unfolding, a tunneled city yet to be, a flaming sky yet to come.

Fort Moore

Stand on Broadway (originally Fort Street) just west of a parking lot for the old Plaza, just east of another parking lot, and stare straight up into the sky. Focus on the empty space about eighty feet over your head. There was a flagpole there once. It was ridiculously tall, two tree trunks joined together, jabbing another 120 feet into the sky.

The flagpole is gone. The fort around the flagpole is gone. The hill where the fort stood is gone. You are standing beneath their deepest foundations. The streets now flow through the absence of a hill, submerged roads settled on the floor of forgotten caverns.

Fort Moore was dedicated on July 4, 1847, and named after Captain Benjamin Moore who was killed at the Battle of San Pasqual the previous December. In 1941, the *LA Times* falsified his death as a swashbuckling adventure: "Moore engaged the general in a duel, but his sword snapped at the hilt after the first few parries. He was about to draw his revolver, when a nearby Californian plunged a lance into his heart."

What actually happened was the Americans, mostly mounted on mules, were confused in the early morning fog. Capitan Moore thought he heard a charge called—he heard wrong. Galloping away from the rest of his troops, he was soon surrounded by Californios, excellent horsemen armed with lances. San Pasqual was the bloodiest American defeat of the conquest of Alta California.

Looming over the church from its hill, Fort Moore's eastward bastions held the pueblo in a pincher of overlapping howitzer fire, yet its walls were completely open to the west. The fort was not built to protect the city—it was built to protect the American occupiers from their newly conquered city.

The only military action Fort Moore ever saw was on the night of December 7, 1847, when a stray cow wandered past the guards in the dark. They successfully repelled the cow's attack, but in the confusion, someone tossed a still-smoldering fuse into a box of ammunition. Pieces of the exploding guardhouse landed three blocks away. Four soldiers were killed on the spot, and were buried on Fort Moore Hill.

The fort was abandoned soon after, and officially decommissioned a few years later. The site became an informal cemetery, which was also abandoned. And the city grew over the hill, streets and houses erasing the fort's remains, basements and tunnels winding around forgotten bones.

Los Angeles Mall

Just south of Aliso Street and the 101 freeway, the dungeons of the Los Angeles Mall crouch beneath the pale shoulders of City Hall. This strange bunker was built on the site of the "government house," the last capital of Alta California.

The first American occupation force was garrisoned here. And on the night of September 22, 1846, just a few weeks after occupying the city, they were surrounded by the residents of Los Angeles rising up in rebellion against their oppressive martial law. The next day, the Americans fled the government adobe to a nearby hill overlooking the Plaza, and dug in for a siege. After a week without water or shelter, surrounded by hundreds of angry townsfolk, they "remembered the Alamo"—in particular, the gruesome deaths of its failed defenders—and surrendered Los Angeles back to the locals.

When the Americans recaptured Los Angeles, the government house was the first administrative capital of conquered California. When this building was demolished in 1940, it was a low-rent hotel. The site remained a parking lot for decades, until the Los Angeles Mall erupted from the underworld in the seventies.

The "mall" was supposedly built as a parking garage, but the stairs leading down to the alleged garage are always locked. A sign next to the doors reads: "In case of emergency, chant the holy names." There is a running stick figure, a series of arrows pointing in a circle, and an icon that might represent a glaring eye.

In the "mall's" sunken courtyard, there's a dry fountain with an obelisk covered in the glyphs of a culture that never existed. A tunnel of blank storefronts beneath First Street are flanked with always-lit lamps which imitate an imitation New Orleans. You see no one. But you know you are being watched.

The concrete rooftop of this torpid sepulcher is named Fletcher Bowron Square, in perverse honor of the mayor of Los Angeles when the capitol building on this site was demolished. Mayor Bowron, who cheered on the internment of his Japanese citizens, who oversaw his brutal police force during the Zoot Suit Riots, who presided over the bulldozing of Chavez Ravine and the 101 freeway's swath of destruction. They say Fletcher was actually a pretty nice guy.

Legends claim that this place was also the original location of the Tongva village of Yaangna. But that is a lie.

Yaangna

Drive southbound on the 101, under the shadows of the overpasses, into the gathering dusk in the east. Just as you pass beneath the Gold Line bridge, jam on the brakes and skid to a stop. Put on your hazards. Get out of your car. Please be cautious of the vehicles around you. LA drivers can be so aggressive.

You are standing on the site of the Tongva village of Yaangna. The tranquil beauty of this riverside place was the reason the Spanish first chose to settle here, resulting in the elimination of the Tongva society and their village. Today, the nearest habitable structures are a strip club and the looming tower of Metropolitan Water District headquarters.

Cars in the northbound lane are slowing to gawk at you. The air is thick with the smell of rubber. Rise into the air about seventy feet above your car. To your left, you see the battlements of LAPD's helicopter landing pad rising above the concrete bank of the river. Over the clashing din of horns, screams, and screeching tires, you hear approaching sirens from the west. Now, travel back in time about two hundred years.

The grass along the river is the color of bread. The hills glow violet in the smokey orange light. Just beneath your feet are the vast green shadows of a sycamore tree. It is centuries old. This is the council tree. Tongva tribes from the entire area would meet here. The Spanish didn't know what a sycamore was, so they named the tree with their word for alder: "El Aliso." Jean-Louis Vignes built his winery around the tree. Then Aliso Street paved over El Aliso's roots. Then the Philadelphia Brewery bought the winery and expanded the buildings. When a branch of the suffocating tree fell on a wagon, the brewers cut the rest of the limbs off. And that was it for the council tree.

There is no memorial of this place. It was destroyed with such total ferocity, it is as if it never existed.

Return to your car. Turn to your fellow drivers and the gathered representatives of law enforcement, face your palms outward in a gesture of peace and understanding. Expressively mouth the word "sorry!" Point the fingers of your right hand to your left breast, and mouth, "My bad!" Then shrug with palms upward. As you pull away, be sure to check your blind spot and guard your face from projectiles.

This concludes your tour of the Tongva village of Yaangna.

Fort MacArthur

Deep within the hills overlooking San Pedro lie the barrows of Fort MacArthur, its long tunnels leading to the empty concrete amphitheaters of gun batteries where massive cannons pointed at the horizon, guarding the West Coast's largest port. The only action this fort ever saw was ninety-six years after the American military conquest, when Los Angeles was attacked for the second time.

On the night of February 24, 1942, radar caught an unidentified aircraft off the coast, headed straight for the heart of America's aerospace industry. The operators smacked their scopes in disbelief, trying to knock the signal off their screens, but there it stayed. With shaking hands they reached for radios and pneumatic tubes to make the call.

At 2:25 a.m., all of Los Angeles County was plunged into darkness, as sirens wailed and 12,000 air-raid wardens leapt out of bed. Just after 3:00 a.m., something drifted over Santa Monica, and all the cannons of the 37th Coast Artillery

Brigade opened fire with twelve-pound shells. Witnesses said the air over Los Angeles "erupted like a volcano." Yet the thing drifted on.

The official military account says that from this point, all reports were "hopelessly at variance."

There were reports that a guardsman died of a heart attack while he was behind the wheel of an ammunition truck. There were reports that a plane had landed in flames at a Hollywood intersection. There were reports that a dairy herd was caught in the rain of flaming death. There were reports that the cows donned their helmets and ran for the shelters, just as they'd been drilled, but some of them were not fast enough. There were reports of heavy casualties among the cows.

The *LA Times* got their front-page photo of the thing as it floated past the 65th Coast Artillery regiment in Inglewood, pinned by spotlights, surrounded by flak bursts. Some said it looked like a tree in flames. Some said it looked like a vast flock of crows, their black wings flashing silver and red in the searchlights. Some said it looked like the eye of a monstrous owl.

Ignoring the impotent hellfire, the thing hooked a gentle right turn and headed south, trailed by a shimmering cowl of metal and smoke. Deep within the hills of San Pedro, the guns defending the port turned away from the sea, targeting the thing bearing down on them from the city. And as it passed overhead, Fort MacArthur opened up with everything they had. Uselessly.

As the thing floated back out to sea, witnesses said they felt an immense sadness from it, like a lost whale tormented by Lilliputian harpooners. It was never seen again.

The blackout was lifted at dawn. More than 1,400 shells were fired into the sky over Los Angeles. Six humans and an uncertain number of cattle died in the barrage. The property damage was spectacular. It was the most destructive military assault in the history of Los Angeles. Yet no one had any idea what had happened.

The Navy said the Army was shooting at absolutely nothing due to "war jitters." The Army said there definitely *was* something and that the Navy should shut their stupid Popeye mouths. After the war, the Japanese said they never sent any aircraft of any kind to the area. The U.S. Department of Defense eventually concluded that the unknown thing was not a mass hallucination, but they also didn't bother with a decent cover story. "Indestructible weather balloon," a spokesperson mumbled. "Or whatever. I mean, there's a war on!"

According to unnamed officials, the Battle of Los Angeles was simply a moment lost in time, like tears in rain.

October's Diaphanous Battlements of Speed and Illusion

When the Americans first invaded Los Angeles on August 13, 1846, an old woman—her name was probably Inocencia Reyes—took the city's ceremonial cannon from the Plaza and buried it near her house. Cause you just never know. After the besieged Americans fled to their hill, the Californios dug the cannon back up and used it to encourage their retreat from the city on September 30.

When the Americans marched back towards Los Angeles on October 9, the Californios stopped them with the "Old Woman's Gun." Mounted to a wagon and hitched to fast horses, they'd fire at the invaders, then quickly ride out of range. Getting blown to pieces, and unable to seize the constantly moving gun, the

Americans retreated back to San Pedro. They buried six soldiers on a small pyramid of clay just offshore called Dead Man's Island, and sailed off to regroup.

On October 28, the Americans once again landed in San Pedro to march on Los Angeles. The city's defenders wanted a truce in Alta California until the war in Mexico was settled. But hoping to negotiate more favorable terms, they tried to make it look like they had a huge cavalry by herding wild horses back and forth through the hills overlooking San Pedro, visible to the Americans anchored at the port below. The dust kicked up by the horses hid the fact that almost none of them had riders. The trick worked too well. Instead of negotiating, the Americans avoided this mighty cavalry, and sailed to San Diego for reinforcements, resulting in the battles of San Pasqual, Rio San Gabriel and La Mesa before a truce was finally signed.

On Halloween of 1914, Fort MacArthur was formally dedicated in the hills overlooking San Pedro. They do not memorialize the Californios' cavalry masquerade. But in honor of that one time they shot at that one thing in 1942, they do hold an annual costume ball and air raid, complete with vintage searchlights and a merry barrage of artillery fire over the port.

In January of 1910, the battlefield of the Old Woman's Gun was the site of the first air show in America. A quarter-million people came to see impossible new machines wheeling through the hazy air. Today, the site is a nondescript industrial area in Compton.

As for the Old Woman's Gun itself, some say the Americans seized it with the city and used it in Mexico in 1848. Some say Juan Sepulveda hid it in his ranch and fired it from Dead Man's Island on the Fourth of July in 1853. Some say it was on display at the New Orleans World's Industrial and Cotton Centennial Exposition in 1884 as Naval Trophy Number 53. Some say it was transferred to the Annapolis Maritime Museum in 1925, where it still sits today. Some say it's still buried in someone's backyard, long forgotten.

When Dead Man's Island was dredged out of the harbor in 1928 (killing two workers), three redwood coffins lurched out of the clay, and the bones inside were posed for the papers in the romantic style of old pirate maps. Some say they were the remains of American soldiers killed by the Old Woman's Gun. Some say that is impossible because they were reburied with honors, somewhere, at some point. Some say that under a full October moon, you can still find bones leaking from the repurposed charnel earth of Dead Man's Island, which now lies beneath the shipping containers of America's busiest port.

Fort Moore Pioneer Memorial

The scale of the Fort Moore Pioneer Memorial is inhuman. Occupying the length of a city block, its sheer brick battlements

rise nearly a hundred feet above Hill Street, separated from the sidewalk by a dry moat, fed by a dry waterfall. It is not immediately clear what memory this monstrous structure is defending. While it claims to be in honor of Fort Moore's Fourth of July dedication in 1847, the fort itself is not explained or described on the memorial. Only the fort's flagpole is shown, and that is too mythopoetically huge for the huge edifice to depict, its mighty staff erupting off the top of the central bas-relief.

It is also not a literal memorial to American pioneers. The only reference to them is a vague dedication inscribed on an eagle-emblazoned pylon:

> *To the Brave Men and Women, Who with Trust in God Faced Privation and Death in Extending the Frontiers of Our Country to Include this Land of Promise.*

The rest of the memorial makes it clear that these brave people are, for the most part, the Mormon Battalion—the only religious unit in United States history. Their march to California is described in foot-high letters as "one of the longest, most arduous infantry marches in history." Though as an infantry march, it was also entirely pointless, since fighting in Alta California ended well before they arrived. Aside from the "Battle of the Bulls" in Arizona (two soldiers wounded, eleven wild cows killed), the Mormon Battalion did no fighting at all. They *did* do most of the construction work on Fort Moore, and the Church of Latter-Day Saints helped pay for the Pioneer Memorial, so the Mormon Battalion's labor gets major billing. But this also makes the absence of the fort on the memorial even more odd.

It's not as if there weren't plenty of pioneers inside Fort Moore Hill itself to memorialize. In 1951, the excavation of the

101 freeway even turned up the remains of a soldier in full uniform. Scientists poked at the bones with a stick. "That guy," they said, clipboards in hand, "is dead. He looks pretty old too," they added, while jumping out of the path of an earthmover.

But that pioneer soldier—perhaps one of the few killed at Fort Moore—is not mentioned on the Fort Moore Pioneer Memorial. Even Benjamin Moore, the martyred namesake of the fort and hill, is not mentioned. And it goes without saying that none of the Californios killed by these brave men and women are referenced in any way.

The only person who's death is specifically memorialized on the memorial is Doyle Strong, a construction worker mentioned on the plaque for artists and sponsors. He was killed by the memorial itself when a wooden wall holding back the hill collapsed, burying him in heavy yellow clay.

But if not the fort itself, or the soldiers who died there, or any of the people who died in the conquest of California, what *does* the Fort Moore Pioneer Memorial memorialize?

It is a monument to forgetting. Of the fort, of the hill, and of all that came before them. It does not preserve their memories—it preserves their erasure. Its mighty Fourth of July flagpole does not indicate a now-absent place. It is a towering pin dropped onto the timeline of history, marking the zero point from which memories of Los Angeles are allowed to happen.

Fort Wilderness

On January 8, 1847, at a ford of the San Gabriel River, the locals shouted from the west bank, "¡Viva los Californios!"

The American soldiers wading towards them shouted, "New Orleans! New Orleans!"

What a random thing to yell, thought a young Californio, just before a bullet shattered several of his ribs.

The Americans yelled this in honor the Battle of New Orleans, fought thirty-two years before on that day, when Andrew Jackson defended the city from an invading British army. There is no record of the invading American army recognizing the irony of using this as a battle cry against the residents of the city they were attacking.

Once the Americans got their cannons across the river, it really wasn't much of a battle. And the next day's battle at La Mesa was more of a slaughter. Two days later, the Americans marched into Los Angeles for good. California was conquered.

There is a small monument in the city of Montebello for the battlefield of Rio San Gabriel—a modest red-tiled awning, and two canons pointed over the river. But twenty miles southeast, in the middle of Disneyland, there was a far more complicated memorial of the American conquest of California.

On Tom Sawyer's Island, across the river from an imaginary New Orleans, a dusty mannequin of Andrew Jackson used to sit at a desk, commanding the hewn-log redoubt of Fort Wilderness. The gun towers of the fort mostly pointed their cheerful rifles towards "Indian Country" in the woods out back and out towards Aunt Jemima's Pancake House. But a few of the rifles could aim over the river at the city they were allegedly defending. As a young child, with the lumbering denizens of simulacrum New Orleans locked in your gunsights, you might ask yourself: *What is this fort guarding? Is it an outpost of civilization in the wilderness? Or is it an outpost of wilderness, beset on all sides by the savage forces of civilization?*

After a young child lost part of her finger in a 2002 rifle mishap, Disneyland foreclosed the physical and epistemological trauma of the fort's gun towers. They shuttered the whole fort soon after, its authentically unsealed logs rotted and riddled with termites. And in 2006, the original Fort Wilderness was demolished when all of Tom Sawyer's Island was rebranded as Pirate's Lair.

Children still romp through the same labyrinths of pseudo-historical conquest narratives, but now in a swashbuckling pirate style. Instead of morally ambiguous colonial outposts, now the bones of treasure hunters clutch in eternal desperation for lost gold. And instead of the embarrassingly overt racism of Injun Joe's Cave—whose only special effects were the sound of a screaming Native American ghost and the smell of pee—there's now Dead Man's Grotto, with fully interactive human remains. And when you reach for the pirate gold, the life-size bones now offer witty banter:

> *Arr! Who dares lay hand on me treasure!* say the bones of the pirates.
>
> *We be the Forgotten Civilization!* say the bones of the pirates.
>
> *Keep ye ruddy mitts off me gold!* say the bones of the pirates.
>
> *Ye lives in the city of ye own passages!* say the bones of the pirates.

When you emerge from the darkness, the colors of the above world feel alien. The transhistorical riverboats, built in the old shipyards of San Pedro, slide past on the fathomless jade of the fake river. These boats have sailed far longer than the originals they copied, imaginary histories far more powerful than the ones replaced. You've heard there is a secret cave hidden in this pirate enclave. You turn back toward the darkness.

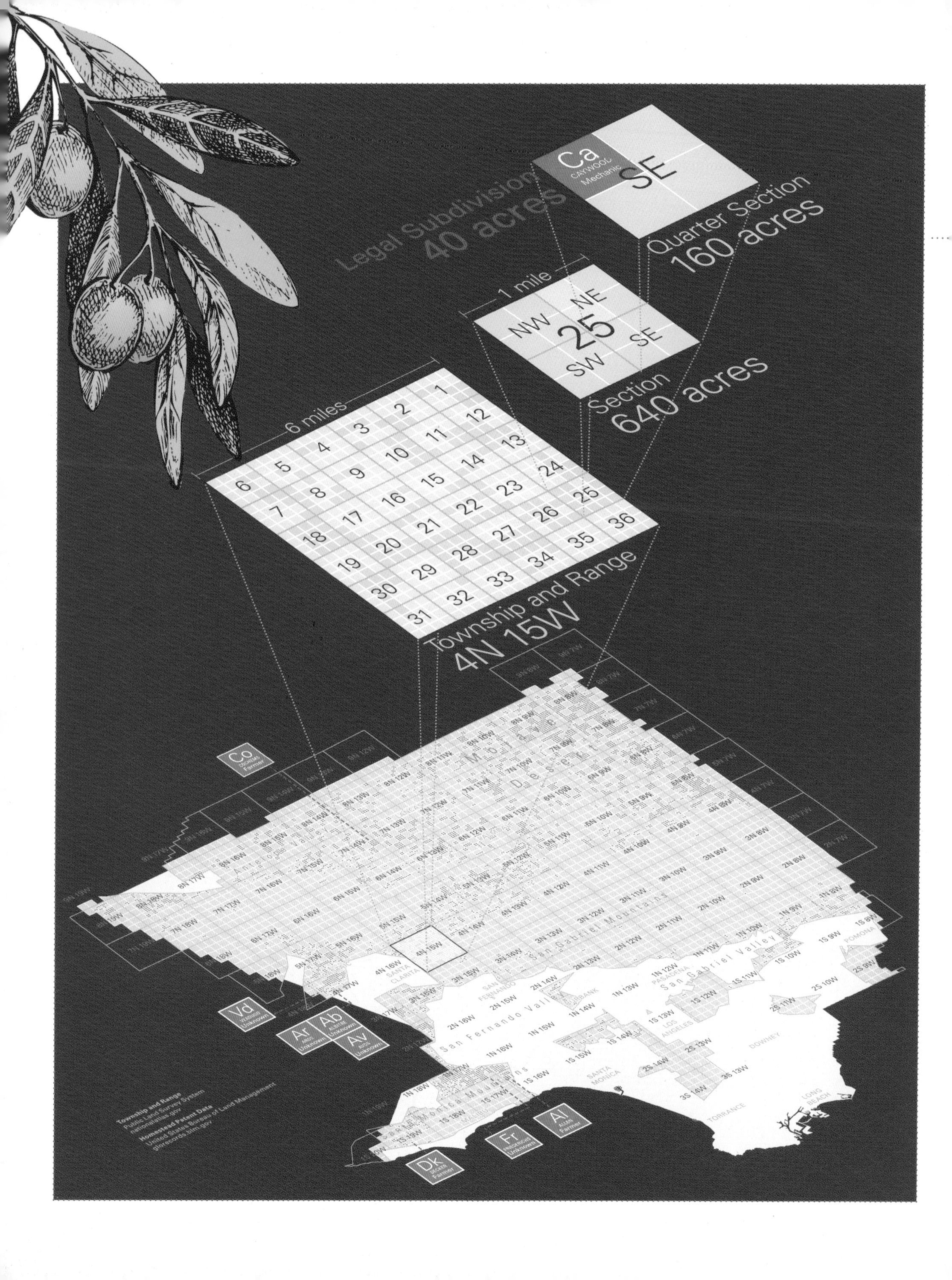
Ca
CAYWOOD
Mechanic
SE
Legal Subdivision
40 acres
Quarter Section
160 acres
1 mile
NW
NE
25
SW
SE
Section
640 acres
6 miles
1 2 3 4 5 6
7 8 9 10 11 12
13 14 15 16 17 18
19 20 21 22 23 24
25 26 27 28 29 30
31 32 33 34 35 36
Township and Range
4N 15W
Mojave Desert
Antelope Valley
San Gabriel Mountains
San Gabriel Valley
San Fernando Valley
Santa Monica Mountains
SANTA CLARITA
SAN FERNANDO
BURBANK
PASADENA
LOS ANGELES
SANTA MONICA
POMONA
DOWNEY
TORRANCE
LONG BEACH
4N 16W
Co
Farmer
Vd
Unknown
Ar
Unknown
Ab
Unknown
Av
Unknown
Al
Farmer
Fr
Unknown
Dk
Farmer
Township and Range
Public Land Survey System
nationalatlas.gov
Homestead Patent Data
United States Bureau of Land Management
glorecords.blm.gov

It has long been assumed that the Homestead Act of 1862 applied almost exclusively to the Great Plains region of the United States. However, the mountains and plains that make up the rugged majority of Los Angeles County were indeed divided into six-mile-square townships, then further sectioned and quarter-sectioned into the forty-acre subdivisions given to settlers for "free" under the law signed by President Lincoln. Although the initial wave of homesteading in LA was relatively slow, this changed when groundwater specialists from the U.S. Geological Survey discovered a substantial artesian water belt underneath the Antelope Valley in 1910, triggering a mass migration of pioneers eager to capitalize on speculative fantasies over land, oil, and agrarian opportunities. This diagram shows the manner in which surveyors sectioned land down to the forty-acre parcels homesteaders would receive. A handful of notable homesteads are called out with periodic table–style labels.

Emperors of Dust

THE FORGOTTEN HOMESTEADERS OF LOS ANGELES COUNTY

Anthea M. Hartig and Josh Sides

Elizabeth Friederich was sixty-one years old and short on luck when she and her daughter, Lizzie, stepped off the train in Los Angeles in 1906. Born in Switzerland, Elizabeth had immigrated with her husband to St. Louis, Missouri, in 1880, but he died shortly thereafter, and she was forced to take work as a domestic servant. Struggling to provide for herself and her daughter, Elizabeth's determined eye caught a promotion in the *St. Louis Republic* that there was free "government land" to be had in California. Their first stop in Los Angeles was at the Land Office, where Elizabeth identified two adjoining parcels in Topanga Canyon, almost thirty miles away. She and Lizzie walked the whole day and into the night, pushing through the oak woodlands and chaparral of the Santa Monica Mountains until they found the lots, marked them with sticks, and fell asleep on the ground. The next morning, they walked all the way back to the office to make their homestead claim official, bought some tools, and headed back to their plots. A well intentioned if condescending reporter from the *Los Angeles Times* marveled at the spectacle of the "gray-haired woman, with her pathetically slight figure, going out into the mountain wilds to build herself a home with her hands." But within four months, and without any assistance, the duo cleared the land, built a cabin, dug a well, and cultivated a garden of lettuce, peas, radishes, corn, and potatoes. They "proved up" their claim and received the land patents, free and clear, in 1912 and 1913.

The Friederichs would not have understood the way historians have told LA's history, for it has always been told from the center, or thereabouts. It has been a story of Hollywood, a story of the Westside, the Eastside, or South Central. But consider this: today, more than 60 percent of "LA" residents live outside the city limits and on the fringes of Los Angeles County. And another significant proportion of the populace lives in far-flung areas like Topanga Canyon that fall within the official boundaries of the city, but exist largely independent from it. In one of the most surprising developments of LA's surprising history, it was the Homestead Act that first brought folks to the city's backcountry after Anglo conquest in 1848.

Signed by Abraham Lincoln in 1862, the Homestead Act gave any American citizen the right to claim 160 acres, solidify that claim by improving it in five years, and file for an official homestead patent granting them ownership for perpetuity. Typically associated with the Great Plains, the act had a profound effect on Los Angeles County's growth and cultural geography. Between 1862 and 1976, when the act ended, more than 2,900 families claimed more than 451,837 acres of Los Angeles County land, equivalent to the total land area of the cities of Sacramento, San Francisco, Bakersfield, Fresno, and San Diego combined. If you want to understand Los Angeles, you need to understand its forgotten homesteaders.

As envisioned by Lincoln and his Republican allies, the Homestead Act would hasten the settlement of the American West by small farmers. The realization of "Free Soil" ideology that had given birth to the Republican Party, the Homestead Act rang an unapologetically populist tone. As a result, Southern Democrats vigorously refused to listen to Free Soil arguments in the late 1850s because they sought the expansion of slavery and the large plantation system in the West. The secession crisis in 1861 resulted in the depletion of vociferously oppositional Southern Democrats in Congress, allowing for easy passage of the Homestead Act, which Lincoln saw as a silver lining to the wrenching divide. Two months later, Lincoln signed the Pacific Railway Act and the Morrill Act, providing federal subsidies for transcontinental railway construction and federal land for agricultural colleges, respectively, permanently reshaping the American West.

It is a fair guess that neither Abraham

Lincoln nor his congressional allies had given much thought to Los Angeles in 1862. With a population of just over 11,000 souls, almost all of whom lived on or around the plaza, it was not a city destined for greatness, as it lacked a functional port, a manufacturing sector, or easily extracted natural resources. Instead, Anglo investors and attorneys frantically subdivided the once vast Spanish and Mexican ranchos during the 1870s, paving the way for waves of land speculation that would crest first in the 1880s and again in the 1920s. "Every city has had its boom," Carey McWilliams wrote in 1946, "but the history of Los Angeles is the history of its booms."

Then, as now, booms rewarded men and women with significant capital, speculative sensibility, and great luck. And during the booms of the 1880s, 1900s, and 1920s, investments in central city property made a handful of folks fabulously rich. But most immigrants and migrants to the pueblo lacked that good fortune: some were just unlucky; others nurtured agrarian dreams but lacked the capital, the skin color, or the citizenship eligibility for entry into the blooming citrus market; still others wanted to create alternative realities or longed for isolation. For them, the undeveloped fringes of Los Angeles County beckoned. In the remote and arid Antelope Valley, the rough and contentious terrain of the Santa Monica Mountains, and the bucolic Santa Clarita Valley, Angelenos, both newcomers and old-timers, claimed thousands of acres of "free land" under the Homestead Act. The distinctive geographies of these three regions deeply shaped the expectations and outcomes of the homesteaders who settled there, but among all homesteaders there burned a core desire of self-sufficiency. It is a yearning that enjoys renewed—if faddish—enthusiasm today, among home gardeners, urban chicken owners, and DIY-ers. But among the homesteaders of Los Angeles County, self-sufficiency meant survival. And in the process of surviving in these different landscapes, homesteaders profoundly shaped the cultures of the regions in ways that remain evident today.

About forty miles northeast from Los Angeles City Hall, and across the jagged terrain of the Angeles National Forest, lies the last frontier of Los Angeles. Minimally developed, covered by sparse patches of yucca trees, and with an average of 350 days of sunshine and only seven inches of rain per year, the Antelope Valley has always been remote. Even in the boom years, few Angelenos were brave or crazy enough to settle the region. "Many people in the county arrived at the definite conclusion," California journalist and scholar George Wharton James wrote in 1917, "that this was part of the irreclaimable desert, was totally unfit for agriculture, and therefore had no future." However, when groundwater specialists

from the U.S. Geological Survey came to the valley in 1910, in efficient order they identified a massive artesian water belt. As it always had in the arid West, capital followed water, and savvy investors soon installed pump engines powered first by gasoline and later by electricity. "The water," Wharton wrote in a promotional tract for the Antelope Valley in the early 1920s, "is pure and sweet, free from all injurious admixtures, either of lime or alkali, therefore admirably suited for domestic, as well as stock and irrigating purposes." All of a sudden, the Homestead Act, about sixty years old at this point, portended great futures. Eager souls deluged the Land Office in Los Angeles with claims, and soon pear orchards, honey farms, almond groves, hog and cattle pasturelands, and wheat fields flourished, creating agricultural hinterlands for the City of Los Angeles.

Peter Nicholas Cochems typified the new zeal for agricultural development in the Antelope Valley. A German immigrant and struggling farmer in Central Los Angeles, Cochems claimed homestead land in the valley in the 1880s, even before the discovery of the artesian water belt. Drawing only from wells on his homestead plots, Cochems planted dozens, and later hundreds, of almond trees. He soon became the leading booster of the Antelope Valley, sending his nuts, as well as a loaded almond branch preserved in embalming fluid, to the Los Angeles Chamber of Commerce, the Los Angeles County World's Fair, and the 1893 Chicago World's Fair. After the artesian water belt discovery, Cochems welcomed new neighbors into the valley, many of whom homesteaded their way to large-scale livestock operations. By the 1920s, almonds, apricots, alfalfa, and cattle were the leading exports from the Antelope Valley hinterlands into the city of Los Angeles, where they arrived by rail.

For men like Cochems, the Antelope Valley may have offered more than free, irrigable land and new commercial networks to the city of Los Angeles. It also represented the moral counterpoint to the degeneracy of Los Angeles. "The Antelope Valley regards itself as superior to many regions in social conditions," Wharton wrote. "In the first place there are no saloons, with their almost certain accompanying evils of gambling dens and haunts of vice. And such is the vigilance of the county officers that there have been few complaints, even, of blind pigs." Indeed, a close reading of the reminiscences of homesteaders and Bureau of Land Management records bears out Wharton's assessment about the rectitude and emerging personality of the region. One of the Antelope Valley's earliest and most prominent residents was a beekeeper and frontier preacher from Ohio named Reverend John E. Robbins, who settled in 1888, claimed a 160-acre homestead plot in 1900, and presided over parishioners in the dusty town of Acton for another twenty years. Simultaneously, residents of Acton, Agua Dulce, Ravenna, and Soledad Canyon founded The Union of Moral and Religious Association of Acton. According to founding articles, the function of The Union was to uphold the "'In God We Trust' principles of our early-on pioneers who were building rural America, U.S.A." It is worth noting that Peter Nicholas Cochems's only known run-in with the law was when he was charged with defamation of character for describing a drunken woman as "lower than the lowest woman" when he encountered her leaving a restaurant during one of his business trips to the city.

About seventy miles southwest of the Antelope Valley, homesteaders were simultaneously claiming land amidst the coastal sage, scrub oak, and chaparral of the Santa Monica Mountains between Topanga Canyon and Ventura County. But if the homesteaders of the Antelope Valley sought free, abundant, land in a godly country of sober, community-minded souls, the homesteaders of the Santa Monica Mountains were individualistic and downright ornery. The topography, the abundance of wildlife, and the scarcity of public infrastructure in the Santa Monica Mountains both lured and intensified this character. Unlike the homesteaders of the Antelope Valley, for whom land scarcity was unimaginable, the homesteaders of the Santa Monica Mountains encountered the limits of public land before they even arrived: because tycoon Frederick Hastings Rindge claimed ownership of what is today a large stretch of Pacific Coast Highway, many aspiring homesteaders had to wait until low tide to haul their belongings across the Pacific shoreline at the base of the mountains.

Indeed, battles between homesteaders and the Rindge family created a culture of perpetual legal and extralegal dispute in the region. Rindge, the sole heir to a vast estate, traveled from Cambridge, Massachusetts, to Los Angeles in 1887, settled in Santa Monica, and with his bride May Wright Rindge purchased Rancho Topanga Malibu Sequit as a 13,330-acre "weekend home" in 1892. In addition to blocking coast access, Rindge hosted weekend hunting excursions for wealthy Angelenos that angered aspiring homesteaders, particularly Marion Decker. A Kentucky-born farmer, Decker claimed his 160-acre plot adjacent to Rindge's property in 1901. Dependent on the Santa Monica Mountains' wildlife for sustenance, Decker was astounded by the brutality and wastefulness of Rindge's guests, who killed hundreds of deer each weekend for sport. The parties regularly shot does and fawns, discarding their bodies in the bushes, in a ritual of violence that was abhorrent even by the standards of the time. When one of the "nimrods," as the *Los Angeles Times* described the hunters, shot Decker's burro twelve times, Decker brought what would be the first of many suits against Rindge. Any hopes that Rindge's sudden death in 1905 would bring peace to the land were quickly dashed by his widow, May, who blocked the coastal road and stationed armed guards there in what would be the beginning of a near twenty-year legal dispute with the county that wound its way all the way to the United States Supreme Court. Finally, in *Rindge Co. v. County of Los Angeles* (1923), the court affirmed the right of eminent domain, allowing the state to pave what would become the Roosevelt Highway, later renamed Pacific Coast Highway in 1941.

But even when the Rindges were not involved, homesteading in the Santa Monica Mountains and Malibu was cantankerous business. When an English-born gardener named George Fremlin acquired his free plot in the hills above Calabasas in 1912 at the age of thirty-three, he appeared to have made the transition to imperious land baron very quickly, by regularly terrorizing his neighbors. Shortly before acquiring his homestead, he organized an armed posse to catch a man whom he believed had stolen his English bulldog, and started a fight with another homesteader onto whose property the dog had ambled. In 1919, the gun-wielding Fremlin chopped down a tree across a stream to divert water from his neighbor's to his own property. When brought before the court, he was impudent, and the judge warned him that his attitude toward the court was "ill-advised."

When they weren't busy fighting, the homesteaders of the Santa Monica Mountains were simply surviving. Cattle ranching and horse training became important enterprises, but the Santa Monica Mountains homesteaders never became large-scale agricultural producers in the way that Antelope Valley homesteaders did. Although the Malibu Creek watershed provided significant water for irrigation, very few acres of the Santa Monica Mountains landscape were actually arable: too many were rocky, hilly, and thickly wooded. As a result, once they'd "proved up" their claims by erecting crude houses, most Santa Monica Mountains homesteaders simply farmed their own plots for survival. "Absolute self-reliance was an essential," Lauretta Houston, a Santa Monica Mountains homesteader from the 1920s later remembered. "Yet when circumstances caused anyone bad luck, the rest of us were there to immediately help." When your neighbor's chickens stopped laying, you gave them eggs. When rabbits pulled out your beets under the cover of night, your neighbors gave you vegetables. "It was the only way we people could have survived in the mountains."

Meanwhile on the northwestern edge of the county, an unlikely band of homesteaders laid claim to the fertile Santa Clarita Valley in the watershed of the Santa Clara River. A tight-knit colony of Mexicans claimed more than 1,700 acres in prime agricultural land between Piru and Castaic creeks. Theirs was a tale of resilience in an era of overwhelming Anglo dominance. One of the first to claim land there under the Homestead Act was a Mexican-born farmer named Macedonia Aros, about whom we know very little other than that he established an outpost there in 1891 when he was in his late forties. However, he soon acquired a neighbor of prestigious pedigree: Juan de Dios Verdugo. Juan Verdugo was the great-grandson of José María Verdugo, the original owner of Rancho San Rafael, a 36,000-acre

Spanish land grant that stretched across modern-day Glendale, Eagle Rock, La Cañada, and Montrose. However, when great-grandfather Verdugo died, his on Julio made a mess of things. He mortgaged the vast property in 1861, according to historian Leonard Pitt, "for sprucing up his casa, buying provisions, and paying taxes." That spree, coupled with ballooning debt, ended in "foreclosure, sheriff's sale, and ruination." Naturally, Verdugo's lawyers were the first to the auction house and bought the entire ranch. "Verdugo thus deserved the penalty for the worst real-estate deal of the decade, and his children inherited very little." Indeed, his great-grandson was forced to take up free government land in an untested valley to reclaim any Verdugo glory. But Juan Verdugo made a respectable go of it, encouraging other relatives from the Verdugo clan to claim homesteads, including Adolfo Albitre and several members of the Aros family, and contributing to the region's burgeoning lima bean production.

Ironically, while the Verdugo and other Mexicans labored on in their obscurity, Anglos in Los Angeles became increasingly enamored with an idealized Mexican past.

The Mexican homesteads in Santa Clarita were fewer than seven hundred feet from the original property line of Rancho San Francisco, the vast Mexican land grant once owned by Mexican solider Antonio del Valle and then his son, Ygnacio del Valle. It was Ygnacio's Rancho Camulos that set the stage for Helen Hunt Jackson's 1884 book, *Ramona*, widely credited for sparking regional interest in the Mexican fantasy past and stimulating tourism. Jackson stayed at Rancho Camulos during the research phase for her novel, and drew inspiration from Camulos in her creation of the Morena Ranch of the novel. Charles Lummis and other boosters quickly seized on the connection and advertised Rancho Camulos as "home of Ramona." In 1910, D. W. Griffith directed the film adaption of *Ramona* with Mary Pickford, and today visitors can stand inside the chapel where she was wed in the film. Neither Jackson nor Lummis would have known what to do with Luciano Chavez, a Mexican homesteader and neighbor to Verdugo, who acquired his free homestead only after enriching himself through extensive land speculation in the central city. The typical Anglo imagination of the era could not easily accommodate a Mexican like this.

Today, the homesteads and homesteaders of Los Angeles County are largely relics. Trees blazoned with claim indicators were felled long ago, and tracts have been subdivided into countless plots. Mini-mansions climb the hillsides of Calabasas, across the flats of Lancaster, southward from Castaic toward the former Verdugo homestead. There's a lonely stretch of road in the Antelope Valley that passes a signpost reading "Cochems Ranch," but there's not a structure to be seen for mile. In Topanga Canyon, the land first broken by Missouri Homesteader Claude Allen in 1901, and occupied by his family through the 1960s, was sold off in 1968, at which point it became home of Elysium Fields, a nudist camp and massage "sensorium" that contributed to the canyon's reputation as a counterculture haven.

But the certain strains of the culture created by homesteaders live on. Today, Chip Mandeville, a descendant of the Santa Monica Mountains Decker clan, earns his keep calming horses. The "horse whisperer," as equestrians refer to him, keeps the Decker spirit alive. "I am tied to these people that are of homestead clans," he recently said. "I am tied into people that were raised in these mountains and literally had to eat off of what they were able to harvest, whether it was deer or rabbit or quail or fish. They lived off the land." Enabled by populism and imperialism, forged by a range of individuals and families, these landscapes and their peoples reveal a forgotten moment of LA history, but one that we may revisit every time we claim a patch of soil in Southern California.

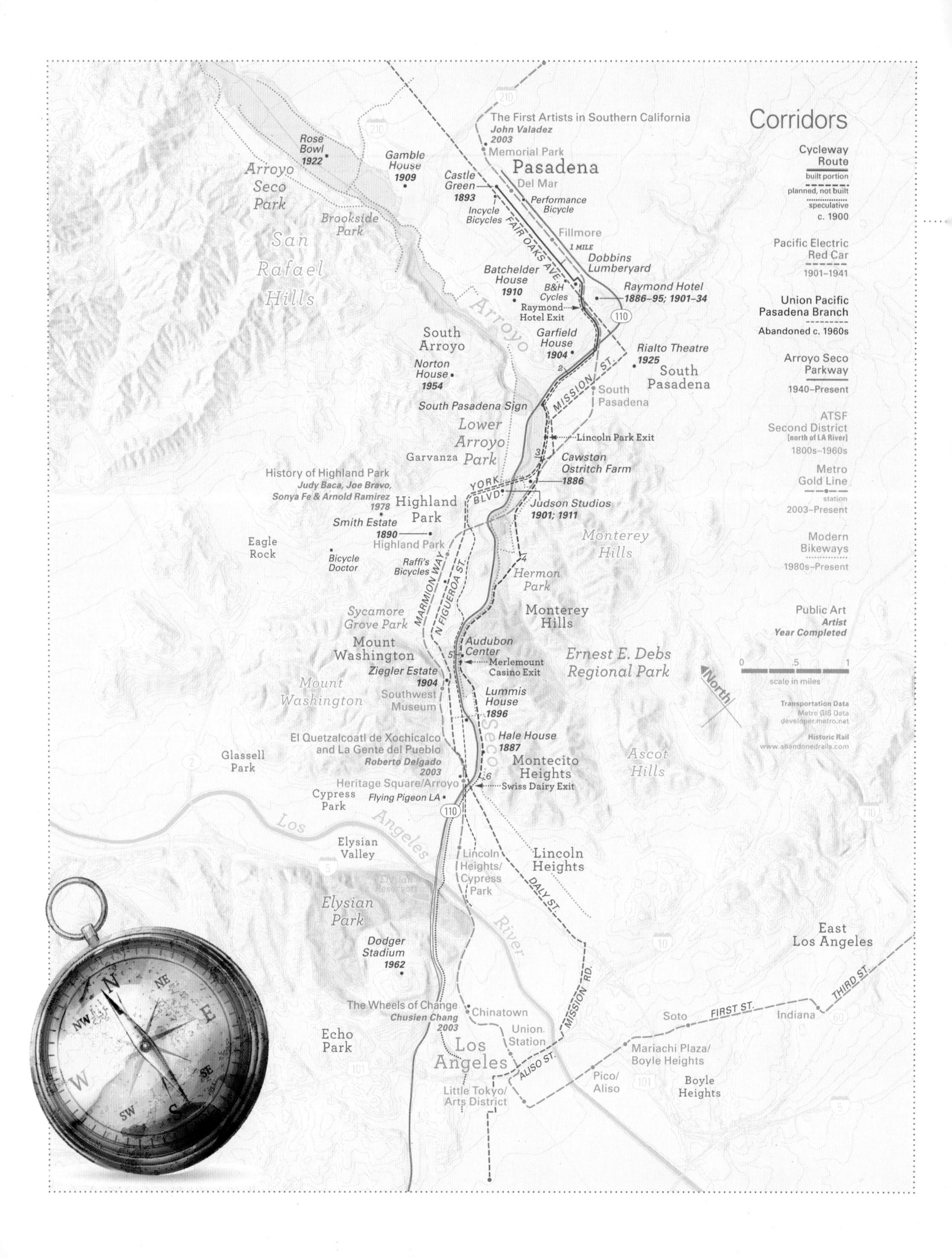

Corridors
Cycleway Route
built portion
planned, not built
speculative
c. 1900
Pacific Electric Red Car
1901–1941
Union Pacific Pasadena Branch
Abandoned c. 1960s
Arroyo Seco Parkway
1940–Present
ATSF Second District
[north of LA River]
1800s–1960s
Metro Gold Line
station
2003–Present
Modern Bikeways
1980s–Present
Public Art
Artist
Year Completed
scale in miles
North
Transportation Data
Metro GIS Data
developer.metro.net
Historic Rail
www.abandonedrails.com
The First Artists in Southern California
John Valadez
2003
Memorial Park
Pasadena
Rose Bowl
1922
Gamble House
1909
Arroyo Seco Park
Castle Green
1893
Del Mar
Performance Bicycle
Incycle Bicycles
Brookside Park
San Rafael Hills
FAIR OAKS AVE
Fillmore
1 MILE
Dobbins Lumberyard
Batchelder House
1910
B&H Cycles
Raymond Hotel Exit
Raymond Hotel
1886–95; 1901–34
Arroyo
South Arroyo
Garfield House
1904
Rialto Theatre
1925
South Pasadena
Norton House
1954
MISSION ST.
South Pasadena
South Pasadena Sign
Lower Arroyo Park
Lincoln Park Exit
Garvanza
Cawston Ostritch Farm
1886
History of Highland Park
Judy Baca, Joe Bravo, Sonya Fe & Arnold Ramirez
1978
YORK BLVD
Highland Park
Judson Studios
1901; 1911
Smith Estate
1890
Highland Park
Eagle Rock
Bicycle Doctor
Raffi's Bicycles
Monterey Hills
Hermon Park
MARMION WAY
N FIGUEROA ST.
Sycamore Grove Park
Monterey Hills
Mount Washington
Audubon Center
Merlemount Casino Exit
Ernest E. Debs Regional Park
Ziegler Estate
1904
Mount Washington
Southwest Museum
Lummis House
1896
Seco
Hale House
1887
El Quetzalcoatl de Xochicalco and La Gente del Pueblo
Roberto Delgado
2003
Montecito Heights
Ascot Hills
Glassell Park
Heritage Square/Arroyo
Swiss Dairy Exit
Cypress Park
Flying Pigeon LA
Los Angeles River
Elysian Valley
Lincoln Heights/Cypress Park
Lincoln Heights
DALY ST.
Elysian Reservoir
Elysian Park
Dodger Stadium
1962
East Los Angeles
MISSION RD.
THIRD ST.
The Wheels of Change
Chusien Chang
2003
Chinatown
Soto
FIRST ST.
Indiana
Echo Park
Union Station
Los Angeles
ALISO ST.
Mariachi Plaza/Boyle Heights
Pico/Aliso
Boyle Heights
Little Tokyo/Arts District

The Arroyo Seco corridor, connecting Pasadena to downtown Los Angeles and thus a significant commuter thoroughfare, is an appropriate lens through which to examine a slice of the city's complex transportation history. Horace Dobbins's never-completed bicycle "Cycleway" path, the subject of this essay, is depicted alongside the Red Car line, once part of the most extensive public transit system in the country before tracks were demolished to make way for automobiles and freeways. The old Atchison, Topeka, and Santa Fe Railway track is now repurposed as the Metro Gold Line. For future-minded Angelenos with a renewed passion for public transit, bicycle commutes, and even trekking through the city on foot, these memory maps of old routes tantalize us with the question, "What if?"

Cycleway

Dan Koeppel

The South California towns, Los Angeles and Pasadena, are now connected by the strangest and most interesting of links—a magnificent, elevated cycle-way, with a smooth surface of wood, running for nine miles through beautiful country, flanked by green hills and affording views at every point of the snow-clad Sierras....On this splendid track cyclists may now enjoy the very poetry of wheeling. At Pasadena, they may mount their cycles, put their feet on the foot rest, and sail down to Los Angeles without so much as touching the pedals, even though the gradient is extremely slight. The way lies for the most part along the east bank of the Arroyo Seco, giving a fine view of this wooded stream, skirting the foot of the neighboring oak-covered hill.

—"California's Great Cycle-Way," by T. D. Denham, *Pearson's Magazine*, September 1901

The California Cycleway wasn't just the first freeway in Los Angeles. It was also the best, because it envisioned a more perfect version of this city—a place where bicycles, not cars, ruled the road. The first time I heard about the Cycleway, I was captivated and stricken with disbelief. It was the mid-1990s, and I was with Dennis Crowley, a bike activist who believed that the old pathway could be—had to be—rebuilt. Crowley took a group of us into the Arroyo Seco, the dry creek bed whose route the Cycleway was to have paralleled. A modern bike path had been cut into the concrete-lined waterway, but to Crowley, it was an abomination.

"That's no Cycleway," he told me. It was too short, and besides, during rainy winters, the path would need to be closed to keep riders from being swept away by floodwaters. In the years since I met Crowley—his dream went unrealized after he passed away in 2008—I've become almost as much of an impossible idealist as he was. My life in Los Angeles has, more and more, become one where travel is primarily under my own power, by bike or on foot. And over and over, on the ground and in my fantasies, I've returned to the Cycleway. With maps, old and new, in hand, I've explored the terrain the old bicycle highway was to have skirted, trying to overlay this turn-of-the-century creation onto a landscape radically altered by the construction of highways, the flattening of hillsides, the shifting of waterways, and, most of all, the arrival of millions of people with their own Los Angeles dreams.

Twenty thousand miles of road crisscross the county of Los Angeles, spreading across an area as big as the state of Connecticut. The region is frequently thought of as oversized, unmanageable, even ugly—a heartless, soulless array of mini-malls and blacktop.

Here's what I tell people—and I say it a lot, so much that my friends and acquaintances are tired of hearing it: If that's the Los Angeles you see, you're probably looking out the windshield of a car. Released from our steel-and-glass enclosures, the size of Los Angeles suddenly becomes the source of its power; the city transforms into the world's biggest game board, with endless variation and permutation, infinite opportunities for exploration and revelation.

I have been "playing" this Los Angeles for over two decades. The game involves searching, finding passages that span both physical place and time, and then bringing people along. I lead walks through the city along themed or idealized passages, trying, for example, to ring downtown along dirt roads, back alleys, and networks of public stairways. To me, there's soul-nourishing discovery, even beauty, in Los Angeles's infamous sprawl.

Early on, most of my explorations were speculative—a search with no particular object in mind, other than discovering things I didn't know about and hadn't seen. I opened my walks to the public, hoping that they would attract people to walking in a city that, to say the least, was unwelcoming to the activity. But over the past few years, an almost shocking transformation has begun. Pedestrianism and bicycling are undergoing a renaissance in Los Angeles. Much of that activity is focused on the neighborhoods between Pasadena and Los Angeles, among the region's most densely populated, polluted, and traffic clogged. Those communities—and I live in one of them—are in desperate need of cleaner, calmer ways to get around. Over the years, I came to view the Cycleway, as described to me by Crowley and then, especially, as depicted in the *Pearson's* article that I discovered several years later, as a template, a vision of Los Angeles as it once was and maybe could be again.

There was only one problem: The British magazine *Pearson's* was a reputable publication, but when it came to Denham's story, its London editors were hoodwinked, something I discovered as I turned my explorations toward the Cycleway, looking for traces of it in the modern landscape. The California Cycleway was a real thing, but the project the article described—majestic, visionary, and especially complete—never happened.

Horace M. Dobbins plunged the shovel into the ground. It was November 1899, and in the decade since he'd arrived in Southern California, the Philadelphia native had become a prominent citizen in Pasadena, the city of which he would later be elected mayor. But for now, the thirty-one-year-old entrepreneur was launching what he believed would be a revolutionary and lucrative venture.

"The earth turns," he intoned, tossing a clump of dirt to the side, "and we turn the earth."

The crowd cheered. Bugles rang out. Within a year, Dobbins promised, something similar to Columbus's short route to the Orient would rise above the hills of the Los Angeles basin. His "Cycleway" was designed to swiftly and conveniently transport people between a pair of key urban centers: the old colonial plaza in Downtown Los Angeles, and Pasadena, the burgeoning, modern suburb to the north that then rivaled the older city in size and ambition. The Dobbins route—which neatly anticipated and presaged the automotive freeways that now stretch across the region—would be a modern marvel. It would boast a state-of-the-art toll-collecting system. It would be elevated fifteen feet above the ground; the limited access would ensure that traffic flowed smoothly. "It can be said," wrote the *Los Angeles Times* of the ground breaking, "that none of the new Southern California enterprises will...be more certain of financial success. The wheel must have a path of its own between these two cities."

In the years leading up to the twentieth century, the idea that such a wheel would be a bicycle's was not surprising: There was no alternative. America was in the midst of a massive bike boom. Over 3,000 American cycle manufacturers were founded in the final decade of the 1800s. Tens of thousands of bike clubs were formed, especially in Southern California, while mild weather made the activity a year-round pursuit.

Dobbins began building, promising that the entire thoroughfare—nine miles long and studded with diversions, amusements, and places of repose—would be completed within two years. For a while, it looked like he'd succeed. The only surviving photographs of the Cycleway's first section show something resembling an idyll; the boardwalk-like track curves gently beneath shimmering arbors. A more hardscrabble image depicts the Cycleway reaching majestically above ramshackle homes and dust-laden surface roads. But the most telling picture is one that implies not how visionary the project—or its founder, who is the subject of that photograph—was, but how quickly it all went awry.

The location of the northernmost piece of the Cycleway, the path's first section, the one featured in those dozen or so extant pictures, is easiest to find. That's because plenty of landmarks seen in those images are still there. But the farther one gets from the route's Pasadena start point, the harder it is to follow the Cycleway's path or find any traces of it. I decided the best thing to do would be to begin in Pasadena, on foot, and head south. I carried along a copy of B. O. Kendall's *Official City of Pasadena Real Estate Guide,* printed in 1900. The Cycleway is one of the map's most prominent features, depicted with a thick double line, the same designation used for railroads and major streets.

In addition to the old map, I was holding a photograph of the Cycleway's Pasadena start point (or end point, depending on your direction of travel), where Dobbins had erected a tollbooth.

Raising the image, it was easy to square it with a building that still stands, or at least partially stands, just south of the city's restored "Old Town" shopping district. At the end of the nineteenth century, there was no more elegant place to spend the night in Pasadena than the Castle Green, which opened a few months before Dobbins broke ground. During those early days, the hotel consisted of mirror-image Moorish structures, connected by a footbridge. In 1924, the eastern building was demolished. Today, the remaining structure is part of a condominium complex, though it retains the oddness of the original design. The photograph I held shows the Cycleway and the exit

kiosk, high above the ground, nearly dead-ending into the hotel's brick facade.

From the Castle Green, the Cycleway extended south, according to the map, paralleling a set of railroad tracks. Those tracks were once used as the approach to Los Angeles for the transcontinental lines run by the Atchison, Topeka, and Santa Fe Railroad. They've been heavily modified in the past hundred years, but the same basic right-of-way today accommodates the Metro Gold Line, part of a regional light-rail system that began operating in 2003. The proximity of the Cycleway to the railroad gives a hint of Dobbins's marketing strategy. It wouldn't be enough, he knew, to offer an unimpeded journey between the cities at both ends of the Cycleway. The thoroughfare would also have to connect existing, established attractions. About a mile south of Castle Green stood the establishment's main rival, South Pasadena's Raymond Hotel. The facility was built by railroad mogul Walter Raymond and offered two hundred rooms to accommodate "particular people"—well-heeled passengers who needed to bathe, relax, and refresh after the long journey across America.

Dobbins saw Raymond's inn as the perfect "second exit" on the Cycleway, and set up a tollbooth directly in front of the hotel's driveway (in his business plan, Dobbins predicted that he'd garner about $30,000 annually in tolls, equal to about $2 million today). Walking from the Castle, it took thirty minutes to reach the Raymond site, where only a single structure survives, the caretaker's cottage where Walter Raymond and his wife, humbled by the catastrophic losses of the Great Depression, lived out their days.

From the Raymond, Dobbins's wooden boardwalk turned briefly west, curving into a lumberyard built to process the thousands of feet of oak planks needed to build the elevated structure. It crossed through Lincoln Park, once an independent town that's since been absorbed by South Pasadena, before reaching the Arroyo Seco. The Kendall map shows the Cycleway extending from there to the Cawston Ostrich Farm, a tourist attraction widely considered to be the region's first theme park, though with a rather odd theme that included several hundred live, flightless birds and the products made from them, including (elegant) feather hats and (delicious?) oversized omelets.

The site of the Cawston farm is now occupied by a pod of modern apartments (going rate for a one-bedroom in the Ostrich Farm Lofts: about $700,000). From here, Dobbins hoped to extend the route another seven miles into Los Angeles. The conventional view, expressed to me by the owners of a coffee house that stood at the dividing line between South Pasadena and Los Angeles from about 2000 through 2008, is that Dobbins got no further, that he never actually entered the city he hoped to connect with his adoptive hometown of Pasadena (the owners were cyclists, named the Cycleway Café after the Dobbins construct, and claimed that their location stood at the Cycleway's southern boundary). But a story published in the *Los Angeles Times* on February 19, 1899, hints that construction of the lower portion of the Cycleway was ongoing even as Dobbins struggled with financing the already-built segments. The article included a conceptual illustration of the Cycleway's midpoint, along the narrowest section of the Arroyo Seco. Because of the way the river cut between hillsides, there was a lack of flat, navigable terrain, making this the only section of the route that would sit on a slope, a potential negative for bike riders (Dobbins had promised, in defiance of physics, that the route would be downhill in both directions).

There were no fancy hotels or established tourist destinations between the Ostrich Farm and Los Angeles, so Dobbins had to invent them himself, and what he proposed would be more populist—and more grand—than the existing attractions along the route's northern segment. "Among the most attractive features of the enterprise are the plans for the 'Merlemount Park and Casino,' an up-to-date pleasure ground and resort about midway on the line," the *Times* wrote. The article continued: "The company has secured 115 acres of desirable land for this purchase, situated on the hills east of Highland Park, three and a half miles distant from the plaza in Los Angeles."

Today, the spot where Merlemount was to have stood is within another utopian construct—this one an actual success. Debs Park consists of two distinct halves. On the east, over an 800-foot hilltop and away from the river, is a traditional city park, with basketball courts and baseball diamonds. The Arroyo side, on land flattened by Dobbins, had been overtaken by nature during the following decades, a patch of chaparral lonely enough to have become habitat for a marvelous assortment of native plants, and, at its lower reaches, a less salutary enclave that sometimes attracted prostitutes and drug dealers. The proposed casino site was reclaimed in 2003, when the California Audubon Society took control of the park and built a nature center. It isn't quite a casino, but the grounds are pleasurable enough.

By the summer of 1899, Dobbins had fallen behind in his promises to complete the route. Though workers continued to excavate, money was tight. By the fall of 1900, Dobbins was having trouble paying his bills, and on October 8 of that year, the *Pasadena Daily Star* reported that the "Cycleway will do no more work now."

Over the next two decades, Dobbins tried mightily to complete his route. But the bike boom was ending. In 1901, the *Pearson's* article appeared, leaving the impression that the pathway was complete, that bike riders were zipping between the two cities, except when they were stopping to dine, gamble, and take in the spectacular views. In reality, the Cycleway was doomed. In 1902, an entrepreneur named Ransom Olds introduced a cheap, reliable motorcar, the "Oldsmobile." A year later, Henry Ford began producing his first internal combustion engines. The Pasadena section of the Cycleway stood, unused and deteriorating. In 1908, the California Supreme Court ruled that Dobbins had to return some of the land he'd received via eminent domain. A year later, under threat of losing more property, Dobbins made a last-ditch proposal for the route, which he'd rechristened "The Air Line." This time, it would be a monorail to Los Angeles. For a decade, Dobbins pushed the project. On March 30, 1919, the citizens of Los Angeles voted on it.

Dobbins lost.

There would be new routes along the Arroyo. Construction on what would eventually become the Pasadena Freeway—"the 110"—would begin that same year, but Dobbins wouldn't be a part of it. Could he have known? I think he did know. The telling photograph—one that was hung, framed, in the old Cycleway coffee house, and which is the only known photo of Dobbins himself on the pathway—provides evidence of the optimism, foolishness, and fate of the project. Dobbins is smiling. He's proud. He's on the Cycleway. And he's driving a car.

Certainly, Dobbins engaged in speculation, and maybe fabrication, too, if the *Pearson's* article is any evidence. Dobbins was sometimes seen as a huckster, but his true place in history isn't easy to determine, even a century later.

I wanted to believe that Dobbins was a visionary, that the vision he imagined, if fulfilled, would have led to a Los Angeles more humane, more functional, and more beautiful than the one we have. I spent hours poring over maps, then following them through the streets and alleys and along the riverbed, searching for traces of a Cycleway whose most prominent written testimony—the *Pearson's* story—was a work of fiction.

But maybe there was a little bit of truth in that fiction.

I'd become obsessed with the idea of finding a piece of the Cycleway within the boundaries of the City of Los Angeles. To me, such a remnant would be proof that Dobbins's vision extended far enough that his legacy, his dream, could be taken seriously—and could, perhaps, be embraced in a Los Angeles that is currently thinking about more gentle ways to move people from home to work, suburb to city.

In other words, I wanted to find something—something, no matter how tiny—in the *Pearson's* article that felt true, that I could touch, or see. I didn't exactly expect Merlemount to be some modern Machu Picchu, a lost city that would reveal itself only to the explorer dedicated and discerning enough to find it (or just somebody slightly obsessed, like me). But there had to be *something* there.

It wasn't an entirely crazy notion. On one of my earlier walks, I scrambled up a slope familiar to many regional commuters; if you're driving north on the 110, you'll notice a steep hillside just as you exit the city of Los Angeles. The words "South Pasadena" are sunken into an incline on your right, formed out of carefully placed boulders. On foot, you exit the riverbed and then pass through a concrete passage below the freeway. Traffic thunders overhead. Climbing, you step alongside the stone letters, eventually reaching a chain-link fence.

Looking over the barrier, you first wonder what the fence is guarding. There's nothing but a thirty-foot-wide strip of land. Thick oaks buffer the freeway's din, and looking north, you can peer a half mile into the distance, where a second fence blocks the strip's northern edge. I didn't know I was actually going to boost myself over the barrier until I held up two maps, the 1900 Pasadena guide, which showed the Cycleway, and a modern roadmap, which listed the closed-off space as a real, navigable street. Layering one image over the other, I was able to line up the bike route perfectly with the modern view. The gentle path the route followed, almost exactly, the bend seen on the old photographs of the Dobbins route. It remains the only remaining segment of the Cycleway that stands clear and undeveloped.

Or so I thought.

I'd also found a dusty map dated 1921 sitting in a poster-sized folio in the archives of the Los Angeles Public Library. On that document, far south of where the elevated boardwalk ended, was another narrow line. Written alongside the line, in perfect draftsman's script, was the word "Cycleway."

I made a copy of the map and took the Gold Line train to the Southwest Museum station, which sits directly across the Arroyo from the proposed Merlemount site. Five minutes later, I was looking at a row of homes—all of which were built and noted on the nearly century-old document. Somewhere above, perhaps in the backyards or on the hillside, I hoped to find proof that Dobbins had very nearly reached downtown Los Angeles.

Halfway down the block, I found a way up. A narrow sidewalk ran perpendicular to the street. I followed it up the slope. Just beyond the row of houses, the sidewalk turned into a set of stairs. Alongside the stairs was a thick stand of trees and bushes. Thirty feet up, those bushes gave way to the backyards of the houses on the street above. The stairs covered exactly thirty feet of terrain—the width Dobbins had set as a standard dimension for his rights-of-way.

When I got home, I pulled up the Google satellite view of the pathway. What I saw astonished me: The right of way was easy to see. The thick stand of vegetation alongside the stairs actually extended for blocks. With houses on either side, the path wasn't accessible, but it was a path, overgrown and therefore obvious.

The next step was to consult the Los Angeles County Assessor's Office maps database, where you can click on a tiny image and capture block-by-block surveys of the city's five hundred square miles. I opened each printed segment as it downloaded, zooming in. The overgrown pathway was clearly marked as city property. It was clearly marked with a name. The maps I was looking at were less than ten years old, but the designation they bore reflected a purpose assigned more than a century ago: "California Cycleway."

If you want to ride a bike from Pasadena to Los Angeles today, you have to cobble together a route. You can follow the rough path of the Cycleway to South Pasadena on surface streets, pedaling past the old Ostrich Farm, then dropping into the 2.2-mile-long bike path along the Arroyo Seco. If it isn't raining, you can take that modern path halfway to downtown before you're unceremoniously ejected onto surface streets just below the Merlemount site.

Recently, the city has begun trying to find a way to connect the Arroyo path to downtown. The plan is to add new bike lanes to existing streets. As recently as a few years ago, this meant doing little more than painting a stripe and putting up a few "Share the Road" signs. This more advanced lane would give a full three feet of room for bike riders, creating a safe and comfortable path, integrated with traffic. The proposal is controversial, though, with local drivers complaining that it would slow their commutes.

I like the idea of fewer car lanes, and I like the idea of cycling on the main boulevards, where bikes—legally considered full-fledged vehicles—have a right to be. But the spots where these modifications are being proposed are just yards from the overgrown right-of-way I discovered that still bears the Cycleway name. It doesn't seem like it would take that much to clear that strip, pave it, and finally bring it to public use, as Dobbins intended. And the route could be extended along the hillside, passing the nature center, which could provide a Merlemount-like respite for fatigued riders.

The only thing missing would be the final attraction Dobbins dreamt up but never built, his "Swiss Dairy," an ice cream parlor, located just before the route would have reached downtown. The question of ice cream is a serious one, as long as we're dreaming and speculating. Riding a bike in Los Angeles is sweaty, hot work. Luckily, there's no need to build something permanent. Modern Southern California is a paradise of frozen treats, ranging from pushcart vendors serving *paletas*—Mexican popsicles—to marvelous trucks offering soft-serve. Somehow, I imagine, if the Dobbins path were revived and rebuilt, the amenities would come. So would I. And as long as I'm channeling Horace M. Dobbins, I wouldn't be alone. Thousands of others would join me. They'd empty the freeways and take to their bikes. And they wouldn't just be playing on the great game board that is Los Angeles. They'd be living on it. They'd be creating it anew.

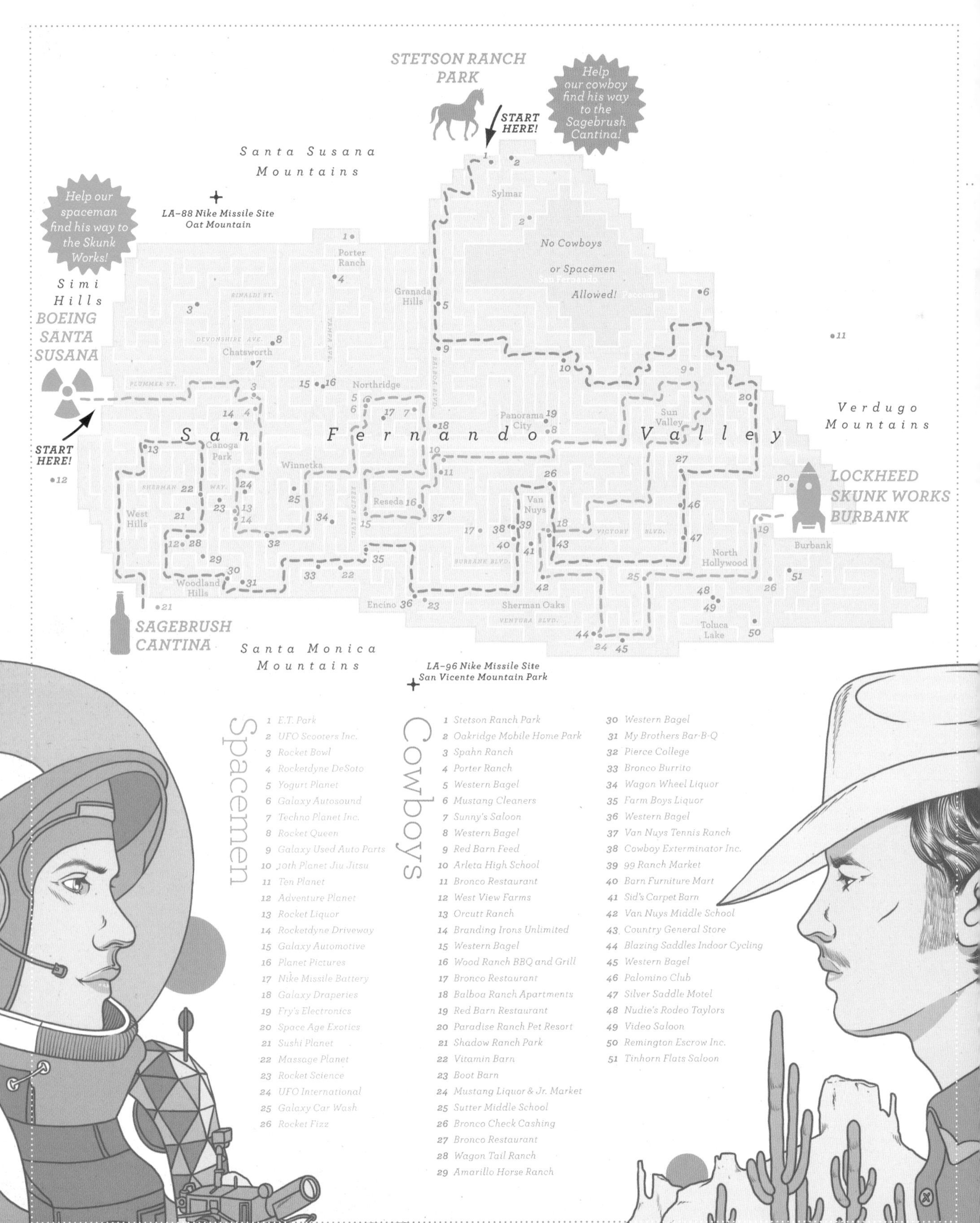

STETSON RANCH PARK
START HERE!
Help our cowboy find his way to the Sagebrush Cantina!
Santa Susana Mountains
LA-88 Nike Missile Site Oat Mountain
Help our spaceman find his way to the Skunk Works!
Simi Hills
BOEING SANTA SUSANA
START HERE!
Sylmar
No Cowboys or Spacemen Allowed!
San Fernando
Pacoima
Porter Ranch
Granada Hills
Chatsworth
Northridge
Canoga Park
Winnetka
Reseda
West Hills
Woodland Hills
Encino
Van Nuys
Panorama City
Sun Valley
North Hollywood
Sherman Oaks
Toluca Lake
Burbank
San Fernando Valley
Verdugo Mountains
LOCKHEED SKUNK WORKS BURBANK
SAGEBRUSH CANTINA
Santa Monica Mountains
LA-96 Nike Missile Site San Vicente Mountain Park
Spacemen
1 E.T. Park
2 UFO Scooters Inc.
3 Rocket Bowl
4 Rocketdyne DeSoto
5 Yogurt Planet
6 Galaxy Autosound
7 Techno Planet Inc.
8 Rocket Queen
9 Galaxy Used Auto Parts
10 10th Planet Jiu Jitsu
11 Ten Planet
12 Adventure Planet
13 Rocket Liquor
14 Rocketdyne Driveway
15 Galaxy Automotive
16 Planet Pictures
17 Nike Missile Battery
18 Galaxy Draperies
19 Fry's Electronics
20 Space Age Exotics
21 Sushi Planet
22 Massage Planet
23 Rocket Science
24 UFO International
25 Galaxy Car Wash
26 Rocket Fizz
Cowboys
1 Stetson Ranch Park
2 Oakridge Mobile Home Park
3 Spahn Ranch
4 Porter Ranch
5 Western Bagel
6 Mustang Cleaners
7 Sunny's Saloon
8 Western Bagel
9 Red Barn Feed
10 Arleta High School
11 Bronco Restaurant
12 West View Farms
13 Orcutt Ranch
14 Branding Irons Unlimited
15 Western Bagel
16 Wood Ranch BBQ and Grill
17 Bronco Restaurant
18 Balboa Ranch Apartments
19 Red Barn Restaurant
20 Paradise Ranch Pet Resort
21 Shadow Ranch Park
22 Vitamin Barn
23 Boot Barn
24 Mustang Liquor & Jr. Market
25 Sutter Middle School
26 Bronco Check Cashing
27 Bronco Restaurant
28 Wagon Tail Ranch
29 Amarillo Horse Ranch
30 Western Bagel
31 My Brothers Bar-B-Q
32 Pierce College
33 Bronco Burrito
34 Wagon Wheel Liquor
35 Farm Boys Liquor
36 Western Bagel
37 Van Nuys Tennis Ranch
38 Cowboy Exterminator Inc.
39 99 Ranch Market
40 Barn Furniture Mart
41 Sid's Carpet Barn
42 Van Nuys Middle School
43 Country General Store
44 Blazing Saddles Indoor Cycling
45 Western Bagel
46 Palomino Club
47 Silver Saddle Motel
48 Nudie's Rodeo Taylors
49 Video Saloon
50 Remington Escrow Inc.
51 Tinhorn Flats Saloon

Allusions to cowboys and spacemen are deeply encoded into San Fernando Valley's residential, commercial, and industrial landscape; the gun-slinging past and rocket-ship future imagined by Cold War–era Valley residents are still etched in the environment today, selling everything from alcohol to used cars to insurance. The Valley's center-less surface grid inspired this map maze, offering playful (and intersecting) traversals from two "cowboy" sites, the equestrian-friendly Stetson Park Ranch and the restaurant Sagebrush Cantina, and two "spaceman" sites, a former Boeing field laboratory and Lockheed's Skunk Works, where classified aviation work continues to this day.

Woody and Buzz

LANDSCAPE MOTIFS IN THE SAN FERNANDO VALLEY

Steven M. Graves

When my kids were toddlers, they loved watching the computer-animated feature *Toy Story*. For those who haven't seen it, *Toy Story* recounts the adventures of a group of toys, who, when no humans were around, would come to life. It is a brilliant storytelling device that no doubt confirms the imaginative suspicions little kids have regarding their toys. *Toy Story* is largely a "buddy tale" in which rival toys, a cowboy doll named Woody and a spaceman action figure named Buzz Lightyear, become fast friends after a series of thrilling journeys across town.

It occurred to me shortly after I moved my family to Los Angeles in 2003 that Woody and Buzz provide excellent metaphors for exploring the landscape of America's classic postwar suburb, the San Fernando Valley. Cowboys and spacemen are *everywhere* in the Valley: the former evoke a romanticized past and the latter a romanticized future as dreamed by those living in the 1950s and '60s. Over and over, Woody and Buzz—and their tensions and ultimate similarities—tell the story of the Valley during its adolescence, narrating a story about past and future as they were understood during the Cold War. Other places in the United States also feature cowboys-and-spacemen landscape motifs; Houston, Roswell, Area 51, even other parts of LA come to mind, but no location anywhere matches the San Fernando Valley in terms of the sheer volume and intensity of this iconic and ironic imagery.

Today, though, one wonders if their tale can be heard, or even be understood, in the cacophony of the postmodern landscape crowding around, slowly displacing or rendering illegible their once hegemonic dualism.

Woodyland: America's Suburban Cowtown

Cowboy iconography is deeply woven into both the domestic and commercial landscape of the San Fernando Valley. Loads of businesses leverage Western terminology to sell products, like "Mustang Liquor" in Canoga Park, or the "Silver Saddle Motel" in North Hollywood. Many signs around the Valley are painted in "rural" paint schemes, or feature the one of dozens of variants of "Old West" fonts—even on plastic backlit signs. In the Valley, it's still easy to find huge neon-framed cowboy hat signs in front of Arby's restaurants. They are rare elsewhere in the US. Developers have built entire neighborhoods with fake cowboy themes, complete with street names like "Stagecoach Road," "Silverspur Lane," and "Wrangler Court." Some of it is kitsch, some of it is just dated, but the recently reconstructed gateway entry arch to the hyper-exclusive Hidden Hills neighborhood at the western end of the Valley still features a cowboy. Cowboy rusticity is one of America's favorite motifs: it's quintessentially American, especially as it was framed by Hollywood. We Americans like to think of ourselves as rugged, individualistic, independent, and competent, and our desire to craft this self-image has been heightened by the emasculating effects of living in a densely packed urban area. The astounding success of the Marlboro Man marketing campaign in the late twentieth century stands testament to the power of that imagery. The extraordinary popularity of this imagery in the San Fernando Valley may have been a product of the way land developers marketed the Valley as a wholesome, rural escape from the perceived dangers rapidly integrating postwar inner cities.

Unlike, for example, the cultural messages at play in King Arthur Liquor, cowboy iconography is rooted in this place: cowboys have an exceptionally long history in the San Fernando Valley. Francisco Reyes, a former alcalde of Los Angeles, established Rancho Los Encinos, a massive cattle-grazing venture during the 1780s to go alongside several other hide-and-tallow operations on Spanish land grants in the Valley. For nearly two centuries, the Valley would remain a largely agricultural realm, complete with cowboys on dusty horses. When Mulholland brought water to the Valley in 1913, it was clear to many that homes and small farms would eventually replace sprawling ranchlands, but it wasn't until the after World War II that the threat became reality.

Before the war ended, Bing Crosby unintentionally initiated the first major marketing effort to snuff out Valley cowboys and replace them with suburbanites when he sang dreamily about the charms of the rustic lifestyle of the Valley in his number-one hit, "San Fernando Valley." One of the verses goes:

> So I'm hittin' the trail to the cow country,
> You can forward my mail care of R.F.D.,
> I'm gonna settle down and never more roam
> And make the San Fernando Valley my home.

While Crosby was singing about loping around the Valley on a lazy horse, engineers in Nazi Germany were quickly advancing the science of rocketry in an effort to rain death across Europe. The shocking contrasts between the comforting imagery of a pre-modern rural lifestyle and the horrific potential of modern science unfolded vividly in the Valley during the war years as well. At the beginning of the war, only around 150,000 folks lived in the entire Valley. There were dozens of working cattle ranches, hundreds of small farms, and places like Van Nuys and Canoga Park were still considered "farm towns." Many Valley residents didn't even realize they were citizens of Los Angeles. Few streets were paved. Sewers were generally nonexistent. It was rural.

Buzzland: Rocket City USA

Nearly as ubiquitous as Western motifs in the San Fernando Valley are landscapes evocative of astronauts and planetary travel. Space Needles, starbursts, chevrons, UFOs, early satellites are incorporated into hundreds of signs used by retailers and service providers. You can get your automobile cleaned at "Galaxy Car Wash" in Valley Village, take martial arts lessons at "10th Planet Jiu Jitsu" in Van Nuys, and buy candy at "Rocket Fizz" in various locations in the Valley. Fry's electronics in Burbank, near the site of the old Lockheed Skunk Works factory, carries the motif furthest by incorporating a "crashed" UFO into the facade of the building. The interior of the building pays homage to 1950s-era sci-fi movies and space invasion hysteria. It's no wonder that Spielberg set *E.T.* in the San Fernando Valley.

These spacey landscapes were even more common a generation ago. Space motifs signaled to passersby the promise of a bright shiny happy future, free from the hassles of work, illness, grief, and even dirt. Futurescapes began popping up during the Great Depression mostly in Art Deco buildings, which frequently leveraged machine imagery, streamliners and steam liners, to evoke a hygienic world of tomorrow. The ebullient optimism of 1930s Art Deco evolved as designers adopted jet aircraft and rockets as the latest-and-greatest iconography of the future. For thousands of young Valley families, living in brand-new homes full of miraculous home appliances, sprawled across a brand-new suburb, the unbounded promise of the future was no doubt easy to imagine. For the business community, the metaphor of space was easy to leverage for profit, even if World War II had taken some of the shine off the imagery of the machine age.

The imagery of space was especially salient in the Valley during the Cold War because here is where much of the machinery of the space age was designed and built. Even while the region was primarily dusty ranch land, several of the world's most high-tech factories and research facilities were operating in the Valley. Prime among them were Lockheed (still today one of the largest defense contractors in the world) headquartered in Burbank, and Rocketdyne/Atomics International out in the western end of the Valley. After the war, the promise of good jobs in defense industries and affordable suburban housing attracted thousands of veterans and their sweethearts to the Valley. Within a decade, many, especially those working on rocketry and jet aircraft, found their wartime-defense industry jobs had evolved into longer-term careers in the aerospace industry. Thousands more moved in. By 1950, the population of the Valley had topped 400,000, making the Valley one of the top ten most populated "cities" in the US, and perhaps the top city for space-industry jobs. The landscape that emerged from this high-tech-city-on-a-dusty-ranch is one of deep irony and cartoonish frivolity.

Old West, the Outer Rim, and the Ironies of the Age

Perhaps only in the 1950s San Fernando Valley could you so readily find factories full of rocket scientists springing up among sprawling ranchlands. Cowboys and spacemen worked and lived in the Valley alongside each other for decades. The spatial juxtaposition of the Old West and the Outer Rim was intense during the 1950s. Consider, for example, that Rocketdyne, the designer and manufacturer of the rockets that both put Russia in peril, and Americans into space and onto the moon, was established in 1949 in sleepy Canoga Park. Just a few blocks down the street, employees of Rocketdyne or their children could take classes on animal husbandry at the newly opened Pierce Agricultural College. Across the Valley, Lockheed's infamous Advanced Development Projects division, affectionately known as the "Skunk Works," developed the U2 spy plane, the rocket-shaped

F-104 Starfighter, the Mach 3-capable SR-71 Blackbird, and later the F-117 Nighthawk stealth bomber. Just blocks from the Skunk Works was the seventy-five-acre Los Angeles Equestrian Center, where rodeos and barrel racing continue to this day. In 1955, Atomics International (a division of North American Aviation) began setting up shop alongside Rocketdyne in the Simi Hills at the west end of the Valley. It was there that nuclear power production was first commercialized in 1957. Two years later, it was the site of the first partial nuclear meltdown, a secret kept from everyone for decades, including the cast and crew of the TV series *Gunsmoke* being filmed just a quick mule ride away in Box Canyon. Today, Pioneer Street runs through the middle of Jet Propulsion Laboratory, which overlooks the Flintridge Riding Club on the eastern rim of the Valley.

Valley historian Kevin Roderick notes that during the Cold War, nine out of ten of the biggest manufacturers in the Valley were defense contractors. They included, in addition to Lockheed and Rocketdyne, Litton Systems (later Northrop Grumman), Bendix, RCA, Marquardt, and Radioplane, among others. Still, the Valley clung to its Western-themed past. G. Henry Stetson, the cowboy-hat impresario, still operated the huge Rancho Sombrero, part of which is now Stetson Ranch Park in Sylmar. Nudie Cohn, the tailor to the most famous cowboys and cowboy wannabes in the nation for forty years, ran his shop on Lankershim Boulevard in North Hollywood. There was a cowboy theme park in the Santa Susanna Pass operated by B-Western legend Ray "Crash" Corrigan. Looking down on the park no doubt were soldiers stationed at the Nike missile batteries on Oat Mountain. The intended target of the Nike missiles was a Soviet bomber called "The Bison." Even the Soviets were playing along. Straddling both sides of the cowboy-spaceman divide was J. D. Hertz, owner of the car rental company. He raised world-class thoroughbreds in Woodland Hills on his spread called Amarillo Ranch, while his foundation supported research in ballistic missile systems. Perhaps this strange hybridization of past and future was perfectly captured by the epigrammatic ode to Rocketdyne sang by Valley school kids to the tune of the campfire standard "My Darling Clementine" (also a John Ford Western movie):

> When there's thunder, on the mountain
> Every evenin' just at nine
> And your walls begin to tremble,
> It's not God
> It's Rocketdyne.

Of all the landscapes that capture the duality of cowboys and spacemen, the ever-present ranch-style home is most noteworthy. I live in one. Every house on my street is a ranch. Built largely in the twenty years following World War II, the ranch-style home seems the perfect domestic setting for the San Fernando Valley. Ranches built during the 1950s were built to appeal to suburban cowboys and cowgirls. Board and batten siding, weathered brick chimneys (largely useless), and fieldstones were common design elements. Built largely in a sprawling L or U shape, with large glass doors at the back of the home, single-story ranch homes directed families to spend time out-of-doors, even if it was only in the backyard. Here Dad could make a proper cowboy dinner (steak and beans?). At the same time, the design of the ranch directed family life away from the streets or front porches that marked the communal, anti-cowboy qualities of life back East, or even in LA proper. Ranches were in many ways an adaptation of the Spanish/Mexican adobe rancho, but refashioned to appeal to a generation raised on Hollywood Westerns.

Merry Ovnick argues compellingly that the ranch-style home was well suited to house "GI Joe" and "Rosie the Riveter" who wished to settle down in a safe location. To anyone who witnessed the horrors of Iwo Jima, Utah Beach, or the Ardennes Forest, a little ranch house on a sleepy suburban street in the Valley provided servicemen back home from the war a cozy and safe domestic space without sacrificing their masculinity. Ranches were safe and secure, but not too emasculating. Women, also having contributed mightily to the war effort, especially in the Valley, building, among other weapons, the deadly P-38s, also probably found the ranch a suitable homestead, one that permitted some room to explore their newly won, yet still modest expansion of their gender role. Both cowboys and cowgirls no doubt found the ranch an appealing stage upon which to live out their Hollywood-inspired rides into the sunset.

The great paradox underlying the notion of Woody's ranch home as a sanctuary from the memories of the war years was that Buzz's rockets and jet fighters were largely what folks in the San Fernando Valley built while at work away from their cozy ranch homes. The hundreds of war factories were largely the reason so many job seekers flocked to the Valley, in turn boosting land values and in time laying waste to the ranch culture that had originally inspired the appealing home-on-the range lifestyle. The presence of so many critical elements of America's war-fighting machinery in the Valley also darkened the clouds of nuclear terror over the sea of ranch homes. The Valley was surely high on the list of Soviet nuclear targets. As a result, thousands built fallout shelters in their backyards. Air raid sirens wailed on Fridays, a haunting reminder that Woody was never safe from Buzz's future gone mad.

Despite the deep antithesis of Woody and Buzz and the threat that the latter would displace the former, the characters were in many ways two sides of the same coin. Buzz's catch phrase was "To infinity and beyond!" but he never really escaped the gravity of American cultural norms that bound Woody to the ground. The spaceman narrative in both *Toy Story* and on the landscape of the San Fernando Valley is little more than a spin-off of the classic Western meme, just reset in an interplanetary Wild West. Buzz Lightyear was, after all, a "Space Ranger." Unable to properly fashion a character from new cloth, Americans simply traded white hats and chaps for white helmets and spacesuits. The spaceman remained hypermasculine, white, gender certain, and paternalistic throughout the Cold War. The iconography of spacemen integrated seamlessly into the Western landscape narrative of the Valley in the 1950s. Woody and Buzz were brothers after all.

The End of an Era

The space race was largely won by Americans when Neil Armstrong took his one small step, but the glittering prize promised by modernity turned out to be a booby trap. The world of the future never really materialized as it appeared in the dreams of Americans in 1950s. We were awakened cruelly by the carnage in Vietnam and the ghetto riots at home. It would seem an opportunity for Woody to extract revenge on Buzz, the charlatan who couldn't *really* fly.

Rather, both icons were partially supplanted by new messages on the landscape. Rusticity roared back in the 1970s, but Woody the Sherriff was replaced by Woodsy the Owl. Cowboys on the landscape were joined by Mother Nature. Thousands of commercial and domestic spaces adopted the "environmental look," plastering on (frequently plastic) mansard roofs, incorporating stressed brick, and relying heavily on earth tones to sell everything from hardware to hamburgers. The exterior design features of fast food giants McDonald's, Wendy's, and Burger King come most easily to mind, but the shift in vernacular landscape was seismic. Woody and Buzz were out of style.

Today

The multigenerational gap between the children who grew up in the Woody and Buzz era and the children of the 1990s who were the primary audience for *Toy Story* made Woody and Buzz a puzzling pair to scaffold a hit movie around. Because I'm not a boomer myself, I wondered if the characters resonated less with me than with those older than me. Spacemen and cowboys may be passé among millennials, but much of the landscape erected during the Cold War remains in the Valley. Are these landscapes, imprinted with Woody and Buzz, illegible, if not irrelevant, to younger generations?

Part of the problem is that Woody and Buzz are white. *Really white*. They had to be, because they represented an imagined past and an imagined future; not of Pixar circa 1993, but of mid-twentieth-century Hollywood (excepting perhaps Mel Brooks). The Valley was mostly white, just like the imagined past/future portrayed by Hollywood. The imagined past erased the reality of the Valley's clearly multiethnic rancho era. The imagined future clouded the vision of what *could be* by steadfastly portraying the future as largely the domain of white males. During the Cold War, multicultural sensitivities were few in the Valley. Restrictive covenants, and unofficial but effective steering practices, kept the Valley super white until deep into the 1960s. Until the mid-1970s, the Valley was surely the least ethnically diverse large urban area in the US. Only Pacoima had a significant minority population, and perhaps not surprisingly, is one of the few areas on the accompanying map that is largely devoid of landscape references to cowboys or spacemen. Today, the Valley's exceptional diversity threatens to make much of the narrative of Cold War landscapes anachronistic, like Shakespearean English to mideighties Valley Girls. It's hard to imagine a new business that isn't selling boots or barbecue utilizing a cowboy motif. Ranch homes are derided nowadays. Spacemen are nearly as unpopular.

Though they still dot the landscape, traditional landscape narratives attached to cowboys and spacemen will continue to slide toward illegibility because Hollywood no longer provides a Rosetta stone. Space-set science fiction evolved away from the 1950s Western-in-Space formula in large part due to the genius of Gene Roddenberry. Today, Hollywood spacemen are relatively rare, but when they appear, they are as likely to be evil as good, female as male, white as brown, and prisoners as liberators. Westerns are even rarer today, and they too are far more complex than they were in the Cold War. The nationalistic romance of the cowboy has been undone as we have come to grips with the violence and chaos of frontier American imperialism. Good guys and bad guys are harder to distinguish. Postmodern uncertainties have pulled Woody and Buzz from their cultural moorings.

So what is the future for the mainstays of the Valley's landscape iconography? Woody's legacy on the domestic landscape seems secure as long as the ranch-style home continues to stand in vast swaths across the Valley. Whether folks continue to recognize its connection with cowboys is less clear. However, Woody is disappearing quickly from the commercial landscape of the Valley. My favorite dive diner recently pulled down its wagon-wheel interior lighting and began serving sushi. Contemporary uses of cowboy imagery are largely restricted to the marketing of country (but ironically not western) music. Cowboy hats remain a staple of Nashville stage costumes, and because the music genre remains overwhelmingly white, conservative, xenophobic, and bound by traditional gender codes; most Valley residents can't aspire to join Woody's Roundup. Other than a few feed and seed or tack stores, where else would it make sense to market a product with cowboy imagery? It's a missed opportunity because many with roots in Latin America can lay claim to vaquero culture. So, the imagery is not foreign to Latino youth, but as it has been cast on the landscape of the Valley, there is little chance to appropriate it for a diverse audience.

Buzz's legacy is clearly threatened as well. The end of the Cold War eliminated thousands of jobs in aerospace, particularly in the San Fernando Valley. Fiscal realities and anti-science politicos jeopardize the future of space exploration. Astronauts don't capture the imagination as they did when kids asked their moms to buy Tang for the breakfast table. Few businesses today try to leverage imagery of the future as they craft their retail landscapes. The future remains before us, yet our expectations of it have long been tempered. Buzz has little future, but the "past of the future" has managed to live on in the 1950s-nostalgia landscapes scattered throughout the Valley. It's another irony that we use futuristic landscapes to sell nostalgia for the past.

Conclusion

In *Toy Story 3*, Andy, who owned Woody and Buzz, is leaving for college and all his toys find themselves in a box heading for the attic, or to a yard sale. Andy had long outgrown Woody and Buzz. It's the same way on the floor of the San Fernando Valley. We've outgrown cowboys and spacemen. Woody and Buzz lent certainty to people's lives long affected by the brutal uncertainties of the Great Depression and World War II. Twenty-first-century Americans are not confronted with the apocalyptic possibilities presented to the "Greatest Generation." We're both absent the threats (the Bomb, Nazis, starvation, e.g.) and we're blissfully, sometimes willfully, ignorant of the threats that do loom. We don't look to heroes to save the day. It's not certain that we are capable of hero worship any more. If we do worship heroes, then our landscape, our "unwitting autobiography," provides no hint of how or where we're searching for inspiration. Much of the newly built environment suffers from the sort of twenty-first-century uncertainty that characterizes the rest of our cultural systems. No developer would dream of building a huge neon sign in the shape of a boot, or a rocket, or any other iconographic representation of the sort that was common in the postwar era. To do so would imply certainty about good and bad, right and wrong, truth and falsehood; certainties that we would rather not engage in—even in the San Fernando Valley.

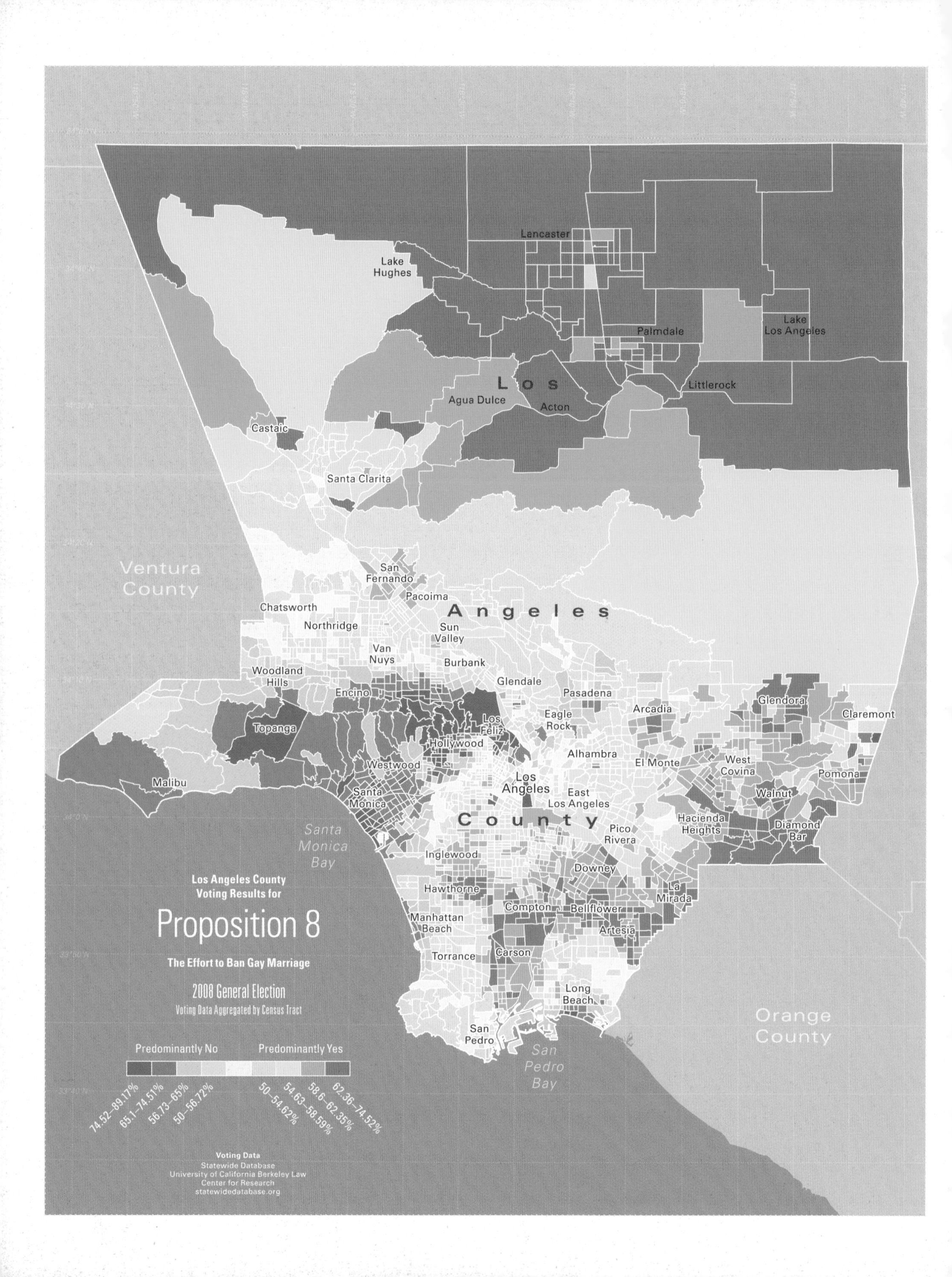
Lancaster
Lake
Hughes
Lake
Los Angeles
Palmdale
Los
Agua Dulce
Acton
Littlerock
Castaic
Santa Clarita
Ventura
County
San
Fernando
Pacoima
Chatsworth
Angeles
Northridge
Sun
Valley
Van
Nuys
Burbank
Woodland
Hills
Glendale
Encino
Pasadena
Arcadia
Glendora
Claremont
Eagle
Rock
Topanga
Los
Feliz
Hollywood
Alhambra
West
Covina
Westwood
El Monte
Pomona
Malibu
Santa
Monica
Los
Angeles
East
Los Angeles
Walnut
County
Hacienda
Heights
Diamond
Bar
Pico
Rivera
Santa
Monica
Bay
Inglewood
Downey
Los Angeles County
Voting Results for
Hawthorne
La
Mirada
Compton
Bellflower
Proposition 8
Manhattan
Beach
Artesia
Torrance
Carson
The Effort to Ban Gay Marriage
2008 General Election
Voting Data Aggregated by Census Tract
Long
Beach
Orange
County
San
Pedro
San
Pedro
Bay
Predominantly No
Predominantly Yes
74.52–89.17%
65.1–74.51%
56.73–65%
50–56.72%
50–54.62%
54.63–58.59%
58.6–62.35%
62.36–74.52%
Voting Data
Statewide Database
University of California Berkeley Law
Center for Research
statewidedatabase.org

More than two decades before the Stonewall Riots in New York City, the modern gay rights movement arguably began in Los Angeles. However, the voting results of California's Proposition 8, created by opponents of same-sex marriage, shows that support for homosexual equality remains far from universal in Los Angeles County. Though the proposition passed in 2008, it was subsequently ruled unconstitutional, and same-sex marriages have been legal in the state since June 2013. This map intentionally destabilizes for-or-against polarities with a celebratory palette.

Pioneers on the Frontier of Faith

HOW A HANDFUL OF AUDACIOUS ANGELENOS SPARKED THE MOVEMENT FOR LGBT INCLUSION IN MAINSTREAM RELIGION THAT LED TO A NATIONWIDE CIVIL-RIGHTS SEA CHANGE

Sylvia Sukop

"No one moves to LA for church," a friend of mine quipped. Yet this improbable city, popularly identified with hedonism rather than piety, gave rise to the fervent aspirations and tentative first steps of LGBT people of faith. Because the churches and synagogues in which they grew up refused to embrace them, gay and lesbian Angelenos of faith joined together in DIY spirit, not to invent new religions but to reboot the old ones. Never in history—not until the founding of the Metropolitan Community Church (MCC) in 1968 and of Beth Chayim Chadashim (BCC) in 1972—had gays and lesbians so forcefully and, with the help of countless allies and hidden angels, so successfully asserted their desire for full participation in church and synagogue life.

Los Angeles lays rightful claim to a number of firsts in American lesbian, gay, bisexual, and transgender (LGBT) history, well before the 1969 Stonewall Riots in New York that ushered in the modern LGBT rights movement. These include the first lesbian publication (*Vice Versa,* 1947), the first sustained homosexual organization (the Mattachine Society, 1950) and, growing out of that, the first pro-gay publication (*ONE* magazine, 1953). Even *The Advocate* was born here; the preeminent national LGBT magazine began in 1967 as a local gay community newsletter in response to a police raid on the LA gay bar The Black Cat.

In their compassionate and richly documented *Gay LA: A History of Sexual Outlaws, Power Politics, and Lipstick Lesbians* (2006), Lillian Faderman and Stuart Simmons explicitly define Los Angeles as a place of sanctuary, taking us inside the donut shops and private dinner parties, the dark bars and later the sunlit parades, that have provided refuge and connection for generations of queers—outliers and outlaws who found a measure of freedom on the Western frontier. As far back as the 1880s, Los Angeles was home to underground gay cultures that flourished despite provincial moralist attitudes and legal prohibition of behaviors ranging, over the years, from "masquerading" (i.e., cross-dressing) and the sale of liquor to "unescorted women" (i.e., lesbians), to oral sex, sodomy, and same-sex marriage.

In one chapter, the authors recount the pivotal people and events in the formative years of MCC and BCC, offering valuable insight into a history that intersects intimately with my own.

Living in Los Angeles was never my dream. In fact I had to move here twice before the transplant finally took—the first time from New York, the second from Boston, both times for a new job. With the first move, I was scarred by a breakup and swallowed whole by the demands of a high-pressure job, resulting in total failure to connect with my adopted city. Rather than living in Los Angeles, for two years I merely transected it like a blinkered animal, emotionally hobbled, passing each day through the same narrow chute from gated apartment complex to gated workplace.

I missed my smaller-footprint East Coast cities, the spontaneous exploration and serendipitous encounters their density encouraged; on sidewalks and subways you rubbed shoulders with fellow citizens and couldn't help but feel part of this concentrated energetic flow of humanity. In wide-flung Los Angeles in the 1990s, you moved through the city alone, sealed inside a car—that profligate living room on wheels, complete with stereo, AC, upholstered recliners, and a place to put your coffee. (Digital screens and mobile phones were not yet part of the decor.) Daily routines were defined by alienation rather than community, congestion rather than flow.

I attribute the success of my second attempt at bonding with LA to finding my village within the metropolis. Like newly arrived immigrant Jews before me, I went shul shopping. And I was surprised at the number of synagogue doors that were open to me as an out lesbian.

Spiritually speaking, I am "trans." Born and baptized in 1961, one of seven children in a Hungarian-German immigrant Catholic family, I completed my journey to Judaism in 5761. That is not to say the journey took 3,800 years. But rather that the first event, my birth in a Paterson, New Jersey hospital, was recorded on a birth certificate according to the Gregorian calendar, while the second, my conversion in a burbling blue-tiled mikveh off the 405 freeway in Los Angeles, was recorded on the Hebrew calendar. The journey took forty years, the same time my adopted ancestors wandered in the Biblical wilderness before they reached *their* promised land.

Why, more than a dozen years ago, did I become Jewish?

Judaism held many attractions for me. Among them: the making sacred of everyday life and the marking of life-cycle events in community; the call to study and prayer, and the insistence that study *is* prayer; the emphasis on ethics and on a direct relationship with God.

But perhaps the most compelling reason I became Jewish is because I am gay, a fact that hit me with sudden and immutable force in my first-grade classroom at St. Catherine's elementary school in Reading, Pennsylvania. I fell in love with a girl named Stephanie who was smart and funny and outgoing, and so generous with her attention to me it made my loner tomboy's heart ache. Her long legs defied the confines of our plaid skirt uniforms, and her dark hair, cut straight and serious across the bangs, fell in two jaunty braids past her shoulders, where every day I resisted touching them as she sat in the seat in front of mine. I continued to fall in love with girls, in junior high, in high school, in college—till finally I stopped resisting.

Judaism welcomes the stranger and so does Los Angeles. Both exist beyond the centers of traditional power, outside of mainstream historical narratives and identities. Judaism and Los Angeles are both "big tent" outposts, intensely absorbed in self-definition while forever open to newcomers. Resisting permanence, Judaism and Los Angeles are always in the act of becoming.

Jews in the Los Angeles Mosaic, edited by Karen S. Wilson and published in conjunction with an eponymous exhibition at the Autry National Center, makes the case that LA epitomized the American West's ethos of unfettered reinvention. The frontier offered freedom from restriction and repression, and physical space in which to pursue that freedom. It was a promised land beckoning ranchers, real-estate moguls, and religious seekers alike.

As California's population exploded—more than tripling since 1950—so did the presence of major religions. Today California has the largest population of

Buddhists, Catholics, Hindus, Jews, and Muslims of any state in the country, and more Mormons than any state except Utah.

As a city, Los Angeles has the largest population of Jews after Jerusalem, Tel Aviv, and New York. Perhaps more importantly, LA is home to one of the most *diverse* Jewish communities in the world. You won't find this full-spectrum Judaism in Israel or Europe, nor in many American cities. The proof is in the purse: LGBT issues, still taboo in many Jewish communities, have been openly funded since at least the 1980s by bedrock Jewish communal organizations like the Jewish Federation and the Jewish Community Foundation of Los Angeles—including the world's first Jewish AIDS-service organization, initiated by BCC. Meanwhile, Angelenos have built not one but two LGBT synagogues, BCC and Kol Ami, each with thriving congregations.

....

Who started the first gay and lesbian church? The answer is simple: the Reverend Troy Perry.

I reached Perry by phone at his home in the Silver Lake section of Los Angeles, where he has lived with his husband, Phil, since 1985. Renowned for his warmth and candor, Perry, seventy-three at the time of our interview, took me vividly back in time to his early days as a Christian Pentecostal minister.

Born in 1940, the son of a Florida bootlegger, Perry became a licensed Baptist preacher at the age of fifteen. In the early 1960s he moved to Southern California with his wife and two children after being thrown out of his church in Joliet, Illinois, "enjoined for being gay," he says matter-of-factly. While hoping to shed his past, the same thing happened at the next church he pastored, in Santa Ana. It was only then, he says, "that I came to terms with my homosexuality."

At a Los Angeles "hippie bookstore," he asked a woman working there if she had anything on homosexuality. She gave him two publications that would change his life: Donald Webster Cory's landmark 1963 book *The Homosexual in America* and a copy of *ONE* magazine. The book, says Perry, "brought me out of the closet. It described me to a T." *ONE* magazine led to a further and equally important insight—the existence of a gay *community:* "My God! I found out there were *organized* homosexuals. I was just *amazed* to find that out. When I read that I knew I was a gay man. And it broke up my marriage. My wife and I separated. I moved into Los Angeles and I said, okay, God, you can't love me and I can't love you, and that's that."

As he began exploring LA's gay community, Perry's impression was that "none of us were from California, we were all runaways from something." Although he found "bad laws" oppressive to gay men and lesbians—"people were arrested all the time out here"—he found the overall culture to be liberal, marked by social mixing and subtle resistance to authority.

"California was liberal in some ways and hard in others," says Perry. "When Anglos arrived in California, the Mexican community was already here. Those Anglos married into Mexican American families. Even though until 1967 you couldn't legally marry members of other races [in other parts of the country], people got married here." (Interracial marriage became legal nationwide in 1967 with the U.S. Supreme Court decision in *Loving v. Virginia*, but by then only Southern states still prohibited it. It had already become legal in California in 1948 with the California Supreme Court case of *Perez v. Sharp*, the first time a state court had invalidated an interracial marriage ban in the twentieth century—a harbinger of the California Supreme Court's groundbreaking decision legalizing same-sex marriage sixty years later.)

The presence of a major navy port also shaped Southern California's LGBT culture. "Gay GIs who met in World War II, they came back and they stayed here," says Perry. "And here we had the movie industry. GLBT people who were artists, who were writers, they loved it here."

But for a newcomer, finding fellowship was not easy. "I went to my first gay bar in Hollywood, it was called the Red Raven," he recalls. "When I went up, there were young people my age, but it was very dark. And there were signs on the wall, 'Don't talk to strangers.' And I thought, *how do you meet someone?* And yet here was this bar full of people. It was very sad. That was my introduction to the gay community."

Experiences like this inspired Perry's return to ministry. Envisioning a safe and welcoming place that would offer more open and meaningful connection, he founded MCC in 1968, the first ever affirming Christian ministry serving the spiritual needs of LGBT people. He actively led the church until his retirement in 2005. With his unwavering belief in the emancipatory power of true Christian values, and the oratorical gifts of great civil rights leaders before him, Rev. Perry has since been called, with loving wit, the "Martin Luther Queen" of gay liberation.

Who started the first gay and lesbian synagogue? The answer is not so simple. But that story also begins with Rev. Troy Perry.

From the very first service in Perry's living room on October 6, 1968, Metropolitan Community Church and its activities were open to everyone, regardless of religious background or practice. The church grew quickly and in 1971 moved in to a permanent home, a refurbished church and former opera house at Twenty-Second Street and Union Avenue in LA's West Adams neighborhood. In addition to Sunday services drawing hundreds of worshippers, MCC held a small weekly drop-in rap group. One night in 1972, only five people showed up and four of them, it turned out, were Jews—all craving spiritual connection, but all unaffiliated at the time with a synagogue. MCC was the one place they felt safe and affirmed within a spiritual context, and they became active participants in MCC, attending services, contributing donations, serving as volunteers.

"We tried to put together a community, just to have something other than a bar," says Jerry Small, who was present that night. At the time, homosexuality was neither acknowledged nor accepted in synagogues; as in mainstream Christianity, it was considered evil, an abomination before God. Homosexuality was classified as a mental illness and criminalized in Los Angeles and other cities, where vice squads regularly conducted raids and undercover operations in gay bars and cruising areas. To be openly gay or lesbian could have devastating consequences—loss of employment, family, community, and, when hatred turned violent, life itself.

Small, who was eighty years old when we spoke and living in Albuquerque, New Mexico, grew up "in a shtetl in New York," in a poor, Russian-Jewish immigrant family. He vividly remembers, at the rap group, the subject of church membership coming up. While welcome at MCC, Jews could not become full members and therefore couldn't vote on church policy—"not unless we accepted Christ, and that wasn't going to happen," he says. "Then someone said, maybe we should form a temple. Okay, so how do we form a temple?"

They started by calling Rev. Perry. "He didn't hesitate," Small recalls. "He said, 'I support you completely.' And he added, 'Just make sure it's *very* Jewish.'"

MCC welcomed its Jewish brothers and sisters with open arms, providing them a safe place to worship where they could fully express both their gay and Jewish identities. The nascent congregation began holding Friday-night services at the MCC church in West Adams. Small went on to become a cofounder of BCC and the chair of its first steering committee. To this day, Small and Rev. Perry remain close friends, and Perry reiterates how wholeheartedly he supported the creation of a gay and lesbian synagogue. "I believe the Jewish covenant with God is just as real as mine," he tells me.

The next step was more audacious: The Metropolitan Community Temple (MCT), as BCC was known in its early days, requested a meeting with the Union of American Hebrew Congregations (UAHC), the national organization of Reform Jewish synagogues. (MCT's founders had ruled out approaching the more traditional Orthodox and Conservative movements.) Without UAHC's official recognition, and the seed funding and other resources that would come with it, MCT was unlikely to survive over the long term.

On the appointed day in September 1972, Small, then forty, drove a black Cadillac convertible to the two-story office building on Ventura Boulevard in Studio City. He became absorbed in a beautiful display of butterflies framed on the wall in the waiting room. *Butterflies are free,* he remembers thinking, taking it as a positive sign.

When UAHC regional representative Rabbi Arnold Kaiman appeared, he offered a warm welcome, which Small was not expecting. A gay and lesbian synagogue was unprecedented, after all, even heretical. At that point the Metropolitan Community Temple had just twenty-six members, with two or three times that attending Friday evening services in a makeshift sanctuary in MCC's basement.

As the congregation's ambassador, Small had come to request the synagogue's admission to mebership in UAHC. He was startled by the rabbi's unhesitating response: "How can we help you?"

Although he had been raised Orthodox on the East Coast, Rabbi Kaiman, it turned out, was an innovator himself, already conducting interfaith marriages in the 1970s, a time when few rabbis were willing to do so. Proudly nonconformist, Kaiman was also known for using popular music in his services, including "Somewhere over the Rainbow." (Whether or not the married Kaiman was aware of it, the Judy Garland song was a veritable anthem for the gay community, and "friend of Judy" code for homosexual.)

By the end of their meeting Kaiman decided to lend the temple not only a helping hand but, that very day, a sacred Torah scroll—the congregation's first, a profoundly symbolic gesture of affirmation.

Holding back tears as he left the UAHC office, Small carried the scroll snug against his torso, "like a newborn baby," he recalls.

At great personal and professional risk, religious revolutionaries like Small and Perry, in their quest for fully embracing faith communities, formed congregations here in Los Angeles whose impact is almost beyond measure. The movement they sparked has helped dismantle once-intractable pillars of prejudice—"God hates gays" and, no less pernicious, "Love the sinner, hate the sin"—raising up in their place ideas of acceptance so fundamental a child could grasp them: "Each of us is created in God's image and worthy of God's love."

MCC now has more than two hundred congregations in over thirty countries, and the number of gay-affirming progressive Christian churches is steadily growing. An online list of "Gay-Affirming Churches" includes 750 in California alone, of which more than 70 are located in Greater Los Angeles.

Today BCC has LGBT sister synagogues in some fifteen cities, not to mention the official embrace of all 900-plus congregations in the mainstream Union for Reform Judaism (URJ), formerly UAHC, in whose membership BCC was accepted in 1974—making BCC the first LGBT congregation of *any* faith to be accepted by a major religious movement.

In the wake of the U.S. Supreme Court's April 2013 hearings on the federal Defense of Marriage Act (DOMA) and California's Proposition 8 (a state constitutional ban on same-sex marriage in California imposed by ballot measure five years earlier), new and unlikely allies emerged at a breathtaking pace.

"Same-sex couples should have the right to civil marriage," said Republican Senator Mark Kirk of Illinois, who had recently survived a stroke. "Our time on this earth is limited, I know that better than most. Life comes down to who you love and who loves you back—government has no place in the middle."

Kirk became only the second sitting Republican senator to publicly support marriage equality. (The first one did so in support of a gay son.) One extraordinary detail in Kirk's announcement reveals the far-reaching impact of LGBT integration in mainstream religion, where to share a pew is to form a friendship, perhaps the ultimate shield against discrimination: "The gay community is larger than ever before," he said, "and it's not in the 1950s closet, so most of us have gay acquaintances at work or *at church,* and we know them, and the thought of legally discriminating against our own friends...is an anathema to me." [Emphasis added.]

A historic tidal wave, first set in motion in late 1960s and early 1970s Los Angeles, is now cresting.

On June 26, 2013, the U.S. Supreme Court delivered twin landmark rulings striking down DOMA and ending Prop 8. My partner, Bonnie, and I, in our living room in northeast Los Angeles County, watched the news at seven that morning, televised live from the Supreme Court steps in Washington. As the jubilant crowd, waving rainbow and American flags, expressed overwhelming support for the California plaintiffs and their legal team, the camera turned briefly to one lone minister who dropped to his knees lamenting the decision.

That evening, a Wednesday, coming from our jobs on the other side of town, we arrived at the victory rally in West Hollywood. An elevated island of TV cameras and journalists stood between us and the action on stage, obscuring our view, but we caught glimpses of—and heard at full volume—the triumphant plaintiffs (one couple from Burbank and one from San Francisco) who had just flown in from Washington. They vowed not to stop here but to continue fighting for marriage equality in the thirty-seven states where it remained illegal.

In the buoyant multigenerational throng we ran into Rabbi Lisa Edwards, one of the first out lesbians to be ordained and, since 1994, the spiritual leader of our congregation Beth Chayim Chadashim. Wearing a kippah and her trademark smile, she passed out colorful fliers announcing "The chuppah is up! Reservations now being accepted!" The fliers featured a sassy illustration of the Statue of Liberty giving Lady Justice a kiss, an Internet meme that had gone viral, based on the famous Alfred Eisenstaedt photograph of a sailor kissing a nurse on V-J Day in Times Square.

Rabbi Edwards disappeared into the crowd, making her way toward the stage to join her fellow clergy from California

Faith for Equality. Just then Metropolitan Community Church's Rev. Neil Thomas stepped up to the microphone. The event's loudest, proudest speaker yet, he cheered the day's momentous events, with a handful of other clerics behind him. But where was Rabbi Edwards? She never appeared and later explained why. "They were afraid the stage couldn't hold all of us," she said. "At the last rally there were so many clergy the stage almost collapsed under our weight!"

As the celebration concluded and the crowd began to thin, Bonnie and I strolled confetti-strewn San Vicente Boulevard, snapping pictures of people with handwritten placards and equal-sign flags, and of American flags lined up like sentries on the now empty stage. Red-white-and-blue was everywhere, from the "More American Today" printed posters to the clothes the two of us happened to be wearing.

That's when we noticed the tall bearded man in a white robe, standing alone beyond the barricades, on the greensward on the other side of the boulevard, silently holding a large sign in his open outstretched palms. Curious, we crossed the street, and others did too, like paparazzi spotting a celebrity. No one expected *this* guy to show up, and if so, not necessarily on friendly terms. But here he was: sweet Jesus (or his Hollywood stand-in). His message, in unequivocal bold type: "**MARRY WHO YOU LOVE.**"

The chuppah, the traditional wedding canopy held aloft by four poles, was up—had already been up for more than two decades in progressive Jewish congregations—and waiting for us to step beneath it. But now, at last, the right to a California marriage license—a canopy of legal protection and recognition—was ours as well.

On this our victory day I leaned into Bonnie, who clutched a small bouquet of roses she had brought from our garden, and planted a kiss on her dimpled cheek.

Author's acknowledgments: I am profoundly grateful to the elders of MCC and BCC for sharing their memories of the founding days with me—Rev. Troy Perry, Jerry Small, Jerry Nodiff, and Tom Johnson; to Rabbi Lisa Edwards and her wife, Tracy Moore, and to all the members of my congregation who encouraged and supported my exploration of this history, especially Stephen J. Sass, Karen S. Wilson, Larry Nathanson, Davi Cheng, Bracha Yael, and Ray Eelsing; to the ONE National Gay & Lesbian Archives at the USC Libraries, which provided generous access to primary research materials; and to Bonnie S. Kaplan, poet, artist, teacher, and my ardent companion on the adventure of life.

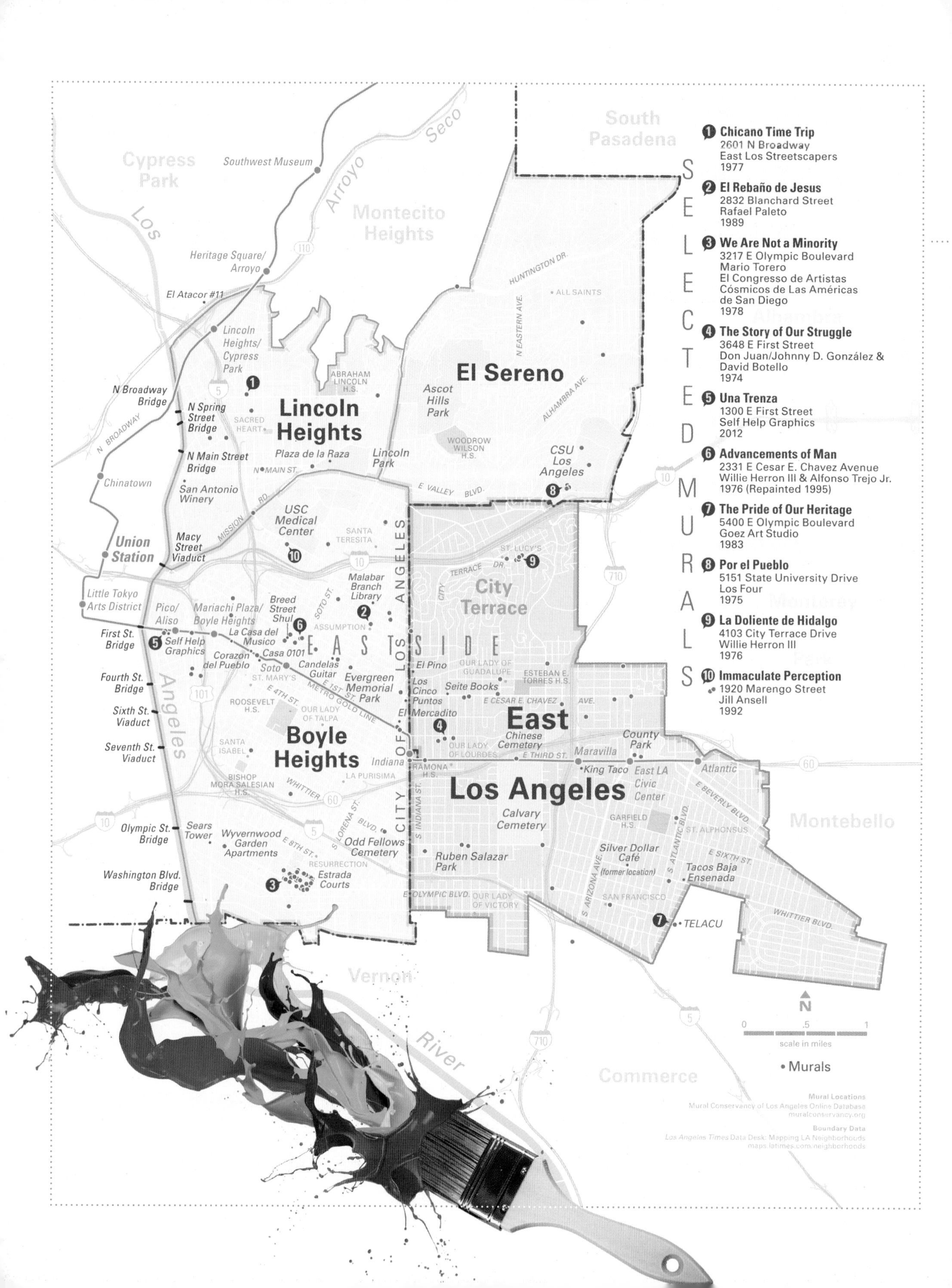
SELECTED MURALS
1 Chicano Time Trip
2601 N Broadway
East Los Streetscapers
1977
2 El Rebaño de Jesus
2832 Blanchard Street
Rafael Paleto
1989
3 We Are Not a Minority
3217 E Olympic Boulevard
Mario Torero
El Congreso de Artistas Cósmicos de Las Américas de San Diego
1978
4 The Story of Our Struggle
3648 E First Street
Don Juan/Johnny D. González & David Botello
1974
5 Una Trenza
1300 E First Street
Self Help Graphics
2012
6 Advancements of Man
2331 E Cesar E. Chavez Avenue
Willie Herron III & Alfonso Trejo Jr.
1976 (Repainted 1995)
7 The Pride of Our Heritage
5400 E Olympic Boulevard
Goez Art Studio
1983
8 Por el Pueblo
5151 State University Drive
Los Four
1975
9 La Doliente de Hidalgo
4103 City Terrace Drive
Willie Herron III
1976
10 Immaculate Perception
1920 Marengo Street
Jill Ansell
1992
Lincoln Heights
El Sereno
Boyle Heights
City Terrace
East Los Angeles
EAST SIDE
CITY OF LOS ANGELES
South Pasadena
Cypress Park
Montecito Heights
Vernon
Commerce
Montebello
Los Angeles River
Arroyo Seco
Southwest Museum
Heritage Square/Arroyo
El Atacor #11
Lincoln Heights/Cypress Park
N Broadway Bridge
N Spring Street Bridge
N Main Street Bridge
Chinatown
San Antonio Winery
Union Station
Macy Street Viaduct
Little Tokyo Arts District
Pico/Aliso
Mariachi Plaza/Boyle Heights
First St. Bridge
Self Help Graphics
La Casa del Musico
Casa 0101
Corazon del Pueblo
Soto
Candelas Guitar
Evergreen Memorial Park
Fourth St. Bridge
Sixth St. Viaduct
Seventh St. Viaduct
Olympic St. Bridge
Sears Tower
Wyvernwood Garden Apartments
Washington Blvd. Bridge
Estrada Courts
Odd Fellows Cemetery
Indiana
USC Medical Center
Malabar Branch Library
Breed Street Shul
Plaza de la Raza
Lincoln Park
Ascot Hills Park
CSU Los Angeles
El Pino
Los Cinco Puntos
Seite Books
El Mercadito
Chinese Cemetery
Maravilla
King Taco
County Park
East LA Civic Center
Atlantic
Calvary Cemetery
Ruben Salazar Park
Silver Dollar Café (former location)
Tacos Baja Ensenada
TELACU
scale in miles
• Murals
Mural Locations
Mural Conservancy of Los Angeles Online Database
muralconservancy.org
Boundary Data
Los Angeles Times Data Desk: Mapping LA Neighborhoods
maps.latimes.com/neighborhoods

Los Angeles boasts the largest Xican@ population in the country, and a jaunt through the Eastside (the unincorporated area of East Los Angeles and the three LA city neighborhoods of Boyle Heights, Lincoln Heights, and El Sereno) reveals a plethora of cultural treasures, from clusters of mariachi musicians to wheat-pasted, silkscreened political art posters. Murals unfurl along the alleyways, freeway underpasses, and storefronts, all part of a vibrant tradition of communicating and commemorating via street art.

How Xican@s Are the Makeweight of Los Angeles's Past, Present, and Future

Luis J. Rodriguez

When I traveled to Appalachia in the 1980s (before Mexicans ended up there), people thought I was Chinese. In Europe I'm often mistaken for North African or Arab. Although I was born in Texas, can someone label me "American" and get the picture? Not likely. Xican@ for generations meant a Mexican born or raised in the United States, but since the 1960s movement days the term indicated any Mexican-descended person who politically and culturally identified with his or her native roots and fought for a change in how this country was controlled by one social class—generally of one race, mostly of one gender and sexual orientation (capitalist, white, male, and straight). Yet today even the word "Chicano" has become adaptable, often incorporating the large numbers of Central Americans and recently arrived Mexicans (if not by name at least in talk, dress, gestures). Most use the term "Raza" for "The People" to include them. Half-Asians, half-whites, half-blacks (there is a Chicano rap artist known as the Blaxican) now call themselves Chicanos. And there is a large LGBT/queer community among Chicanos where identity becomes even more fluid, defying labels and definitions.

And to add to the dilemma, in Mexico the word Chicano was hardly acceptable and has been used for decades as a put-down.

It's complicated. It's weird. It's uncomfortable.

Welcome to my world.

Terms like Hispanic or Latino, created by others to designate us, are misnomers. We may speak Spanish and have Spanish-derived names. But nobody can confuse us with the actual people in Spain. Blond-haired and light-eyed people from Spain have been known to cross the US-Mexico border with little problem. But a Guatemalan Mayan man that police recently killed in the streets of the Pico-Union barrio was mislabeled as "Hispanic." That's the rub, *que no?* Labels.

Today many Chicanos forgo the "ch" and use X for the sound the Nahuatl peoples used (all Roman lettering is alien to native peoples so there is no correct way of doing this). Xicanos also include @ to be inclusive of both male and female (a complement rather than a distinction). Xican@s are more like water, an ocean or wavering river, slithering like Quetzalcoatl through borders, cultures, labels, races, languages. After more than five hundred years of conquests, genocides, wars, discrimination, and criminalization, Xican@s are still here: solid, rooted, yet hard to pinpoint and categorize.

Xican@s are also not small in number, unlike US subgroups such as Cajuns of Louisiana. There are millions of Xican@s in the country. We have been a source of vitality for Los Angeles even when the city grew to resonate with some 250 languages. We're more "Angeleno" than most "Angelenos." Today we exist beside migrants from Asia, Europe, Africa, the Midwest, the South, and other places. In this mix are Mixteco and Zapoteco inflections, Mayan tongues, and various Nahuatl speakers (regions of Mexico and parts of Central America, like the Pipil tribe of El Salvador, speak different kinds of Nahuatl).

For decades, Xican@ graffiti street artist would place the letters *c/s* for "con safos" at the end of their letterings and art. This is street slang for "no one can touch this" (to remove or disrespect).

So be it—*con safos*.

If You Ain't Mexican and You Ain't American, What the F*** Are You?

Los Angeles is a perfect place to extend the conversation about Xican@s—who we are and where we're going. Natives, Africans, and even Chinese (and mixtures thereof), led by their Spanish overlords, founded the city in 1781—a group similar to what makes up Xican@s today. By "race" Xican@s are mostly native (up to 100 percent depending on what part of Mexico). And we include Spanish, African, and in some cases Asian, Irish, Arabic, and Jewish ancestry.

My mother, for example, had a full-blooded Rarámuri mother from the Copper Canyon of Chihuahua, Mexico. The Rarámuri are also known as the

Tarahumara, the second largest tribe after the Navajo north of Mexico City. Her father, however, had blue eyes, considered "special" among all the brown-skinned, brown-eyed family members. My dad came from Guerrero, Mexico, in a Nahuatl-speaking area that also included African slaves and Spanish soldiers. An odd bird, my dad looked like a kind of Frankenstein—with tight wooly hair, Spanish face, and native brown skin.

Any "racial" purity in my case is absurd. The concept of race itself is absurd. Light-skinned Europeans first raised this issue in their clashes with darker-skinned peoples of Cem Ānáhuac (presently known as "the Americas"), Africa, East Asia, Southeast Asia, India, Melanesia, and the Mideast.

Race, as many have said before me, is a social and economic construct.

Nonetheless, like many Xican@s I've gravitated to my native roots. I've been involved with Native American and Native Mexican ceremonies and teachings for over twenty years. My elders have been Mexika (so-called Aztec from Mexico), Mayan (from Mexico and Guatemala) as well as Navajo (Diné) and Lakota from the United States. Even Quechua from Peru. I speak English and Spanish, both languages with only around 500 years in these lands. I also know a few Nahuatl, Rarámuri, Diné, and Lakota words that have been spoken here for several millennia.

In fact, the main indigenous peoples in Los Angeles, the Tongva and Tataviam, have linguistic ties to the Rarámuri as well as the Mexika, Hopi, Shoshone, Arapaho, Paiute, and others.

Still, when I returned to Los Angeles in 2000 after spending fifteen years in Chicago, I walked down a Northeast San Fernando Valley (long known as the "Mexican" side of the Valley) street when a pickup truck with "white" Americans yelled out, "go back to where you came from!" I've heard this many times in my life. I call them drive-by epithets.

The thing is, I am back where I came from. My roots, like all Xican@s, Mexicanos, Salvadorans, Guatemalans, and others, are inexorably linked to this land. Yet, now the brown-skinned are the "foreigners," "strangers," and "illegals." Now we don't belong. This is where the current state of race and migration in the United States has taken us—where everything is turned on its head.

Unseen and Everywhere

In 1986 there was a movie called *Echo Park*. I lived in this culturally rich Los Angeles community northwest of downtown in the late 1970s and early 1980s. Echo Park was then—and is largely now—a Mexican and Central American enclave. Although it has had at least three decades of gentrification, it's still a barrio (now dotted with art galleries, high-end cafés, and a bookstore). It's become hip, although street peddlers, gang members, and women on their way to the garment district still people its corners.

I lived in Chicago when the movie was released, and upon entering the theater I hoped to see familiar sights, sounds, and people. No such luck. The movie was populated with white people. The Mexicans were in the shadows, in the night sounds, out of the frame. Invisible.

This is how I feel about Hollywood movies in general, but I may as well add history books, TV shows, academic conferences. Even in the 1980s when Hollywood High School began to have a majority Salvadoran/Mexican student population, we were nonentities. Hollywood may have been in Los Angeles, but it may as well have been on Mars.

Since 2000, I've done special unpaid tours of the main Mexican barrios of the greater East Los Angeles area (Boyle Heights, Lincoln Park, Maravilla, Highland Park, El Sereno, City Terrace). Mostly streets I've lived on. These places do not exist on tourist maps or on the Hollywood script and screen. I've brought people from Brazil, Japan, Italy, New Zealand, and England. And a TV camera crew or two. These visitors are amazed at how much character and life there is on the Eastside. How poor some of the streets can appear, but also the wonderful smells and sights of taquerías, auto shops, marketas, and musicians with guitars and mariachi suits roving from one eatery to another. They gawk at the old brick buildings and Victorian structures that pop up here and there. And even if the homes are small and wood framed, they are largely clean, with flowerpots, even at times with stalks of corn and chicken coops.

There's a hill in the Juarez Mara gang neighborhood where you can see the skyscrapers of downtown with miles of the Eastside lapping up to them. More than a million people supposedly reside in these neighborhoods. It's about time there was proper recognition. Especially of Xican@s, especially of our complexity.

Murder State, Murder City

In the late 1800s, Mexicans and Natives were living in slums and muddy roads next to the Los Angeles River, which Jacob Riis once called the worst in the nation. Prior to this, Natives and Mexicans were hunted down as bandits and renegades. Tiburcio Vásquez and Joaquin Murrieta were labeled outlaws, but local Mexicans saw them as freedom fighters.

Natives in California—once the largest native population in the country—were systematically killed off and enslaved by the Spanish; by 1818 the percentage of natives who died in the missions was 86 percent. Later more Natives died or were removed under Mexico by anti-Native Mexican governments (a major impetus to remove such a government during the 1910 Mexican Revolution). Indians were hunted down after the 1848 treaty that ceded California and more than half of Mexico to the US following their invasion. In the wake of the 1849 Gold Rush, the state put up bounties—and issued bonds to pay for them—making it legal to kill Natives. There was even a street in my old barrio in South San Gabriel called Graves. I found out later it was named for the graves of Mexicans and Natives killed in the 1800s.

Whole massacres were recorded, including of women and children. Scalps and heads were turned in as proof of Indians killed—twenty-five cents for scalps, five dollars for severed heads. Disease killed many others. The numbers of native peoples in the state dwindled drastically—from an estimated 800,000 to a million before Europeans arrived, to 16,000 in 1900.

Then the Mexican Revolution and other rebellions brought more than a million refugees to the US from 1910 to 1930 when Mexico only had 15 million people (what Guatemala has today). The Native/Mexican population rose in California. The reason was that more than a million people were being killed in the upheavals south of the border, including genocides where whole villages and small tribes were exterminated. My father's own village was destroyed, including records of his birth. He was saved when my grandmother held the infant tightly in her arms as she strode out on a burro through dense shrubbery and cactus as *federales* attacked.

It was during this time that LA's first barrios were created, including the Maravilla District of unincorporated East Los Angeles when city officials in the 1920s sold lots at a dollar apiece (although these lands were largely unwanted, including gullies, ravines, and hills, the refugees exclaimed "Que maravilla!"—what a marvel!). In Boyle Heights, Jewish, Japanese, and Russian immigrants moved out as Mexicans moved in. By the 1950s, the vast Eastside became the largest area of Mexicans in the country (and third in the world after Mexico City and Guadalajara).

Other Mexicans filled the poorest sectors of the Harbor, the Northeast San Fernando Valley, the migrant camps of the San Gabriel Valley, and another refugee stop known as Pico-Union, just west of downtown. Waves of Mexicans moved into Southeast LA and also South Central Los Angeles, then mostly populated since World War II by African Americans. Los Angeles, designated at the turn of the century by the National Association of Manufacturers as a nonunion, cheap labor town, became the largest manufacturing center in the United States—serving as a magnet for migrants to the garment industry, canneries, auto plants, steel plants, foundries, meat-packing, refineries, aerospace, and shipyards. The Los Angeles/Long Beach Harbor became the largest US commercial port.

When civil wars in Central America escalated in the 1980s, resulting in tens of thousands killed in massacres of native peoples and villages, refugees from

El Salvador, Guatemala, and Honduras flooded communities like Pico-Union. The eighties also brought a wave of immigrant Southeast Asians, Russians, Armenians, Koreans, and other Latin Americans to LA; "Gold-paved streets, glitters and glamour" drew them to this monster city by the ocean.

Mostly they found squat apartments, culturally barren streets, strip malls.

With deindustrialization from the mid-1970s, hitting a peak in the 1980s, more than 400,000 jobs were eliminated in the big mills and assembly plants. I worked in this industry from 1972 until 1980, including the Bethlehem Steel Plant, the National Lead Foundry, Chevron chemical refinery, and the St. Regis Paper Company. This was the best means for youth like me to leave the gang life and heroin that had invaded most barrios after World War II and in the 1960s during the Vietnam War era. However, in short order, these plants and mills closed down.

Whole communities, the majority black and brown, saw their livelihoods shuttered away by the rising new technology and the removal of industry to cheaper labor markets in the South, Mexico, Central America, or Southeast Asia.

I also witnessed the influx of drugs and guns that pervaded the inner city during the shift away from big industry. In the 1980s, during the Reagan Administration's Iran-Contra debacle, Los Angeles became the first to have crack. In the midst of four decades of a "war on drugs," other new drugs became available—including now crystal meth and ecstasy. Also in the 1980s firearms from wars around the world ended up in the barrios and ghettos of LA—the result of collusions by gun manufacturers, dealers, and law enforcement. Gangs, which existed here for generations, now became the most cohesive organized force to make the most of this illicit but increasingly viable economy.

Los Angeles soon had more gang violence than any city, followed closely by the second largest manufacturing city, Chicago (and other "rust belt" cities like Detroit, Cleveland, Flint, Gary, Philadelphia, and more). One report estimated some 15,000 young people died from gang and drug violence in the LA area from 1980 to 2000. By the mid-2000s, the murder rate of Latino males ages sixteen to twenty-four in South Central LA was 70 per 100,000, rivaling the world's worse homicide rates in El Salvador and South Africa. But for young black males in the same neighborhood and age group, it was 120 per 100,000.

The official response was even more detrimental—more laws, more police, more prisons. By the 1990s, the US escalated a prison industry that had been growing since the 1970s. Now federal funds helped create new institutions, including the rise of private prison corporations. California went from 15 prisons housing 15,000 prisoners in the early 1970s to 33 prisons with 175,000 in the mid-2000s.

Blacks and Xican@s, unfortunately, filled the juvenile lockups and correctional institutions, becoming up to 80 percent of the population behind bars. Sixty percent of all the state's prisoners came from Los Angeles. The Nidorf Juvenile Hall in Sylmar is now North America's largest juvenile prison.

For dignity and power, Xican@s gravitated toward political organizing. This included uniting with African Americans (despite media portrayals to the contrary), other ethnicities, and with new migrants from Mexico and beyond. Strategic thinking and plans were created. Names like Cesar Chavez, Dolores Huerta, and Sal Castro resonated beyond the barrios and migrant camps. Cultural and political centers were established—including Mechicano Arts Center, Goez Art Studio, Self Help Graphics, and many more. Murals with Xicanesque images, ideas, and imaginations filled many walls, including the Eastside housing projects of Estrada Courts and Ramona Gardens. For a time Los Angeles became the mural capital of the world, with Xican@s at the heart of it.

Many Xican@s thrived. Their influence grew—including the rise of the cholo street style (which can be seen among Crips and Bloods, Cambodian gang members, white skaters, and Salvadoran refugee youth); lowrider car and bike culture; colorful public murals; black-and-grey tattoos; and a street slang that mixed Spanish, Mexican caló, and English words into a kind of LA speak. A Xican@ face—brown, with beret, Day of the Dead paint, cholo stance—emerged in the national consciousness.

Orale pues!

El movimiento

The pinnacle of Xican@ political awakening was in the 1960s and 1970s. Xican@s took part in the civil rights battles that African Americans had been waging since the end of slavery to integrate schools and neighborhoods and end Jim Crow. While an estimated 10,000 black people were lynched following Reconstruction in the South, some 3,000 Mexicans were also lynched, mostly in Texas, along with Chinese, Italians, others. In the 1930 and 1940s, Mexicans also launched lawsuits to outlaw segregated schools. These struggles reached their height during the 1960s with marches, rallies, boycotts, and fiery urban rebellions. Mexicans, Puerto Ricans, and native peoples were also involved with people like Martin Luther King Jr.

The three major areas of protests in California became the antiwar movement, the civil rights movement, and the movement for the rights of farm workers.

I was thirteen years old when I took part in el movimiento during the 1968 East LA "Blowouts" (the largest walkouts of school students in US history) to protest inferior education for Mexicans. Although I attended a school just outside the heart of this struggle, it was known to have the lowest reading scores in the state. A handful of us managed to leave our classes and make it out the gates before we were stopped, sent back in, and promptly suspended.

Then on August 29, 1970, at sixteen, I was arrested and beaten during the Chicano Moratorium against the Vietnam War that brought some 30,000 people to East LA—the largest antiwar protest in a community of color at the time. Sheriff's deputies attacked a largely peaceful crowd enjoying music and speeches at Laguna Park. A riot ensued (this was the worst of nine civil disturbances on the Eastside in the 1960s and early 1970s). Being a tattooed cholo gang member, I was placed with five other cholos on "murderer's row" of the Hall of Justice jail, threatened with murder charges in the deaths of the three people killed by police during the protests, including crusading Chicano journalist Rubén Salazar. I was in a cell next to Charles Manson. I had razor blades pressed against my neck. I was lost for several days in a facility that was supposed to house people over eighteen. But I stood up against all this. Eventually no charges were filed and I was allowed to go home. But this experience proved to be a powerful politicizing act.

Even though I was in a street gang and on heavy drugs, including heroin, I slowly became more active in the Chicano Movement—painting murals at seventeen, learning Mexika dance, and returning to high school (I had dropped out at fifteen) to lead walkouts for Chicano studies and a Chicano student center. I was eighteen and in the county jail, facing a possible prison term for allegedly fighting with police, when I let go of "La Vida Loca" (The Crazy Life) of a Chicano gang member, which included undergoing my first heroin withdrawals. With community backing, including letters of support, a judge gave me time served and I never looked back. Although I was shot at by a couple of homeboys for trying to bring peace, forcing me to leave my old neighborhood, I found out later one of them was a police informant. I moved deeper into Boyle Heights/East LA and organized in the Pico Gardens housing projects. I helped young people, including those in gangs, become politicized. And I took part in efforts to end barrio warfare.

I've been doing this work ever since, accumulating forty years of bringing peace and justice to cities like Chicago (which has the second largest Mexican population in the US), but also with LA's Crips and Bloods; Chicano/Central American gangs in the early 1990s; and in places like northern Mexico, El Salvador, and Guatemala where US deportations since the early 1990s brought many LA-based gang youths to countries with no resources, no jobs, and much devastation due to poverty and wars.

A Circle Completed

My wife, Trini—we've been married for over twenty-five years—was also a Xican@ activist in *el movimiento.* In the mid-1970s, we came together as revolutionary thinkers, teachers, and activists. By then COINTELPRO infiltrated and undermined most social justice organizations such as the Black Panthers, Brown Berets, Young Lords, the American Indian Movement, and antiwar groups. Trini and I, with other cadre, got enmeshed with community, fighting for the rights of new migrants, of labor and the poor.

In Chicago we served as editors of political newspapers and were active in the Mexican/Puerto Rican communities. It was there where our love as friends and comrades blossomed into romance. My own work in Chicago with gangs also involved African Americans, Asians, Natives, and whites. In 2000, we moved back to Los Angeles, to the Northeast San Fernando Valley, where Trini had grown up. It was an area rife with gangs, housing projects, and working poor. It was the second largest Mexican/Central American community in Los Angeles after East LA.

In the Northeast Valley, Trini and I, along with other members of the family and community, created Tia Chucha's Centro Cultural & Bookstore, LLC, in 2001. We established a nonprofit cultural space in 2003, later disbanding the LLC and donating all our equipment and inventory to the nonprofit. We've kept the spirit of the Xican@ movement and extended it. We do this by helping develop the creative/imaginative life of the community, and doing what we can so everyone is truly authoritative, autonomous, and artistic. Independent and interdependent.

Los Angeles is enriched and much alive due to Xican@s—and the future holds immense possibilities with the world seemingly meeting within our boundaries, exposed to a people and a struggle that has long defined another America.

Revolution is in our blood, the land, in our bones. And a vibrant connection to all human beings is being forged daily, freeing us of borders, archaic economic and political realities, as well as strangling belief systems that no longer hold sway or meaning. The illusions of the wage system, of mortgages, of scarcity and power are being stripped away. A global unveiling is revealing our true destinies—and Los Angeles, with Xican@s as key to its soul, can help lead the way.

We are in a time characterized by "In Lak'ech," an ancient Mayan concept that means, "you are the other me; I'm the other you." The way it should be.

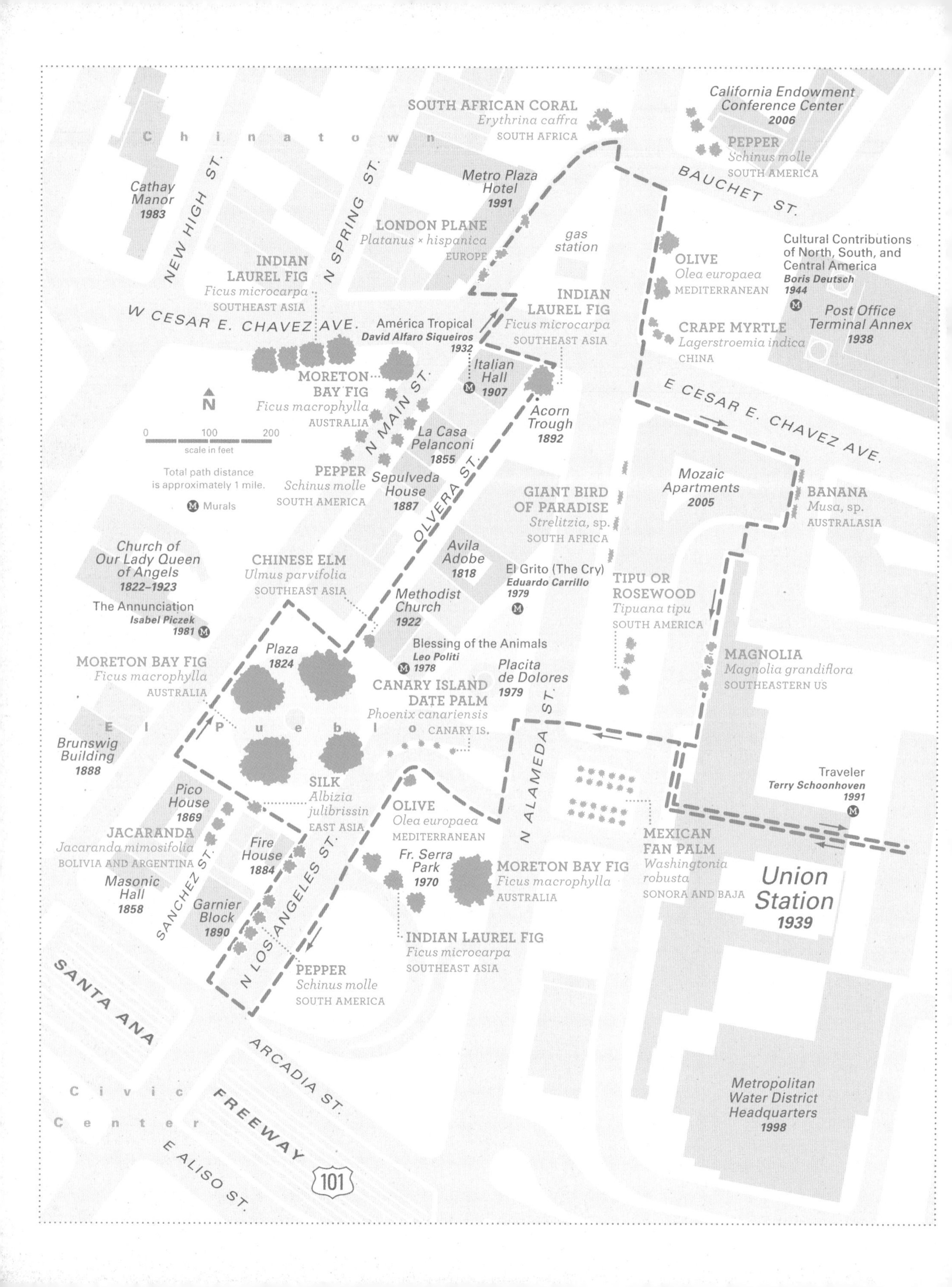

Chinatown
Cathay Manor
1983
NEW HIGH ST.
N SPRING ST.
SOUTH AFRICAN CORAL
Erythrina caffra
SOUTH AFRICA
California Endowment Conference Center
2006
PEPPER
Schinus molle
SOUTH AMERICA
BAUCHET ST.
Metro Plaza Hotel
1991
LONDON PLANE
Platanus × hispanica
EUROPE
gas station
Cultural Contributions of North, South, and Central America
Boris Deutsch
1944
INDIAN LAUREL FIG
Ficus microcarpa
SOUTHEAST ASIA
OLIVE
Olea europaea
MEDITERRANEAN
Post Office Terminal Annex
1938
W CESAR E. CHAVEZ AVE.
América Tropical
David Alfaro Siqueiros
1932
INDIAN LAUREL FIG
Ficus microcarpa
SOUTHEAST ASIA
CRAPE MYRTLE
Lagerstroemia indica
CHINA
Italian Hall
1907
MORETON BAY FIG
Ficus macrophylla
AUSTRALIA
N MAIN ST.
Acorn Trough
1892
E CESAR E. CHAVEZ AVE.
N
0
100
200
scale in feet
Total path distance is approximately 1 mile.
Murals
La Casa Pelanconi
1855
PEPPER
Schinus molle
SOUTH AMERICA
Sepulveda House
1887
OLVERA ST.
Mozaic Apartments
2005
GIANT BIRD OF PARADISE
Strelitzia, sp.
SOUTH AFRICA
BANANA
Musa, sp.
AUSTRALASIA
Church of Our Lady Queen of Angels
1822–1923
CHINESE ELM
Ulmus parvifolia
SOUTHEAST ASIA
Avila Adobe
1818
El Grito (The Cry)
Eduardo Carrillo
1979
TIPU OR ROSEWOOD
Tipuana tipu
SOUTH AMERICA
The Annunciation
Isabel Piczek
1981
Methodist Church
1922
Blessing of the Animals
Leo Politi
1978
Plaza
1824
MORETON BAY FIG
Ficus macrophylla
AUSTRALIA
Placita de Dolores
1979
MAGNOLIA
Magnolia grandiflora
SOUTHEASTERN US
CANARY ISLAND DATE PALM
Phoenix canariensis
CANARY IS.
El Pueblo
Brunswig Building
1888
N ALAMEDA ST.
SILK
Albizia julibrissin
EAST ASIA
Pico House
1869
OLIVE
Olea europaea
MEDITERRANEAN
Traveler
Terry Schoonhoven
1991
JACARANDA
Jacaranda mimosifolia
BOLIVIA AND ARGENTINA
Fire House
1884
MEXICAN FAN PALM
Washingtonia robusta
SONORA AND BAJA
Fr. Serra Park
1970
MORETON BAY FIG
Ficus macrophylla
AUSTRALIA
Union Station
1939
Masonic Hall
1858
SANCHEZ ST.
N LOS ANGELES ST.
Garnier Block
1890
INDIAN LAUREL FIG
Ficus microcarpa
SOUTHEAST ASIA
PEPPER
Schinus molle
SOUTH AMERICA
SANTA ANA
ARCADIA ST.
FREEWAY
101
Civic Center
E ALISO ST.
Metropolitan Water District Headquarters
1998

It is little known but true: Los Angeles has great trees. They mark former property lines, tell stories of dreams failed and achieved, and green up the backgrounds of a thousand movies and television shows. Some LA trees achieve record size; some surprise even botanists with their tenacity; some come from as far away as Patagonia and New Zealand; all do their bit to turn bad air into good. Take a walk around Union Station—at the heart of the city's historic core—with this map to familiarize yourself with some of these "usual suspects."

Orphans, Dwarfs, Strangers, and Monsters

THE URBAN FORESTS OF LOS ANGELES

Charles Hood

What is a tree? A tree is a big plant with a stick up the middle.
—Collin Tudge, *The Secret Life of Trees*

Trees Flow Out of Mountains Like Water

Contrary to the folderol about Los Angeles being a concrete jungle and postapocalyptic wasteland, current tallies estimate 15 million trees, distributed over 3,000 species. Like the people themselves, many of these came from elsewhere—about which, more in a second—but the thing is, there always have been trees here, and, almost certainly, there always will be.

Five hundred years ago Los Angeles was a savannah floodplain with riparian corridors following half a dozen rivers down to the sea. These arroyos and rivers were green with willows, sycamores, mule fat, and cottonwoods. Headwater canyons brimmed with alder. Many places, the water flowed year-round and the trees just followed the water. There were wild grapes and a native, edible walnut.

Away from these forests, the savannah—a mix of tussocky grassland and xeric chaparral—was home to pronghorn antelope and condors and burrowing owls and grizzly bears and First Nation gatherer-hunters who fed the multitudes not with loaves and fishes but with acorns and jackrabbits. They gardened with fire to cultivate the coast live oak, many specimens hundreds of years old and all handier than a Trader Joe's. One theorist suggests that the Native Americans in California didn't need to build Mayan temples or Sumerian ziggurats because they didn't need a theocracy to control food distribution—plenty of acorns for everybody: just go out and scoop some up.

Was it originally an Edenic landscape? Depends what you expect. Stepping out of a time machine, at first it might look odd. Missing would be most of the semiotic markers we're used to—orange trees and palm trees and a certain casual abundance of tropical foliage. In fact, the land might seem strangely altered: no pigeons yet, no starlings, no rats, no opossums, no fire ants. No eucalyptus trees. No contrails in the sky. Ravens maybe, but fewer crows. No snails, or at least not the pest kind your garden has now. No cockroaches. No tumbleweed. Even the flies would be different.

Trees change as population regimes change: missions imported pepper trees from Peru, and some of the better-watered *tuna* cactus tangles grew taller than horses. The first olive trees. The first oranges and lemons. Wine grapes. Date palms, for fruit and for fronds on Palm Sunday. Maybe the first fan palms, originally from Baja Sur. Three-hundred-year-old sycamore snags adzed into chunks for firewood and charcoal. Here and there Los Angeles began to look a bit more Mediterranean, a bit transformed, but most of the current arborscape hadn't yet arrived.

Soon, but not yet.

And when they did come, the new trees, they came in trends and fads, as dateable as any other fashion preference. Which individual *kinds* of trees got planted in LA changed decade by decade—some things came into favor as other things cycled out—but the one constant was a raid-the-cookie-jar internationalism.

Part of this reflects broader cultural trends, such as the City Beautiful Movement that suggested urban plantings didn't just provide aesthetic balance, but promoted civic virtue and social harmony. To take a simple and small example, even from its start Beverly Hills wrote ordinances requiring lawns—an absurd, Victorian indulgence in a land of little rain. More so than elsewhere, though, in creating Los Angeles, these newest Californians needed to quiet their Midwestern fever dreams and lessen the constant ache of childhood's loss, but they also needed to build a *gabacho* fantasyland just as tropical and surreal as could be. They would plant elms and chestnuts, yes, but also bizarre exotics and wildly inappropriate water-hogs. For most Los Angeles residents, when designing a yard, it didn't matter where a tree came from so long as it looked taller and more exotic than the neighbor's tree.

Los Angeles began to look like "Los Angeles" by the early 1900s. Each day the ships and railroads brought new plants, while enterprising people of many ethnicities nursed them, sold them, planted them, watered them. And more water was coming, as everybody knew. The year before the aqueduct opened in 1913, exotic trees were as popular as new-model iPhones. Prices dropped and sales boomed. You could buy a three-foot-tall jacaranda for thirty-five cents, and in an even better bargain, a eucalyptus sapling barely cost half that. People wanted magnolias, but at first they were too expensive. No matter: If Texas won't work, try Mexico. If Mexico won't work, try Australia. George Irvine in 1888 imported 12,000 eucalyptus seedlings at fifteen bucks per thousand. The new "mahogany of California" all this eucalyptus was going to be, other than it turns out that the oil makes the tree explode in wildfires and the grain twists up more contrary than a mule on crank. Okay, so much for a lucrative timber franchise, but they grow fast and make okay windbreaks, so have at it. Pretty soon they were everywhere, as they still are today.

On Colorado Boulevard in Old Town Pasadena, native oaks gave way to pepper trees and, in time, those were replaced with queen palms. Then we had Taiwan Fig (*Ficus retusa,* also called Cuban-laurel), and the latest tree to show up is ginkgo, or as some local business owners call it, the el stinko tree. You want something that looks nice but won't buckle the sidewalk like a spoon cracking crème brûlée or spread a violet mess, as jacarandas do, so slippery the street becomes a lawsuit just waiting to happen. Don't like the mix of trees right now? Wait a bit longer and trends will change again.

Meet the Usual Suspects

To understand the urban forest, first we have to be able to see trees as discrete and separate objects: we need to be able to locate the specific within the general. Let's do a short walk together, just to learn some trees. Take the Gold Line or Amtrak to Union Station, rub in some sunscreen, and we're ready to go for a walk.

Our trip begins with a palm tree. Step outside the main entrance and the palms to your left and right as well as the rows just ahead of you in the median are all Mexican fan palms. Our native palm—the palms for which Palm Springs was named—never occurred naturally in Los Angeles; almost all the current palm stock originally came from Baja.

These at Union Station look like they're supposed to look because crews help them look right. The hula skirt thatch of dead fronds just below the living foliage has to be maintained by frequent trimming; on their own, they would look shaggier, bushier, messier. From the city's perspective, dead fronds are a hazard—if they come off in a windstorm, their serrated edges spin down like ninja saws. Rats nest in them, and it just looks untidy. Nature always has a plan, so in the wild, a beard of fronds has a purpose, since it acts as a fire retardant—dead fronds burn up, but in doing so, protect the green crown.

Los Angeles shows off more than just one kind of palm, of course. The lower, squatter, thicker types, the ones with broad, vigorous fronds and whose trunks sometimes crisscross in a heavy diamond pattern, these are Canary Island date palms. But most of the svelte palms of Hollywood (and Santa Monica and Beverly Hills and most everywhere else) are Mexican fan palms, same as the ones in front of you now. Fan palms have fronds that are broad and (hey!) "fan-shaped." Date palms have fronds more like long, green feathers.

If you want to "do" palm trees, LA is the place to be—by the 1890s, eighty-seven varieties of palms were sold commercially, with prices ranging from twenty-five cents to ten dollars. A row of graceful palms creates an expected look of quasi-tropical prosperity, and you will find this species planted now in Phoenix, Tucson, even Seattle. Mature palms these days go for a thousand bucks a foot, so if you're building a new office tower, a thirty-foot tree will cost as much as a good car.

Most of the palm trees around Los Angeles are heading towards being one hundred years old, so many may be reaching the end of typical lifespans. On the other hand, maybe not. The conditions here are not the same as nature, and in nature, nobody really was counting. Wait and see, the gods tell us. Like the Lakers, they may have another hundred years in them after all.

When a palm tree dies, if it is not removed by city workers or burned up by a passing fire, the trunk can stay upright for years—a strange, topless swizzle stick poking up out of the ground like failed sculpture. Probably the oldest palm tree in LA is at Exposition Park, a twice-transplanted tree that Nathan Masters of the USC Libraries believes came to Los Angeles in the 1850s. The ones here at Union Station most likely are not much older than the station itself, which opened in 1939.

Turn right to see magnolias. Native to the American South, the primitive magnolia tree produces a showy white blossom; leaves are large, glossy, and dark, with a sort of fuzzy and sometimes tan underside. It can be a common street tree, and in Glendale or Burbank you can find entire blocks with nothing but these. By leaf area, some counts rank this as the most common tree in LA.

Ahead and to the right, Parking Lot B's row of feathery-leafed, acacia-looking trees with yellow blossoms adds spring color to the view. The tipu tree or rosewood likes hot, interior places like urban

Los Angeles or the better-watered suburbs of Phoenix; originally from South America, an alternate name is "pride of Bolivia," which makes it seem like a Miss World winner or perhaps a particularly fine grade of coca leaf.

Cross Alameda now, aiming for the obvious, oversize Moreton Bay fig dominating the small park often used by homeless people. This is the immense tree with the buttress array of aboveground roots, a tree native to Australia that was first planted in Los Angeles in the 1870s. On the park's top end, near the war memorial, waits a single, token olive tree, a species descended from host plants first domesticated 5,000 years ago. Around the top near the statue are more figs of a different species than the big one, almost all of them Indian laurel. This is one of the most common street trees in LA: if you see a straight, pale trunk and a bushy green top, just tell out of town guests it's a fig.

Cross uphill to the bandstand. More recently planted, other trees fill out our list, including our first jacaranda. Best identified in spring, this is the delicately branched tree from Brazil that looks sort of acacia-ish and whose blossoms fill the tree with a spray of lavender or lilac or blue (depending on whose description you trust).

Look instead to the firehouse on the left, and then from it, left along the street. The small weeping willow-looking trees by the benches all are pepper trees, *Schinus molle*. People call these California pepper though they come from South America; they have been part of the flora here at least since 1800. The leaves filter the light in a soft, fluttery way, as if you're being shaded by the beating wings of hummingbirds.

The tour office features a few small silk trees out front. Another name for this is mimosa; it's abundant in Los Angeles and arrived in 1918, ready to celebrate the end of the war to end all wars. The delicate red flowers look a lot like bottlebrush.

From the tour office, cut back through the plaza towards the church. The large

tree between the Methodist church and the entrance to the Olvera Street shops is a Chinese elm, and you know you have the right one if you are standing by a tree with a sort of puzzle-piece park that blends olive green with some outlined squiggles of dark orange.

For once, this one's name matches reality; it indeed is an elm, and it even comes from China. If the tree dies in your lifetime, try to be the first on site with a chainsaw and a large backpack, since the dense, fine-grained wood makes great baseball bats and tool handles. For now, it shades a small cross sanctifying the entrance to the shopping arcade, which is one definition for *alameda*.

Follow the main pedestrian alley past the many incarnations of the Blessed Virgin to exit onto Cesar Chavez Street.

Look ahead north and a bit left. See the bail bonds office and sign for 99¢ tacos? There's a Subway too and a hotel, but our target is the row of London plane trees, our first of the trip. Growing up in Atwater, I learned to call these the itchy bomb trees after the fuzz we rubbed out of the seed balls and stuck down other kids' shirts.

The plane tree is a hybrid of Old and New World sycamores that has become one of the most widespread urban trees in the world. It's been cultivated since the late seventeenth century, and you can find them by the thousands in London (hence the name) and in most other big cities—Madrid, Paris, Boston, Santiago. The bark has a mottled, watercolored appearance, just asking to be portrayed with a loving blend of pale blues and warm creams, while the leaves have a sort of hand-shaped, maple-leaf kind of look, pointed and bright green.

Crossing Alameda to the Post Office Terminal Annex takes us past a thoroughly Roman mix, as a row of lush but low olive trees has been underfilled with a very rich bed of rosemary. A few young crape myrtles have been tucked into the far corner, easy to overlook. Last stop, the Mozaic apartments just north of Union Station. Those banana tree–looking tropical plants lining the side of the building are all giant birds of paradise, from South Africa.

Going home, out the window of the train you may spot a willow forest in the river at the Glendale Narrows, or perhaps spot a cluster of California sycamores, pale-barked trees that look like London plane trees but more often will be tucked away in seeps and well-watered parks near riverbeds, sometimes hosting a bright crown of mistletoe. Kumeyaay Indians used sycamore bark to treat asthma; the leaves can be used to wrap meat for baking. It looks superficially similar to sweetgum or liquid amber, a southern species planted just about everywhere. Sweetgum's leaves are more sharply star-shaped, and its seed ball has more of a pockmarked, burned-out asteroid look. Don't step on it barefoot.

Tallest, Oldest, Strangest, Ugliest

It turns out that some tree people—and just as trains have their trainspotters or Inverted Jennies their ardent philatelists, so trees have their tree people—look for, celebrate, want to be photographed next to champions. Obviously, if there is such a tree as the snot apple *(Azanza garckeana)*, somebody will want to know which one is the biggest snot apple. Maybe not you—you probably have better things to do on a Saturday morning—but *somebody*. Somebody will have driven around counting branches and can tell you which trees bulge with the best girth or stretch taller than any rivals.

According to the Urban Forestry Ecosystems Institute, "California has 327 Big Tree listings, 112 National Champions, and 37 Co-Champions." It's a points thing, like trophy antlers on an elk. Maybe you have one of these champs in your local park, don't even know it. Get out your surveyor's measure. Here's the formula: *Trunk Circumference (inches) + Height (feet) + ¼ Average Crown Spread (feet) = Total Points*. To get circumference (or "dbh," diameter at breast height), you measure the trunk four feet up, unless there is a branch or the tree is on a hill or the tree grows on level ground but at a crazy-ass slant.

How perfect that one of our local national champions is the flower fence tree, and the other, a silk floss, hides away inside the Hotel Bel-Air. Or rather, it did, past tense, the silk floss, up until a hanging chad recount. *Exceptional Trees of Los Angeles* nominates the Hotel Bel-Air's silk floss tree as a national champion, but some spoilsport found a big sprawling mess of a rival on the side of the road in Fallbrook and now he puffs that *that* is biggest. Who's right? Probably neither: probably there's one in some crotchety gardener's backyard that would bust the buttons off both of those, only he doesn't want to say so out loud—might have strangers knocking on the door, wanting to trample the Dichondra.

Either way, we do seem to attract the Liberaces of the plant world, don't we? Flower fence has other names: peacock flower, Mexican bird of paradise, caballero. Silk floss is also floss silk is also ceiba is also drunken sailor. Related to the mighty kapok of Mayan cosmology, it is a food tree for our screeching hordes of yellow-chevroned parakeets, one of a dozen species of feral parrots nesting and feeding in Southern California's urban canopy. You can make life-jacket stuffing from the cottony kapok seedpods, if you hanker for a sort of retro, World War II look. Pollinated by butterflies, the hibiscus-like flowers, in the words of naturalist Matt Ritter, "are showy, deep pink, with long ruffled petals and a white-spotted throat." All the leaves fall off at summer's end to reveal the blossoms, a trait left over from the rainforest when insect infestations become a burden for many trees. (It also may make the blossoms easier to find in the dark and crowded aroma-fest of a rainforest night.) Young silk floss trees can photosynthesize just with their trunks, while older ones, at least in the Costa Rican species, used to be made into coffins.

Candidate for oldest tree would have to be one of the Pasadena oaks, though a detour into botanical trivia causes me to mention "King Clone creosote," a scrubby ring of vegetation just over the mountains in the Mojave Desert. One plant growing as a successive series of related branches probably is 11,700 years old, making oak trees in comparison look barely old enough to drink Schlitz. We had a really great oak tree locally, the Lang Oak, supposedly (but probably not) a thousand years old, but it went to the happy hunting grounds in 1998 during El Niño rains. No redwoods, sequoias, or bristlecone pines ever occurred here naturally; in Southern California, most pine trees just last a few hundred years, so turning our eyes to Mount Wilson won't help. Our endemic Engelmann oaks still endure: the Los Angeles County Arboretum has an especially lovely stand. A Central Valley species, the valley oak, can live to six hundred years, and the bottom edge of its distribution ends around Encino ("oak" in Spanish).

Ugliest tree in Los Angeles? We won't include here the option of a diatribe against the topiary in front of It's a Small World at Disneyland. Robert Adams has made a career out of finding smog-ruined trees and turning them into manifestations of the New Topographic sublime. Bruce Davidson, another art world A-lister, recently has been working with trees too. Interviewed in the *New Yorker,* he says he's interested in photographing LA nature because of "what [trees] can tell us about the way we live today."

Thinking about it beforehand, for "ugly trees" I had imagined some ghetto tree tagged up with idiot gang runes, but even there, it's hard to fault the tree for the failings of the primates around it. Ugly maybe just means architecture *without* trees, since there no more could be an ugly tree than there could be an ugly ocean, an ugly moon, an ugly sunrise.

What It All Means

What do our trees tell us about ourselves—indeed, what does any given tree "mean"?

On the obvious level, trees feed birds and squirrels, and trees help make any neighborhood look rich. But we need to go back to seventh-grade science class to explore a deeper, more basic truth: trees help us every day because they scrub carbon dioxide from the air. They shade buildings, buffer street noise, stabilize hillsides, raise the curb appeal of houses. In doing so, they provide scale and balance to architecture. A residential street lined with trees not only looks good, it protects kids, since cars drive slower on streets with trees. It's even good for the pavement itself, since shade (and hence reduced temperature fluctuation) extends the working life of an asphalt street. Hospitals know that seeing a tree helps patients stay calm, heal faster. Seeing a lot of trees does that only more so.

So let's celebrate this abundance. We have easy access to more trees than most of us notice, appreciate, touch. That's easily changed. Just go for a walk around the block and spend five seconds with your hand touching each tree before you move past. Smell the bark—some pines smell like vanilla—or look for fruit. Locavores and foragers will want to investigate the maps available on FallenFruit.org, which detail small, walkable slices of neighborhoods where one may harvest unclaimed fruit. The group offers simple advice: take only what you need; say hi to strangers; share your food; take a friend; go by foot.

We close with a vote for the next official "Tree of LA." No, not a Hollywood fan palm or an Italian cypress, not the magnolia or liquid amber or fig, but I vote for a tree we've not mentioned. A few weeks ago I was surveying plants around Echo Park Lake and I found an abandoned lot completely grown up edge to edge with just one species, *Ailanthus altissima,* or the tree of heaven, named by Matt Ritter "one of the weediest trees in the world." You couldn't even see if there was still a house standing on the lot. Nobody plants it: it just shows up on its own and takes over like crazy. Native originally to Asia, ailanthus came to America in 1787, via Paris via Jesuits who had brought it from China overland via Russia. One common name is stinking ash; this is a rangy, green, fast-growing tree that others call ghetto palm. It once was cultivated as a host for silk worms. The novel *A Tree Grows in Brooklyn* features this species; Elia Kazan directed the movie version just a few years before wining an Oscar for *On The Waterfront.* That makes it a show-biz tree and also a history-tells-us-a-story tree, but the main delight is in its persnickety, ornery, darn cussed enduringness. In *A Californian's Guide to the Trees among Us,* Matt Ritter describes it with affectionate honesty: "The tree of heaven has foul-smelling flowers and a suckering habit whereby it produces copious sprouts directly from shallow roots. It manufactures chemicals that kill other plants and is nearly impossible to kill itself."

Some day every tree alive now in Los Angeles will be dead, and yet in the end, Los Angeles will have just as many trees as it does now. Trees grow, mature, die, get cut down and mulched, and a new something or other gets planted instead. Let the droughts come and the earthquake fissures crack and spread, since even if it comes down to just a few final, last-stand, heat-seared stubs of ailanthus and a fencepost cholla deadheading the greasewood, *some* kind of trees will survive.

In Los Angeles, the tree is dead. Long live the tree.

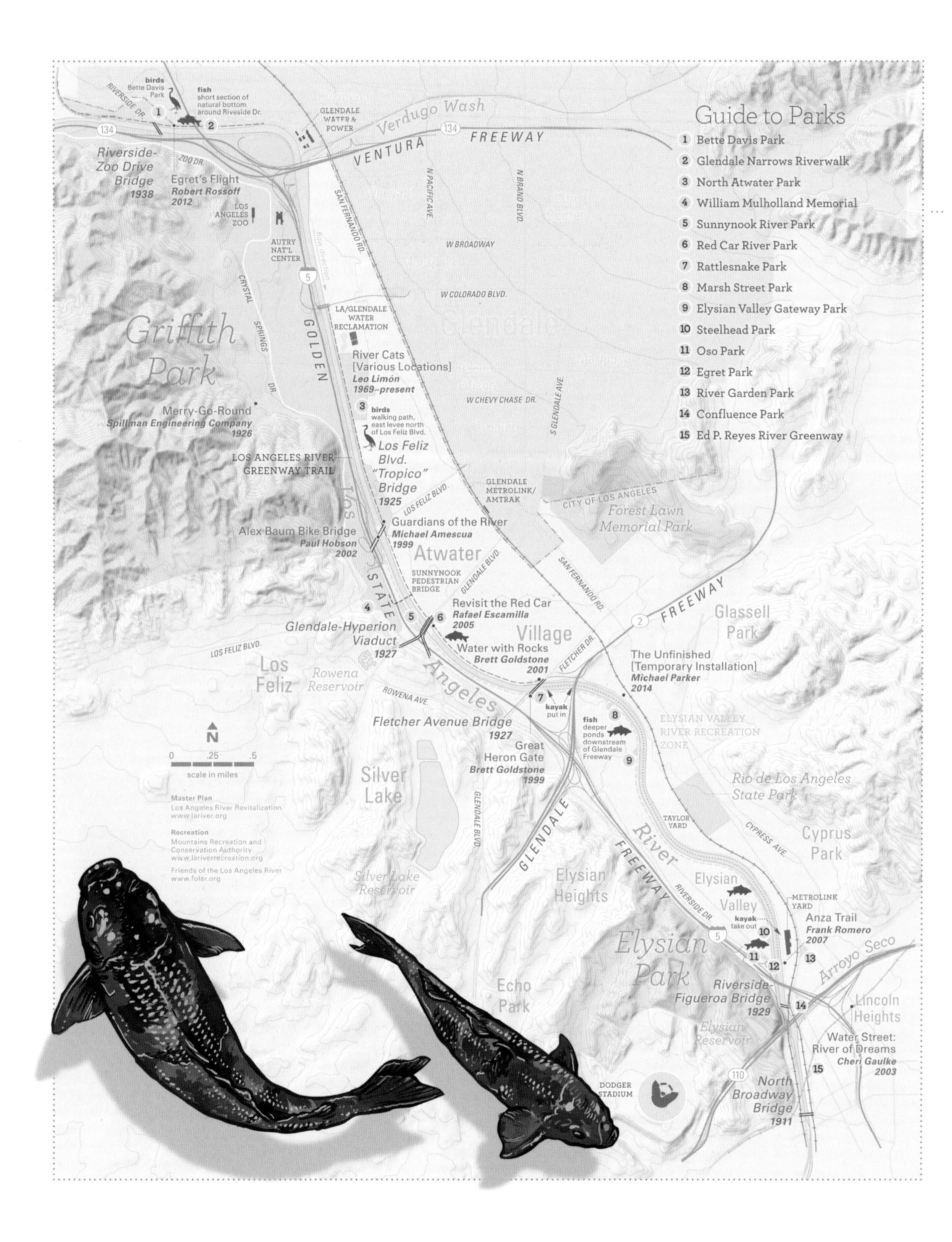

Guide to Parks
1 Bette Davis Park
2 Glendale Narrows Riverwalk
3 North Atwater Park
4 William Mulholland Memorial
5 Sunnynook River Park
6 Red Car River Park
7 Rattlesnake Park
8 Marsh Street Park
9 Elysian Valley Gateway Park
10 Steelhead Park
11 Oso Park
12 Egret Park
13 River Garden Park
14 Confluence Park
15 Ed P. Reyes River Greenway
Riverside-Zoo Drive Bridge 1938
Egret's Flight Robert Rossoff 2012
River Cats [Various Locations] Leo Limón 1969–present
Merry-Go-Round Spillman Engineering Company 1926
Los Feliz Blvd. "Tropico" Bridge 1925
Guardians of the River Michael Amescua 1999
Alex Baum Bike Bridge Paul Hobson 2002
Revisit the Red Car Rafael Escamilla 2005
Glendale-Hyperion Viaduct 1927
Water with Rocks Brett Goldstone 2001
The Unfinished [Temporary Installation] Michael Parker 2014
Fletcher Avenue Bridge 1927
Great Heron Gate Brett Goldstone 1999
Anza Trail Frank Romero 2007
Riverside-Figueroa Bridge 1929
Water Street: River of Dreams Cheri Gaulke 2003
North Broadway Bridge 1911
Griffith Park
Glendale
Atwater Village
Los Feliz
Silver Lake
Echo Park
Elysian Heights
Elysian Valley
Elysian Park
Glassell Park
Cypress Park
Lincoln Heights
Forest Lawn Memorial Park
Rio de Los Angeles State Park
Verdugo Wash
Arroyo Seco
Los Angeles River
Ventura Freeway
Golden State Freeway
Glendale Freeway
Los Angeles River Greenway Trail
Elysian Valley River Recreation Zone
Dodger Stadium
scale in miles
Master Plan
Los Angeles River Revitalization
www.lariver.org
Recreation
Mountains Recreation and Conservation Authority
www.lariverrecreation.org
Friends of the Los Angeles River
www.folar.org

A concrete trough through which effluent ripples past industrial landscapes, the LA River should be an anti-ecology, yet it flourishes. This map is a recreationist's guide to a stretch of river known as the Glendale Narrows, which is dense with parks, vegetation, public artwork, bird life, and, yes, spots to sink a hook into the waters.

Stalking Carp

Andrew O. Wilcox

Many go fishing all their lives without knowing that it is not fish they are after.
—Henry David Thoreau

The Los Angeles River is a strange place—simultaneously icon and iconoclast of wild LA. A soup of intentional engineering and feral ecology, the river is a paradoxical landscape, symbolic of what might be wrong and what might be possible. For some it can be hard to see past its symbolism. Many see a defiled landscape, a river straightjacketed by hubris and concrete. Some see a landscape overrun with "invasive" species of flora and fauna. Some see a cautionary tale of protective triumph over chaotic nature. A dystopian blight. An economic drain—or opportunity. A metaphor. A landscape that cries out for "restoration" to some previous, mythical state. Regardless of ideology, once you've directly and actively experienced this landscape, it is not easily described, imagined, or dismissed.

A corpulent gold lives in the LA River—*Cyprinus carpio,* the common carp. This nonnative species flourishes in the wild outflow from the city's faucets, toilets, and streets. Twenty-pound specimens lurk in the verbal histories of its banks and six-pounders are regularly caught along the eight-mile stretches of the Glendale Narrows and Elysian Valley. Ripples of displacement; thick shadows on sand and concrete floors; reflections and dramatic emergences of hand-sized fins; loud, fat-lipped slurps—all bespeak the pounds of flexing muscles and the quivering barbel mustaches of the fish that navigates this novel ecology of shopping-cart islands and riprap beds.

Walking the Glendale Narrows and Elysian Valley sections of river, squinting in the reflected heat of the channel, fishing for carp is an intentional and open endeavor. Stalking them you must be careful and quiet. You must look at and see what's actually there. The water has an earthy smell. Wet mud clings to your shoes and algal seeps slick your soles. Herons watch warily. Cyclists call out their passing. Plastic bags make fish-shaped shadows. Traffic rumbles on.

Stalking is a way of seeing. There is no nostalgia in stalking carp; it is a search for what *is.*

The River

Most carp fishing occurs in the eight-mile Glendale Narrows/Elysian Valley stretch of the river. This section gets much attention, as the other miles are, for the most part, more difficult to envision and access. The LA River Master Plan places a great deal of focus here; most major river events are launched here; this is the section that gets the majority of new parks and programming; and this is the section that most bicyclists know. These miles, along with the Sepulveda Basin, the Queen's Bay estuary, and very small section of Compton Creek, present the image of a river that we like best, the one that is most *river-like.* These miles may not exactly run "free," but any time spent in them will reveal an untamed, undomesticated, mixed-origin, and thriving ecology—a river in the Los Angeles form.

The Los Angeles River runs a fifty-two-mile course from its headwaters at the north end of the San Fernando Valley, where the Arroyo Calabasas and Bell Creek meet, to where it slides into the Pacific Ocean at the Port of Long Beach. Prior to channelization the river ranged widely across the broad alluvial plain of the Los Angeles basin. It flowed quietly and narrowly in the summer sun then wildly and broadly with winter rain. It, along with the San Gabriel and Santa Ana rivers, made the Los Angeles basin the fertile location it was.

From the earliest accounts it is clear the Los Angeles River was a landscape in contrast to a broader, more arid region. It supported a vibrant riparian plant community amongst the coastal sage scrub: a mix of cottonwoods, sycamores, oaks, willows, sage, buckwheat, grasses, and wild roses. Padre Juan Crespí noted this wealth of life along the river corridor in 1769 in his journal account of the Portola Expedition.

Numerous nineteenth-century photographs provide compelling visual accounts of this landscape.

As Los Angeles grew, the fixed patterns of Spanish and Western settlement and agriculture were not in congruence with the general hydrology of the LA River. The early zanja system of aqueducts transferred water across Los Angeles but did not, and could not, control the seasonal fluctuations of the river. The flood of 1815, and numerous floods after, caused significant losses to the emerging agricultural and real-estate economies. Los Angeles could not afford a river that moved like the LA River did. In 1915 the Los Angeles County Flood Control District was formed. After the flood of 1938, the most damaging to date, a twenty-year channelization process began.

The Army Corps of Engineers took the lead in channelizing the river. Box channels, trapezoidal sections, and industrial feats of concrete manipulation came to define the river. No longer would the sediment-producing flows off the San Gabriel, Santa Susana, and Santa Monica mountains or the Verdugo Hills deposit their fertile wealth across the alluvial plain of the Los Angeles river watershed. The twenty-year process of building debris basins and dams, fortifying embankments, and laying miles upon miles of concrete left only three sections with soft bottoms. These three sections of the river—the Sepulveda Basin behind Sepulveda Dam, Elysian Valley/Glendale Narrows, and the estuary at the Port of Long Beach—were spared the concrete blanket draped by the corps by geologic happenstance: the water table was too high to pour concrete in the river channel. These locations, now described as "naturalized," were established by default rather than design.

The water in the river we know today is mostly treated effluent from the Donald C. Tillman Water Reclamation Plant. The Tillman Plant, located in Van Nuys, opened in 1985 and doubled its capacity in 1991. The plant releases tens of millions of gallons of reclaimed and treated—"clean"—wastewater into the Los Angeles River each day. (Before it runs through the sinks, toilets, and showers of the San Fernando Valley, this water originally comes from Mulholland's Los Angeles Aqueduct, carried south from Northern California.) According to Los Angeles County Department of Public Works, 80 percent of the flow in the river is this recycled water. The remaining 20 percent comes from street runoff: numerous storm drains still run directly into the river. This was especially evident when a tanker truck crash at the 5 and 2 freeway interchange in 2013 set the river on fire: burning fuel flowed into the river through storm drains.

A Los Angeles Archetype

Gold masses of muscle with toenail-sized scales and blood-red tinted fins the size of a man's hands, carp are beautifully identifiable. Barbel whiskers frame fat orange lips that suck seed-laden foam from the edges of giant cane, making telltale slurping sounds. Orange eyes stare atop rotund fleshy bodies. These citrus-tinted, behemoth omnivores eat all day long, gaining pounds per year. Moving from sun to shadow and free of deep thought, these fish are nonetheless remarkably *aware*. They thrive in the opportunity that is the river.

Carp are not native to here: little of what we have come to associate with Southern California and Los Angeles is. Neither carp nor a city of this population should exist here, yet both thrive. This defiant adaptation and opportunistic resilience is a true LA story and, incidentally, characterizes many of the city's human inhabitants.

It is unclear when the common carp was introduced into the Los Angeles River watershed. The *LA Times* has a story (cited in the Friends of the Los Angeles River 2008 fish report) that mentions carp in the late 1800s. It is safe to speculate, as many have, that some early Angeleno saw the need to develop a carp fishery—or perhaps several carp were washed into the watershed from a farm pond during a big storm. Whatever the reason or method, carp have a relatively long history here. They show no signs of picking up and going back to where they came from. As

have so many other residents, they have found a home in the beautiful mess of LA.

Carp are one of the most common species of cultivated fish in the world. More than 2,000 years ago, the Romans and Chinese were eating them. There are many species of carp and numerous subspecies, from koi to the Asian carp that are jumping into boats and invading the Great Lakes today.

Common Carp are members of the minnow family. As big minnows, they have a schooling habit and are often found in groups; where you see one you can be assured there are others around. They reproduce and grow rapidly under ideal conditions. So prolific is the species that it makes the list of the world's top 100 *invasive* species. Carp can make up for very low levels of dissolved oxygen by gulping air from the water's surface and can live in water that is super saturated. They are very tolerant of pollution and water temperature. Carp are omnivorous and spend their days eating everything from aquatic invertebrates and crayfish to cottonwood seeds and decaying vegetation. They prefer slow-moving water like that of the LA River. They can thrive in the challenging conditions of the contemporary river that native fishes—steelhead, for example—cannot.

In March and April it is common to see the river thick with piles of carp roiling up out of the water in the early spring sun. The spawning of carp in the LA River is a spectacular sight: hundreds of fish entangled in a primal act of procreation. The splashing and cavorting is essential to distributing the millions of sticky eggs an individual female fish can lay. The majority of young carp do not make it to adulthood: they become prey for numerous other species—fish, mammal, and avian alike. Though the carp do not themselves enjoy a reputation for beauty, they feed young egrets, herons, kingfishers, and osprey—the charismatic birds that have become the poster children for a healthy Los Angeles River.

The River Specific: Fly-Fishing the River

All soft-bottom sections of the LA River are fishable. Much of the fishing occurs in the stretch of channel through Glendale Narrows and Elysian Valley. This section of river is easily accessed at multiple points between the 134 freeway and Riverside Drive. The Friends of the Los Angeles River fish study of 2008 identifies a number of species in the river, from the small and effective mosquitofish to the gorgeously large carp. Though carp are the primary game fish in the river, tilapia and the occasional largemouth bass or catfish are also caught, primarily by chance. There are many ways to fish this river: *bait fishing,* using rod and reel with a baited hook; *hand lining,* spooling a tin can with line, tossing it out, and retrieving it by hand *Old Man and the Sea*-

style; the less-than-legal *stick fishing*, using a big stick or stone to ambush and club the fish in shallow water; and the method I prefer, fly-fishing.

Fly-fishing is almost a religion for some (read or watch Norman Maclean's *A River Runs through It*). Whether under wide skies or between concrete banks, it is an active form of fishing and requires rhythm, timing, and awareness. Different than bait fishing, which requires one to cast and wait, fly-fishing is an active exercise requiring a heightened awareness even just to get your line in the water. It requires no more gear than any other kind of fishing, though the gear is highly specialized. Often overly rarified by those who practice it, fly-fishing is easily learned but difficult to master. Practically speaking, you'll need a six-to-eight-weight rod, preferably eight, with a weight-forward floating line, an eight-pound leader, a fly on the end, and a commitment to the art of it.

LA River fly-fishermen commonly use a strike indicator, a special type of bobber/float set below the floating fly line along the leader and above the fly. The fly should dangle below the indicator where fish are holding, usually between three and five feet in the LA River. When you cast into areas you think fish might be holding and the strike indicator drags in the current, it is time to strip-set the hook and hold on.

A direct technique is simply to cast to located fish: rather than casting where you *think* they might be, you cast to carp you clearly *see*. You will need to be stealthy: stay up the bank or behind a tree and look for the signs of their presence. Position yourself to be able to present the fly as delicately as you can, a foot or two upstream of the fish, maybe seven or eight to allow for the current. The bundles of feathers, foam, and fur used to make the flies have no smell to attract the fish so you need to bring the fly across their orange-tinged lips and within the near focus of their glossy eyes.

You will need a fly. The most common fly that accompanies the indicator setup described above is the Glo-bug, a bit of chartreuse or goldenrod yarn tied to a hook to resemble an egg sack. Other flies resemble damselfly nymphs, young crayfish, and cottonwood seeds. Most of the subsurface flies used in trout fishing can also be used on carp. There are a few special carp flies with names as unique as the target species: Hise's Carpnasty, Jan's Carp Tickler, May's Identity Crisis, Rainy's Mulberry, McTage's McLuvin, and the Carp Carrot. Regardless of technique or fly, if you find the right fish and make the right presentation, you have a chance at gold.

Don't just cast your line randomly and hope for the best. You must wait until you can *see* carp—or at least be relatively assured that they are there. Learn their haunts. Look for shadows and for fins. Watch for ripples. Listen for the telltale slurps. Know where they congregate.

Understand their movement across the day. Watch the concrete aprons, the sides of the channel that fold flat and merge with the water where carp slide along the edges, feeding in the sun. In deep pockets, where structural engineering and lost carts create drop-offs and riffles, carp lie in wait. In pockets of calm water that form behind boulders, big carp can often be found tailing, feeding head down and tail up. At the base of the clumps of giant cane, carp are often heard, then seen, feeding on roots and foliage at the water's edge. In broad and shallow concrete slicks, especially below the bridges, the fish will feed in the low-light conditions of the day and reveal their broad, copper backs.

You will run across other fishermen using all the forms of fishing described above. In long, slow, and deep pools, you will often find the corn-and-tortilla anglers. White bread, hominy, marshmallows, night crawler worms, frozen shrimp, and tortillas are favorite baits of these often subsistence fishermen. They bait a hook, cast it out into the shade, crack a cold one, and wait for the subtlest of tugs. The carp's barbel mustache is connected to their scent glands, and the "smell" of tortillas tickles them.

You'll cover many miles walking the river as you stalk carp. Because you need to get your fly within a couple of feet of the scaly beast, you will be presented with numerous challenges of terrain. A day of stalking carp produces sore ankles from miles of slow walking on angled, concrete slopes. Sunburned and thirsty, you hop from concrete aprons onto exposed granite boulders and broken concrete slabs, trying to reach the spot where you just saw a fin. You may elect to climb trees to sneak up on a feeding fish. Nettle patches burn your skin as you push through dense vegetation to peek into a protected pool. Your fatigue is a measure of the miles.

Fishermen like to say carp are spooky—as in, easily scared. Carp have a large lateral line that runs the length of their bodies. This unique nerve allows them to viscerally sense the most delicate of movements. A clang on the bank or even loud talking can spook them. Vibrations from a heavy cast or a misplaced step will send them scrambling. Reflections off a quick-moving person in a white T-shirt can send them flying for cover in no time. Once you scare one, the others are gone, and it is time to stalk on.

Know that carp are very difficult to catch. They have a reputation for sloth and dumbness, an uninformed reading of their form and general behavior, but it is not the case. Even very good fishermen see many more fish than they hook and hook more than they land. A big fish with deep flanks of thick muscle can fight tremendously; a fifteen-minute fight with a ten-pound carp is not unlikely. Imagine flying a kite in a Santa Ana wind with dental floss or walking a rambunctious dog on a kite string and you get close to the idea.

To do this within sight of the crawling traffic of a Friday evening on the 5 freeway is a strange experience indeed.

Most fly-fishers practice catch-and-release, but you can also eat the carp. In the Friends of the Los Angeles River fish study of 2008, preliminary—and admittedly limited—tests revealed that levels of PCBs and mercury in fish found in the LA River are actually below the EPA's accepted levels—lower than levels found in a number of species fished from our oceans for consumption. So yes, you can eat them, and some do. Barbecue and grilling are favorite local preparations. Keep the head on, clean, gut, rinse, and stuff the body cavity with lemon, herbs, and potatoes. Wrap the meaty specimen in foil or lay it straight on the grill. The flesh flakes in large white chunks that have the subtle taste of white fish and the river in which it lived; use plenty of lemon. You can also make soup. Clean, descale, and cut the fish into a few big pieces, add it to a big pot with oil and salt and pepper, and give a strong sear. Add your favorite soup stock, herbs, and vegetables, and boil away; the large bones are easily picked out. Or you can do as I did, carp tacos. Fillet, brine, and give the fish a hard pan sear, then wrap it in a good tortilla with cabbage slaw and a lot of hot sauce.

Carp fishing is growing in popularity in the US. It has been big in Europe for a long time as a sporting endeavor, less so in Asia where it is primarily fished for consumption. There are numerous magazines, websites, and publications devoted to the sport. As a species that grows large and thrives in challenging urban conditions, carp are the perfect quarry for the urbanite. As we progressively urbanize our cities, urban species like carp are enjoying more value.

Lessons

You can observe a lot just by watching.
—Yogi Berra

As much as stalking carp is about catching the gold-leafed river monsters, it is about walking the river, a landscape of mixed and confused origins where volunteers and captives thrive. Mexican fan palms *(Washingtonia robusta)* grow horizontally where they were pushed over by tons of liquid weight and now turn their crowns skyward in phototropic response. Cottonwoods *(Populus fremontii)* and willows *(Salix lasiolepis* and *Salix alba)* crowd the banks, signifying deeper soils. Ash and tree of heaven provide structure for morning glory to find the sun. Thickets of giant cane *(Arundo donax)* and castor bean *(Ricinus communis)* clump and struggle with the bulrushes and fountain grass for gaps and cracks of exposed soils. These highly successful species—some labeled *invasive* like the carp—make this ecology.

The LA River is like any other river. The

flow carries sediment that settles around impediments—shopping carts, car doors, concrete blocks, car tires, trees, and lawn furniture. Islands emerge. In the LA River, sediment-laden shopping carts sprout trees that grow higher than a person can reach. Trees are shrouded in plastic bags and vegetal detritus. Green bubbles are embedded in bark where trees have grown to engulf discarded plastic bottles.

Like the occupants of the dystopian *Concrete Island* created by J. G. Ballard, the river has its own community. These occupants are transient and fluctuate with the seasons. Full encampments exist off the bounty of the river: makeshift hammocks are strung between willows and palms; circular fire pits are scavenged from the river; shelters of tarps are camouflaged with unrecyclable materials; river-washed clothes dry in the branches. These sites are linked by a myriad of winding paths: over, under, and between piled branches and debris from the previous winter's storms, these thin trails are mashed flat by the feet of self-reliant occupiers and reclusive tenants looking for an off-the-grid existence or illicit experience.

In the warm water of the summer, the river becomes thick with vegetation. The banks and islands are worlds unto their own. Hoisting six pounds of carp out of the river after walking for miles is an experience that allows you to engage with this uniquely Los Angeles landscape. Stalking carp reveals the seasons of this city and the cycles of life above, below, and within the mass-media identity of the city. It will take billions of dollars to revitalize the Los Angeles River. While this is a noble endeavor, there is a river worthy of celebration *now*. The Los Angeles River is thriving and wild between concrete and freeway, host to hardy, resilient species—carp, palms, cane, and people alike.

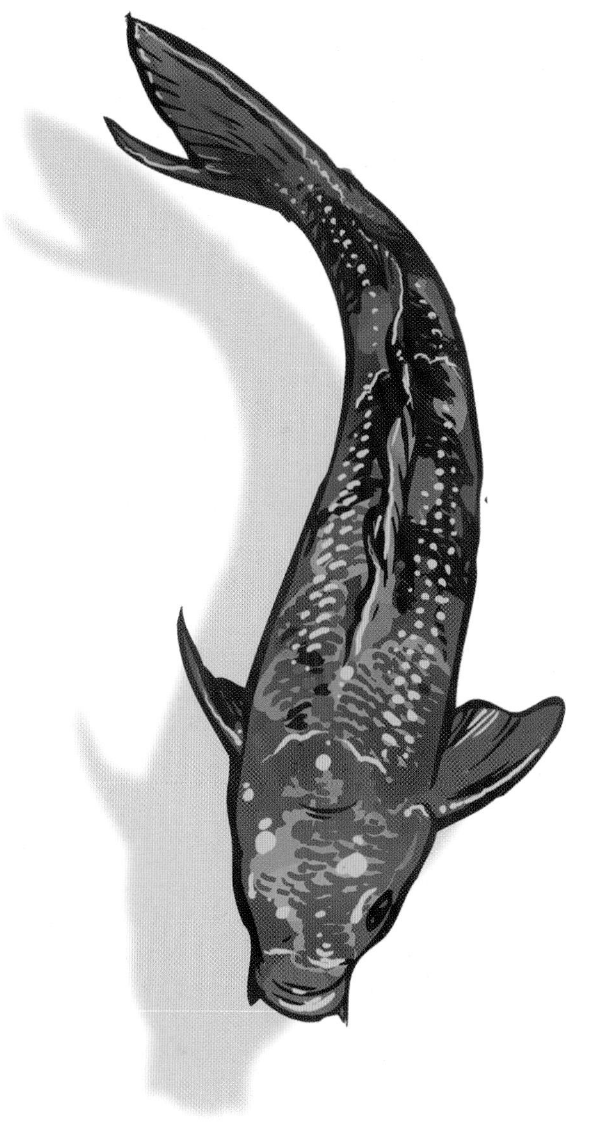

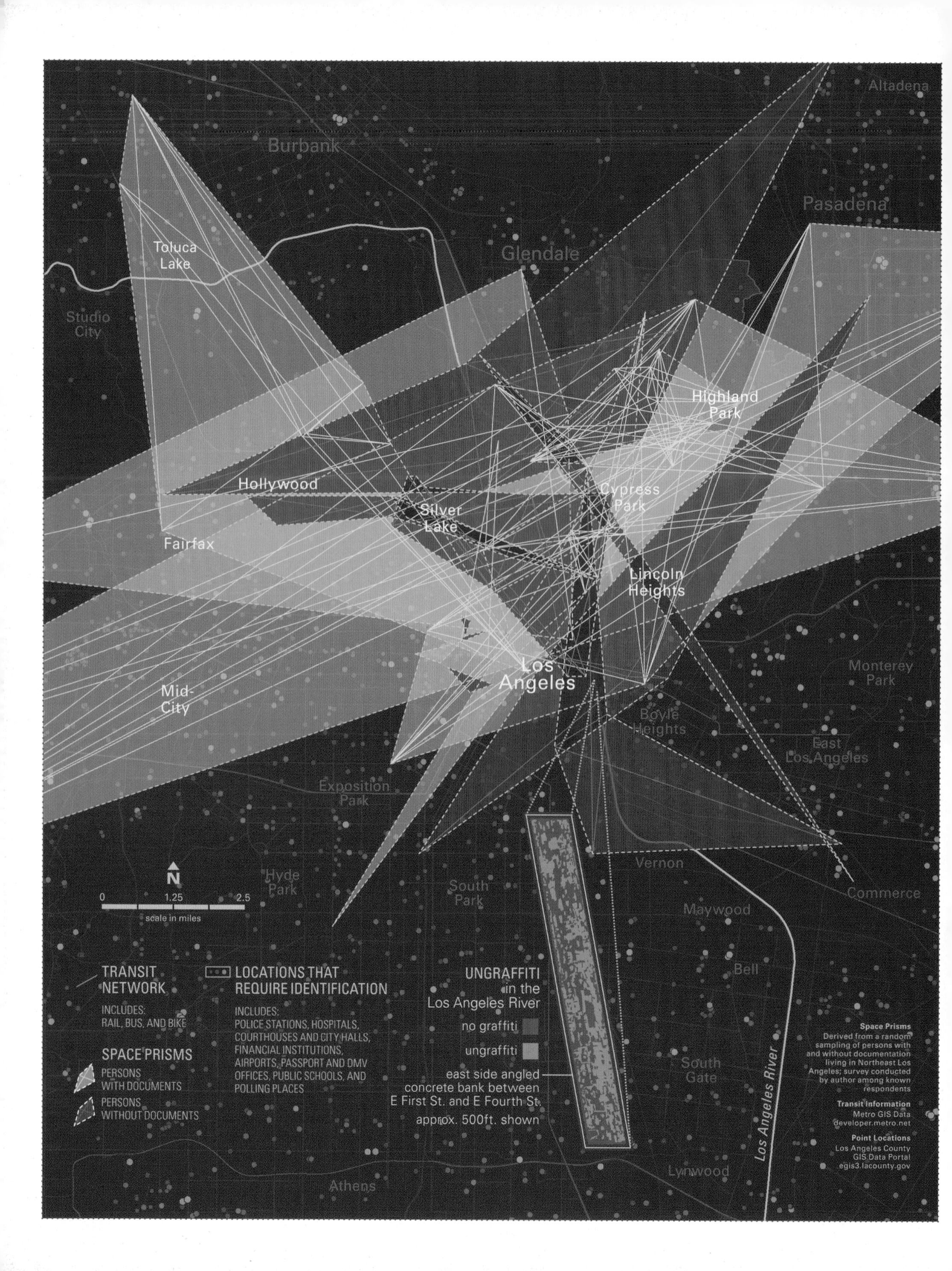

Altadena
Burbank
Pasadena
Toluca Lake
Glendale
Studio City
Highland Park
Hollywood
Cypress Park
Silver Lake
Fairfax
Lincoln Heights
Los Angeles
Monterey Park
Mid-City
Boyle Heights
East Los Angeles
Exposition Park
Vernon
Hyde Park
South Park
Commerce
Maywood
Bell
South Gate
Lynwood
Athens
Los Angeles River
N
0
1.25
2.5
scale in miles
TRANSIT NETWORK
INCLUDES: RAIL, BUS, AND BIKE
SPACE PRISMS
PERSONS WITH DOCUMENTS
PERSONS WITHOUT DOCUMENTS
LOCATIONS THAT REQUIRE IDENTIFICATION
INCLUDES: POLICE STATIONS, HOSPITALS, COURTHOUSES AND CITY HALLS, FINANCIAL INSTITUTIONS, AIRPORTS, PASSPORT AND DMV OFFICES, PUBLIC SCHOOLS, AND POLLING PLACES
UNGRAFFITI in the Los Angeles River
no graffiti
ungraffiti
east side angled concrete bank between E First St. and E Fourth St.
approx. 500ft. shown
Space Prisms
Derived from a random sampling of persons with and without documentation living in Northeast Los Angeles; survey conducted by author among known respondents
Transit Information
Metro GIS Data
developer.metro.net
Point Locations
Los Angeles County GIS Data Portal
egis3.lacounty.gov

Essayist Jen Hofer asked documented and undocumented people she knew to provide a list of the places they frequent throughout a typical week: work, home, shopping, their kids' school, et cetera. The resulting trajectories, or space prisms, are set against the circulatory system of LA's public transit system and bike routes. These maps are overlaid with a constellation of dots that represent locations that require some type of official identification or documentation. Also shown is "ungraffiti" along a section of the Los Angeles River, graffiti that has been painted over by the city and thereby undocumented, rendered both visible invisible. With numerous points of intersection, this map encourages us to consider our own movements through space, as well as the freedoms and constraints that affect them. What would your space prism look like?

Under the Radar and Off the Charts

UNDOCUMENTATION IN LOS ANGELES

Jen Hofer

L., about to graduate high school, gets stopped by the LAPD for driving with a bald front tire. L. was driving the family's beige minivan, running an errand to refill the propane tank for the makeshift kitchen in the backyard; L.'s mother cooks food to sell at factories and swap meets on the south side of downtown Los Angeles. She makes various kinds of pan dulce, bolillos, mole verde, and mole rojo among other dishes, homemade tortillas, and menudo on Saturdays. She used to make birria but the meat got too expensive. L. does not have a driver's license because of repeated failures to pass the written test—multiple choice is not L.'s strong suit. L. gets a fix-it ticket for the tire and an infraction for driving without a license; the car is impounded. The only way to free the car is for someone with a valid driver's license to accompany L. to the police station, and then to the tow yard. No one in the household has a license. All the children in L.'s family were born in the US, after their parents walked across the border from Mexico more than half their lives ago, but all except L. are too young for a license.

This narrative, or some variant of it, happens often, in thousands of versions in thousands of sites across Los Angeles. Many aspects of an undocumented immigrant's life—having a teenage child who gets pulled over, for instance—are potentially risky. The most humdrum activities, like making enough money to pay the bills, driving anywhere, or interacting with authorities, carry with them the possibility of things going terribly awry and ending in detention or deportation. At the same time, many aspects of an undocumented immigrant's life are just as complicated and just as miraculous and just as unremarkable as anyone's life: humdrum activities continue to be humdrum, both joys and frustrations abound, bills get paid or deferred, transit occurs, entanglements with authorities are endured. Living "undocumented" is both different and not different from any living. Los Angeles harbors many forms of "undocumentation," with ramifications that extend far beyond the evident question of immigration status. Undocumentation provides a frame through which to consider a variety of phenomena that fall outside official structures of categorization and legitimation—phenomena that might be experienced by any Angeleno, regardless of immigration status.

Reconceptualizing undocumentation shifts our capacity to see, illuminating what is invisible in plain sight and revealing the structures—and unstructured spaces—that are under the radar or off the charts. For example: myriad systems of oil pipelines extend like a sluggish, lucrative circulatory system under the asphalt beneath much of Los Angeles, though ironically most of the oil pumped out is too dense to refine into fuel so instead, in a seemingly endless echo, it is used to make the very asphalt that covers its extraction pathways. These pathways, these extractions, are not undocumented—and neither are most "undocumented" immigrants, who usually have numerous documents, just not the ones that permit them to live and work legally in the US. However, the moments when these pathways seep to the surface of the city go largely unrecognized, purposefully cloaked by windowless buildings designed to blend in with the architecture of their surroundings or tucked into the far reaches of a cemetery or mall. For example: RVs with names like Cruise Aire, Dolphin, Lazy Daze, Midas, and Minnie Winnie park for months on end behind big-box stores and twenty-four-hour taquerías, on streets with free parking and no street cleaning. These largely stationary mobile homes are invisible nodes of private space in the public eye. For example: Enormous labyrinths of tunnels snake under many parts of Los Angeles. Some, marked by seemingly random chain-link boxes at odd intervals along numerous sidewalks, were built to protect pedestrians from trolleys and cars on the streets above. Others were originally used as subway routes, like the ones running from the old Subway Terminal Building on Hill and Fourth Streets downtown—now "Metro 417" high-end rental apartments—to the Belmont train tunnel—now "Belmont Station Apartment Homes: Experience Deja Nu, Classic Makes a Comeback."

Any city is multiple cities, but Los Angeles, with its vast dispersed terrain, immigrant communities from all over the world, and penchant for self-reinvention, is more multiple than most. The various cities that are Los Angeles shift in and out of recognizability. "Undocumentation" might refer to things we don't see because we don't have a way to conceptualize them. It might delineate things that evade or exceed official impulses to count or map. It might signal sites and lives that are documented one way and manifest in another. The script as conventionally written no longer pertains. Living without the requisite legal documents entails very real limitations; at the same time, undocumentation can function as a space of autonomy and agency outside the confines of official sanction.

The Public Policy Institute of California reports that our state is home to the largest number of undocumented immigrants in the US; of those, the largest number is in Los Angeles. The term "undocumented" can be understood and critiqued from a variety of perspectives. In April 2013, the Associated Press changed their stylebook to remove the terms "illegal immigrant" and "undocumented immigrant," to avoid labeling and to foster precision. People in Los Angeles without legal immigration papers use a variety of terms to describe themselves: "sin papeles/without papers," "undocumented," "undocuqueer," "out of status" (particularly used by immigration attorneys and by people who have overstayed visas), and even "illegal," used proudly: the problem is with the law, not the person, so being "illegal" in relation to an unjust law can be a political statement. E. grew up using the term "wetback," until political consciousness caused a shift to "undocumented," then to "undocumented and unafraid," and then to an expansive and celebratory sense of what E. laughingly calls "undocu-everything." M., a bespectacled grandmother and fierce immigrant rights activist, finds the term "indocumentados" (undocumented) derogatory, and prefers the term "no documentados" (not documented or without documents) as it signals something a person does not possess, rather than something the person is or is not.

Where do you go in a city where you do not have the legal right to live, transit, shop, work, receive medical care, or even walk down the street? S., whose dad crossed the border in the mountains and whose mom crossed in the sewers, describes what happens when your undocumented family moves to Los Angeles and knows no one: you move—"migrating like butterflies"—to areas where there are many people from your country, which in the case of S.'s parents was South Central (as it was called at the time). You might go to Artesia, to Boyle Heights, to Compton, to El Sereno, to Highland Park, to Hollywood, to Huntington Park, to Inglewood, to Koreatown, to Lincoln Heights, to MacArthur Park, to Monterey Park, to Pico-Union, to South Los Angeles, to Watts, to West Adams, to Westwood (also known as "Tehrangeles"). You might go, as O. did, to neighborhoods and apartment buildings where one or two or twenty people from your family or your colonia or your town went before you. You might move nearly every year, as E.'s family did, to follow whatever jobs are available, the only constant the type of neighborhood where you live: black and brown people with low-wage work or no work, gang activity, gun violence. You might go where there are landlords who won't ask for a credit check, slumlords who preside over what S. calls "ghettos of apartments," building after building after building with family after family after family or laborers sharing scant space in exorbitantly priced apartments that function as holding cells between work shifts.

The California Endowment has sponsored ads at bus stop kiosks all over LA, presenting "Undocumented Californian Facts: Number in CA: 2.6 million. Working Households: 92%. Taxes Paid: $2.7 billion. Contribution to CA Economy: $302 billion." Like the oil pumped invisibly and ubiquitously under our city, undocumented workers are a vast, ever-present current that nourishes the city's more visible economy. Contradictions abound: Most undocumented workers pay taxes yet are not eligible for government benefits or legal work permits. LAPD checkpoints are prevalent, ostensibly intended to net drivers under the influence, but often targeting undocumented immigrants driving without a license, impounding their cars and exposing them to risk of deportation. Yet LAPD Special Order 7, currently being contested in the courts, gives police officers discretion to allow any licensed driver to liberate an impounded vehicle as long as it is insured. Recall L.'s confiscated minivan: according to state law it should have been kept for thirty days, at a cost of more than $1,000—a cost that forces many people to lose their cars permanently to the impound lot. Accompanied by a neighbor with a license, however, L. and L.'s father went to the police station, where a detective wearing a brown polyester suit processed their paperwork. The three then drove to the Official Police Garage tow yard; the vehicle was released, and in the parking lot L.'s father climbed in and drove it home. Regarding anxiety around potential deportation, E. remarks, "the fear was always there, but when you do anything and you're undocumented there will always be interactions with authority, with police, so you have to know how to navigate that, how to understand your rights."

Where do you go in a city where you have the legal right to live, yet lack the resources to exercise that right comfortably? People who have slipped under the radar or off the map—the socially sanctioned map of credit-card bills and pay stubs, of rent checks and DMV registration renewals—become invisible in plain sight. A blue milk crate is chained to a post at the end of a bridge over the LA River; a few tomato plants flourish there. P., who has lived under the bridge for years, has no idea who left the crate with the tomatoes, but waters the plants regularly. Most folks who drive over this bridge probably have no idea there is a kitchen, bathroom, and bedroom just below their tires. People without a house are not undocumented in the conventional sense—many of them are US-born veterans or formerly incarcerated citizens—yet the lack of an address or current driver's license or many of the other trappings of normalized identity places them in a congruent state of suspension. J., a college-educated Vietnam veteran who has lived on the streets of various California cities since 1977, lived on the same freeway on-ramp in Eagle Rock for six years, until suddenly one day the police decided to raid. A brief jail stint later, J. found a spot in Northeast Los Angeles with a mattress, a rotting door, and some cardboard, with walking access to various necessities: a 99¢ store, a recycling center, a laundromat, a source of water. J. listens to a small transistor radio, transiting the city by changing the dial. It's not safe to leave the tent for long because of the high probability of theft. In Eagle Rock, J. felt secure leaving belongings for hours at a time, and would ride the bus all over the city, exploring based only on curiosity and whim. Other homeless folks noticed this, and soon there was a group taking small tours by public bus. "There were people who'd lived here their whole lives and hadn't seen the tar pits or San Juan Capistrano or Malibu," J. says.

Undocumented immigrants, too, sometimes choose to censor their own movements. Checkpoints, immigration raids, and overzealous policing of immigrant communities create an atmosphere of insecurity and fear; where might you go to feel at ease? Literally everywhere in the city reminds G. of status and legal citizenship—"gas stations, intersections, diners"—and it's only in nature that G. feels truly released from the pressures of being undocumented: "The river looks like a river everywhere." M., on the other hand, prefers busy public spaces, like Placita Olvera, MacArthur Park, and public buses, where anyone or everyone might be undocumented. Visibility, too, can provide a kind of cover: acting as if you have the right to occupy a space and then occupying it, or being disguised in plain sight like oil derricks behind fake office-building facades. O. resists allowing an abstraction like a line on a map or a laminated piece of paper to restrict free movement, driving across state lines without a license and routinely fetching people at LAX despite the omnipresent checkpoints at the entrance. R. celebrates small groups that gather in parks to share food or play ball or chat in the slanting evening sun with others who share their ethnicity, language, and rituals. For years before it was replaced by condos, the Belmont Tunnel was known internationally as the birthplace of LA graffiti art, and was also used by indigenous immigrants as a space for regular games of Mayan pelota. You "make community inside of community," S. says, in unexpected places, outside the structures of official legitimation and recognition.

The Pocho Research Society of Erased and Invisible History (PRS), dedicated to the investigation of place and memory through archival work and guerrilla public interventions, views DIY art and activist endeavors as "generating a counter-sphere...spaces where people can produce their own knowledges and counter-knowledges." One of their first actions was the placing of commemorative plaques around downtown LA, responding to the narrow representation of Mexican Americans at the city's official Cinco de Mayo celebrations in 2002. *El Otro Ellis,* placed at Placita Olvera, read in part: "An important entry point for migrants of the Americas. From 1910–1930 over a million Mexicans crossed into the US as a result of economic and military upheaval. During the 1980s, over 200,000 Central American immigrants flowed in as a result of heavy political repression and bloody civil wars in their home countries." *The Displacement of the Displaced* commemorates "the fate of the working class Mexican community of Chavez Ravine"—uprooted to make way for what would eventually become Dodger Stadium. PRS puts these sites, and the people they represent, back on the map—in other words, documents these spaces so we see our city more complexly.

O., who followed a brother from Mexico City to LA twenty-one years ago at age sixteen, describes the experience of living here without legal immigration documents: "You live in a bubble, and the bubble is a different dimension. You live in the same city as everyone else but you don't see the same things." Everywhere you go, everything you do, exists within that bubble. But the bubble is iridescent—visible only to some, or only in certain light. The bubble protects you and separates you: you don't delve farther than you need to, but merely skid on the surface of necessity; M. refers to this as the difference between "planeación y resolución." As an undocumented person you experience only as much of the city as you need in order to resolve the myriad problems that arise, but you don't have the capacity to make plans and trust they stand a good chance of coming to fruition. You move through the same spaces as others who are legal residents or citizens, transit the same streets, but you inhabit a different layer of the city. For G., that layer is permeated with loneliness: a bubble of one. G. is convinced that overstaying a student visa and applying for asylum is a more livable alternative than returning to Iran where living openly as a queer person might result in imprisonment, torture, or even execution. In G.'s experience, there is an expectation that immigrants will look a certain way or be from a certain part of the world, and since G. does not fit the stereotype, being undocumented is "completely invisible in my social public life as a person. These are the basics I'm struggling with every hour of every day of my life," and few people in G's life have an awareness of the kinds of tiny split-second assessments G. makes all the time, about whether or not a certain place or conversation is safe. G. is considering grad school, for example, so signed up to take the GRE. After studying for the test, and paying to take it, G. arrived at the test-taking center and the person at the door asked for ID. If G. showed an Iranian passport rather than a California or US ID, might there be consequences?

Fake ID is exceedingly easy to come by in Los Angeles, and is fairly inexpensive. Not long ago in MacArthur Park, just a few blocks away from the last active well on the Los Angeles City Oil Field, you could buy a "simple" fake ID for $50 and a "deluxe" one, with holographic lamination and a magnetic strip on the back, for $110. For more money you could acquire someone else's real ID, but aside from the inconvenience of having an ID in someone else's name, you might expose yourself to that person's criminal history, and/or more serious charges if you were caught using it. To acquire an ID, O. walked around in MacArthur Park and then "went with my gut" and approached someone. After jotting down the relevant info, O. was directed to visit a particular business—a donut shop that was a front for an ID production studio that looked exactly like the DMV, white photo background and all—"and tell them Pedro sent you." O. was then instructed to wait a couple of hours before going to Sixth and Alvarado to find "Pedro," who confirmed that all relevant details were correct, then exchanged the ID for O.'s cash on the spot, in broad daylight in the middle of the afternoon. O. used that ID successfully for years—taking numerous flights for work and presenting it when pulled over by the LAPD—until finally deciding its luck had run out and putting it away for good. E. acquired a fake social-security card in someone else's name, but found it dehumanizing to have to remember, constantly, to answer to that name at a job at Taco Bell. When E. received temporary legal status through DACA (a short-term legalization program for those who entered the

US as children), it "eased the tension" and made all kinds of logistics easier, though didn't change things that much: living in the city as a working-class person of color shapes E.'s experience as much as being undocumented does, and DACA didn't change that.

Undocumentation, for some, becomes a site of solidarity and agency, of community organizing around issues facing poor folks. Four or five volunteers with the Revolutionary Autonomous Communities (RAC) food distribution collective were resting on the tailgate of a truck after filling nearly one hundred food boxes with kale, melons, tomatoes, cucumbers, radishes, strawberries, lettuce, squash, beans and rice, and other items for free distribution. A fellow wearing pressed khaki pants and dress shoes walked up, gave his name, and said he worked with the local neighborhood council. He was excited to find a community-based organization working in MacArthur Park and was enthusiastic about the food giveaway program: "I want to document this!" he said eagerly. He asked if the RAC activists have a business card—no. He asked if RAC has a website—no. He asked who leads the group. The activists said "We're RAC, a mutual-aid food program. People learn about us through word of mouth." RAC coalesced in the aftermath of the police crackdown on community uprisings that took place on Mayday in 2006; the group exists to foster self-sufficiency and open exchange among different people. RAC is about mutuality and creating real-world transformations in people's lives, not about status or naming certain individuals as "leaders." Leaders can easily become targets, and the ethos of RAC is that everyone is a participant. "Waiting patiently to receive your food is participating. Being present is participating," R. said. RAC is made up of immigrants of all types from countries including Cambodia, El Salvador, Guatemala, Korea, Mexico, and the US. No one is queried about their immigration status and few offer that information. RAC embodies undocumentation: unpermitted autonomous action in the here and now to change the ways people relate to their surroundings and to each other.

Any of us might inhabit undocumentation as an extra-official state of observation, consciousness, resistance, and potential, yet it is impossible to ignore the genuine hardships experienced by so many people who cannot access the particular pieces of paper or plastic that indicate they've been correctly filed in the system, or who do not have the resources to keep those official markers of legitimate existence up to date. J.'s tiny triangular encampment under the Metrolink bridge is extremely tidy: gallon jugs with water from the spigot at a nearby park lined against the wall, blankets folded neatly, white plastic buckets demarcating a minuscule patio outside the tent, with a small stack of newspapers beside them that J. uses as bucket covers for visitors who wish to sit. J. comments: "A place for everything and everything in its place." J.'s term for living on the street is not "homeless," it's "without a house at this time"—a distinction congruent to those who would consider themselves "without papers at this time." Though off the radar in this uncharacteristically exposed living spot, J. notes "I'm still in the system. The system is people. That is the system. You can't get out of the system." If "the system is people," then even those without legal immigration documents are part of it, though they are not officially legible to that system even as it seeks to count and categorize them. "Quien te nombra, manda," M. remarks—the person who names you, commands you. "Undocumented," however, is too complex a name to connote any one thing: it's a wide open space where anything might happen.

J. and P. both live within a few yards of the Los Angeles River, where graffiti once spooled out along the steeply angled channelized banks for more than five miles: a river to mirror the river. Now, light grey paint spirals and swoops on darker grey cement in patterns that seem abstracted but are in fact entirely determined by the particularities of the graffiti that occasioned this "ungraffiti" and is now layered beneath it. Graffiti artists inhabit uncharted territories, adorning otherwise invisible public canvases while resisting official structures of permission. The city—and in the case of the LA River, the Army Corps of Engineers, ironically the same body that paved the banks of the river in the first place, providing the perfect canvas for graffiti—covers over the graffiti, undocumenting it. When contemplated as visual artifacts, detached from the political maneuvering that propelled them into existence, the grey on grey patterns are beautiful, though not nearly as beautiful as the graffiti was when it was visible. The literal attempt to undocument the graffiti along the LA River channel results in a new form of graffiti that declares only "we covered up what was here before." Undocumentation is simultaneous invisibility and visibility. Simultaneous unrecognizability and surveillance. Shadow and spotlight. The purpose of the ungraffiti is to return those highly unnatural constructed river walls to their natural constructed state. Yet there is no "natural state" to which the LA River—or any of us—might return; our natural state is one of evolution, cacophony, multiplicity, unexpected developments, and fortuitous or unfortuitous interventions by other forces or beings. A state of mobility.

For a list of sources used in this essay, please visit jenhofer.net/la-atlas-bilbiography.

J.J. JACKSON
KMPC · 101.9MHz
LOS ANGELES
RENÁN 'EL CUCUY' ALMENDÁREZ COELLO
KLAX · 97.9MHz
LOS ANGELES
'HUMBLE HARVE' MILLER
KIQQ · 100.3MHz
LOS ANGELES
KRTH · 101.1MHz
LOS ANGELES
EDDIE 'PIOLÍN' SOTELO
KSCA · 101.9MHz
LOS ANGELES
KIIS · 102.7MHz
LOS ANGELES
LEVI 'WHO LOVES YOU' BOOKER
KJLH · 102.3MHz
COMPTON
KNAC · 105.5MHz
LONG BEACH
CHUCK 'BEBOP CHARLIE' NILES
KKGO · 105.1MHz
LOS ANGELES
RODNEY BINGENHEIMER
KROQ · 106.7MHz
BURBANK | GLENDALE | PASADENA | LOS ANGELES
JED 'THE FISH' GOULD
RICHARD BLADE
KLOS · 95.5MHz
LOS ANGELES
JIM LADD
KMET · 94.7MHz
LOS ANGELES
JEFF GONZER
PAT 'PARAQUAT' KELLEY
BARRET 'DR. DEMENTO' HANSEN
RUSS PARR
KDAY · 93.5MHz
REDONDO BEACH
TOM SCHNABEL
KCRW · 89.9MHz
SANTA MONICA
DEIRDRE O'DONOGHUE
JASON BENTLEY
KCSN · 88.5MHz
NORTHRIDGE
STELLA VOCE
KXLU · 88.9MHz
LOYOLA MARYMOUNT
88 90 92 94 96 98 100 102 104 106 108
MHz
kHz
5.5 6 6.5 7 8 9 10 12 14 16
HUNTER HANCOCK
JOHNNY OTIS
KFOX · 1650kHz
LONG BEACH
CHICK HEARN
KLAC · 570kHz
LOS ANGELES
DAVE DIAMOND
KFI · 640kHz
LOS ANGELES
VIN SCULLY
KMPC · 710kHz
LOS ANGELES
J.J. JOHNSON
KDAY · 1580kHz
LOS ANGELES
STEVE WOODS
NATHANIEL 'MAGNIFICENT' MONTAGUE
KGFJ · 1230kHz
LOS ANGELES
ART LABOE
KRLA · 1110kHz
LOS ANGELES
'EMPEROR' BOB HUDSON
DICK 'HUGGY BOY' HUGG
DICK BIONDI
KFVD · 1020kHz
LOS ANGELES
AIMEE SEMPLE McPHERSON
KFSG · 1080kHz
LOS ANGELES
ROBERT 'WOLFMAN JACK' SMITH
XERB · 1090kHz
ROSARITO BEACH, MEXICO
KIEV · 870kHz
LOS ANGELES
B. MITCHEL REED
KFWB · 980kHz
LOS ANGELES
'LUCKY PIERRE' GONNEAU
CHARLIE TUNA
'THE REAL' DON STEELE
KHJ · 930kHz
LOS ANGELES
XTRA · 690kHz
LOS ANGELES

A diverse assortment of announcers and DJs have graced Los Angeles's radio dial over the years, covering a dizzying array of programming from Spanish-language to gospel music to sports. More than mere entertainers and musical curators, DJs reflected, nurtured, challenged, and defined the tone of life and culture in the area, allowing Angelenos to investigate and experience the city through their ears and imaginations. The graphic that accompanies Lynell George's essay pays homage to a handful of these iconic personalities.

The View from the Air

MAPPING LA RADIO

Lynell George

Between Stations

When did I stop listening?

Really listening?

Five years ago?

Fifteen?

When did the reach of my radio band find itself edited down to news—an every twenty-two-minute meditation on jackknifed big rigs, Nikkei averages, top-of-the-hour roundups, bits and pieces strung together that don't add up to any solid sense of place. Except for the street names and interchanges, it could be happening anywhere at all.

When did I stop tuning in to those late-night atmospheres conjured by DJs pulled by whim and not by corporate playlist? When did radio stop hosting serendipity? When was the last time I connected to a voice—an announcer, a DJ, a

talk jock, those auditory ringmasters who felt so close that I referred to them by first name: Ron, J.J., Chuck, Frazer, Tom, Sergio. They were the ones telling the story of my city in a language that reflected it, with all of its blemishes and bluster, its meltdowns, dead air, faux pas.

They were our connective tissue. We built a community around them, a congregation over the air.

Long before I owned a set of keys, my way of traveling Los Angeles was by coasting along the dial. In a TV age, in the heart of "Filmland," I grew up radio obsessed. Sleep challenged, I'd lie in the dark many nights with my transistor—an LA Dodger/710 AM sponsored giveaway that was forest green with a Union 76 logo separating the silver-tone AM and FM bands. As a rite of spring, I would listen to that radio and wait for Vin Scully to call the pitch—"high and outside"—from Dodger Stadium in Chavez Ravine.

A few years later, I inherited my grandmother's turquoise-and-cream AM tabletop with a gold-sweep dial—the "Trav-ler"—on which I'd tune in to whatever would make its way through the broadcast fuzz. Sometimes I'd land on something "between stations," something from far away that felt like falling through a trapdoor into a scene well on its way: the elegant clink of crystal and silver of "Lunch at the Music Center" or a wild gust of 1940s swing-era music. It would trigger hopes of having slipped through some seam in time, to eavesdrop on a tuxedo-jacketed ensemble set up in a long-shuttered ballroom downtown. Ringside, by way of the Trav-ler, I nursed a vivid imagination.

I was so fiercely radio loyal that when I finally acquired my first set of keys, I proudly affixed the jazz station's green-and-black logo to my car's back bumper. And though at the time I was still quite timid behind the wheel, I knew I was going somewhere, even if it was just on the contours of Chuck "Bebop Charlie" Niles's basement voice back-announcing the history of straight-ahead jazz on KKGO 105.1.

Of late, when I switch into scan mode, hoping to trip onto something, anything, beyond talk or news that feels like it grew up out of this ground, it's made me wonder: What would LA "look like" now if you could navigate it, translate and understand it, by way of its radio air? I'd have to say, probably much like everywhere else—the same six songs, Lap-Bands, call-monitoring centers, "smell-good" plumbers, the works. It feels as second-rate as an off-the-rack suit, built to knock around in but not to make an impression.

The Los Angeles radio market is the second largest in the country in business terms, but in the sense of a medium conveying or speaking for the city, what could you really know about it? Not just headlines and weather, or even the diligent hyper-local call-in forums that thrive on the very left edges of the FM dial, but the spirit and pace of the city, its very style. What would you know about what divides us and where we come to together? Could you locate its soul or heart?

There was a time that you could.

More than a generation ago, Southland radio reflected many of Los Angeles's attendant narratives—a place of reinvention and hope. A refuge. An escape. Radio reproduced that, but it also sent up a signal that echoed what was changing on the ground—city's demographics remade by waves of migration and out-migration, the evolving nature of work, (farming, oil, shipyards, aerospace, and, of course, entertainment). Later, it was white flight, wars on other shores, new immigrants. The new "there to here" stories began to take shape on the band as stations were once again reinvented with each new wave to tell stories to new ears. What you may not have known firsthand you could learn by eavesdropping.

Since the first commercial radio station in LA beamed on in 1921 (KQL), radio evolved into a communication source that didn't just entertain and inform but oriented and immersed you. Because of the region's size, the airwaves served as auditory compendium, an easier-to-navigate representation of a city that was a challenge to traverse, let alone embrace.

Programs and playlists hinted at a place that was different from the one that spread out across the grid of a fold-out gas-station map—one that was nuanced, if elusive, and one that couldn't be charted by longitudes or latitude. It was something we were mapping from within.

Presets

It's "Janet" calling in from somewhere out there.

Like most days, it just feels like another disembodied voice reaching out. This one, though, has a rather unusual question: "Janet" wants to know if Conan, her companion of eleven-and-a-half years, will be waiting for her on the other side in the mists of the afterlife. "Will I be able to see him?" she asks. "Do pets go to heaven?" The loneliness in her voice is as palpable as her grief.

This exchange would seem like old-school call-in radio fare except the host isn't a hectoring radio shrink. This is something entirely different. Janet has leapt over the middle-man and gone straight to the source: the "Holy Host" himself, during the final hour of his program, the eponymous *Jesus Christ Show*.

Of late, I have found myself tuning in and listening in the old, familiar ways: first out of sheer disbelief and then out of bald curiosity. Now I'm hooked. By all of it: the guilelessness of the listeners, the audacity of a host who would call himself Jesus. Some know, I'm sure, that the voice over their speakers is mere mortal, a man named Neil Saavedra, assuming a "what if?" role. But I fret that others, like Janet, think that radio Jesus really has risen for the sole purpose of taking calls every Sunday from 6:00 to 9:00 a.m. over KFI Radio from a studio in Burbank, California.

But when did it come to this? To a lonely on-air space where someone's best or only recourse is to pick up a phone and dial 1-877-HOLYHOST as an antidote to isolation.

These Sunday morning exchanges, beamed beyond the city's borders, resurrect something vital—a shared sense of place created over air. It's been decades since I've heard the easy back-and-forth conversational rhythm of real connection, of empathy. Radio didn't just connect communities, but built them. As early as the 1920s, in an impulse not so far afield from KFI's Sunday morning "Jesus," Aimee Semple McPherson, the "Evangelist from Los Angeles," wanted to connect a vivid and diverse multitude—the shut-in and the far-flung—and minister to their souls. Not just those who gathered under the domed-roof at Angelus Temple in Echo Park, but by broadcasting the Good News across the expanse of the basin and beyond.

Early on, Los Angeles seemed to trade on an inherent facility for attracting charismatics, risk takers, and iconoclasts. Yet even in that realm, the Canadian-born McPherson, founder of the Foursquare movement, stood out. She knew how to find and use a stage, even if it was the metaphorical one.

McPherson was a pioneer in the fledgling arena of radio gospel. By the early 1920s, she was one of the first women to deliver an over-the-air sermon. It was a place where outcasts or vagabond souls could come to worship across borders of time and space. She knew the radio would help her to build a flock beyond what the Angelus Temple could hold.

In February of 1924, she became the second woman to be granted a broadcast license by the U.S. Department of Commerce. She'd raised $25,000 to build her 500-watt station, KFSG (Kall Four Square Gospel), which went live later that year. Her "Cathedral of the Air," as she christened it, linked the region together and set a new precedent. Both in person and on the radio, she wanted to create a true sanctuary with "no boundary line." In her autobiography, *This Is That,* first published in 1919, she elaborated her wishes: "I house the sons of men—the black, the white, the yellow; the brown and red man too. Brothers all sit side by side in my church with no color line." Her in-house and on-air community linked and reflected the multiracial city growing up around it, bringing the Good News, or generally speaking words of encouragement or empowerment, as an across-the-kitchen-table dialogue which reached beyond religion.

Folk singer Woody Guthrie fed the soul in a different but just as crucial way. Broadcasting over KFVD between 1937 and 1939, his show was targeted at recently arrived Midwest migrants, Dust Bowl refugees trying to find their place in Los Angeles. Guthrie and his cohosts—first his cousin Leon "Oklahoma Jack" Guthrie and later Maxine "Lefty Lou" Chrissman—told stories, theirs and those of others, to connect across physical and emotional distances. The soft-play of Guthrie's brotherly back-and-forths through music and conversation was a catalyst: he reminded listeners that no matter how marginalized they felt, their voice mattered. He urged them to exercise their right to speak out against the injustices by voting, strategizing, unionizing, and striking. (Their grassroots community-organizing approach would be mirrored in contemporary radio with hosts like Renán Almendárez Coello—"El Cucuy"—on KLAX and Eddie

"Piolín" Sotelo on KSCA who both spoke to a migrant and working-class Spanish-speaking population navigating Los Angeles in the twenty-first century.)

Powered by the fraternity of the airwaves, radio allowed outsiders to feel like a part of something tangible. It began to close gaps—those of distance, politics, class, even race. It was the view over the fence. As Nathaniel Montague, best known as KGFJ's Magnificent Montague, once observed: "Radio became the place for the curious to "explore a hidden world from the safety of their bedrooms."

Land of a Thousand Dances

Willie Garcia recalls the sounds—of a coronet, a violin, the murmur of an announcer's voice—drifting through an otherwise quiet house. Those bits and pieces made up his formative years and laid a foundation; they were locales in and of themselves. Back in the fifties, he remembers, his father would wander over to KRKD, the "Hillbilly station" and turn up Spade Cooley and Bob Wills on their grand Philco. "It was in a prominent place in our house, that big radio," Garcia remembers. "My father liked the stories in those songs." His mother tuned in to 1300 AM KWKW to find mementoes from an earlier time. "She'd listen to Pedro Vargas and Lola Beltrán and sing right along with them."

His own ears were pulled elsewhere—to the here and now, to the sound of young America. Not just the Motown hits but a galaxy of crooners and soul stirrers. In a few years, he would take his turn behind the microphone as Little Willie G., fronting the band Thee Midniters, his onstage persona styled by the influences he'd first encountered sailing through the dark on the radio: Gene Vincent and his tousled pompadour, the mesmerizing cadences of radio preachers, the punch-in-gut of soul music.

Music built bridges across a city that was taking new shape ethnically and racially. "Really early," Willie recalls, "I was always tuned into KGFJ and Hunter Hancock," who kept his sets moving as he'd spin R&B sides: "He made you feel like you were sitting at the dinner table with him. That voice! I was shocked to find out he was a white guy!"

Garcia grew up in what a generation ago we called South Central and currently refer to as South Los Angeles. Back then, it was known to Willie and his friends as "the neighborhood." Forty-third and Long Beach was one of Los Angeles's micro-communities, one that wasn't hemmed in as tightly by restrictive housing covenants. Before it evolved into a predominantly African American enclave, it was a liberal mix of black and brown, with some Japanese and Filipino and German, Irish, and Italian thrown in.

Through color-blind playlists grouped round feeling, music radio worked its own version of desegregation. Often, black musicians who pulled into Los Angeles worked around the city's racial restrictions dictating who could play where, Willie G. recalls. After a gig at the 5-4 Ballroom on Fifty-Fourth and Moneta or maybe the Old Dixie at Forty-Third and Western, a designated member of some Chicano car club would meet up with the just-in-town musical dignitary and ferry them east, to the next gig, to play the ballrooms and union halls downtown and beyond. "Radio introduced us to these voices and if they were coming to town, we'd want to hear them." Willie recites the roster: Bobby Bland, B.B. King, Barbara Lynn. "One night I picked up Johnny 'Guitar' Watson at the Old Dixie, in my '63 Cadillac Sedan de Ville, midnight blue." They rolled through the dark streets toward downtown, trading stories about the gig, the city, and music: "You know, shoptalk."

Radio could take you places physically and emotionally. All it took was four stations on your presets—KFWB, KRLA, KGFJ, KBCA—and the long stretch of an evening. DJs Huggy Boy, Art Laboe, Tommy B filtered over the speakers and narrated the evening. Drive-ins, casual restaurants that offered carhop service, were destinations, drawing LA teens from all reaches of the basin. Willie enumerates: the hoedads, the stockers, the cholos, the wannabe cholos. All would pull into these fluorescent-lit oases and turn the volume up. They traveled from La Verne, Azusa, Glendora, and "Cucamonga before it was 'Rancho.'" He recalls that "all the cars would be tuned to one station. But if one car changed—found some other good song—suddenly we'd all drift on down there too."

All of those call letters and frequencies were as significant as zip codes. In shorthand, they told other people about where you lived—your allegiances. They were another place you called home. They were more than a little bit a part of you.

Those carefully chosen presets on Willie's car's dash are gone or have been dramatically reformatted. Some of them, I tell him, have become the ones I scan through for news and talk. And those, Willie says, are the ones that hit the hardest: "I *see* news all day," he explains. "But what about the stories?"

"You may not drive a great big Cadillac"

There were versions of Los Angeles along the band that I didn't recognize, rhythms I didn't fall into. Jangly, mono, tinny bubblegum pop that didn't seem tethered to anything. These were spaces I couldn't quite connect with. To my ear, however, black radio still felt like it was rooted in a real place, and by that I mean an emotion. I could spin the dial and still hear the uncut South, a displaced, leisurely drawl. In the late sixties and early seventies, people still sounded like folks who had travelled great distances to be here. But Los Angeles was changing. That optimistic ease with which Willie and his cohort moved about existed less and less. Playlists were changing too. Consequently, where you fell on the dial was a calculation that began in a set of high-rise offices, not inside your heart.

On my side of town, south of the I-10 and east of the 405, the soul stations KGFJ and later KDAY were still the backdrop to everything. Their stories still spoke to us—longing and striving delivered over a dashboard. The stations still felt like a "place" you could walk to: the busy beauty shop my mother visited twice monthly, the cluttered corner market where we purchased big bags of ice for summer parties. The car radios sent out messages from "Loveland" as the teenage boys washed cars for weekend change. Life was still a struggle, and there was a measurable distance between haves and have-nots. Tension was in the mix too, but we pushed beyond.

This was the LA embodied in the voice of DJ Magnificent Montague. In August of 1965, when Watts burned, the whole of Black LA, it seemed, knew whom to tune in to: "We were all mesmerized," says one friend, Darryl Moore. "Will he say it again? Will they kick him off the air?" It was a showdown moment, between the powerless and the powers that be. Montague *was* Black LA. He was poised and suddenly that much more powerful.

His catch phrase, "Burn! Baby, Burn!" was just that. It was a slogan that referenced the hit factor or potential of the records he was spinning, not a charge to set the city afire.

Casual, collective memory erases this, and while he spent years correcting the record, Montague's words are often remembered as a declaration of defiance. The phrase articulated a sentiment that permeated much of Black Los Angeles. No matter its initial meaning, those words marked a turning point: the bridges that needed to be built lay within us. This was a moment of self-defining, and we began to tell our stories in our own voices.

Moore is now an elder statesman of sorts, one of the architects of West Coast Underground hip-hop. As a drummer, he threaded together infectious beats for acts like the Pharcyde and Freestyle Fellowship, and in the process helped to define "conscious hip-hop." These washes of sound—the rhythms, samples, and rhymes, created in garages or rumpus rooms—grew out of that new sense of collective self-awareness, and much of it would eventually bloom out of the radio.

If you're looking for a turning-point story about Black LA, Moore suggests you could point to that era. For a brief moment, the trajectory of life on these streets and the messages in the music over the radio—about passion, pride, and power—were in sync. For a decade or so after, at least within our neighborhoods, black radio remained a unifying soundtrack—not about East Coast/West Coast rap rivalry or stepped-up crosstown gang violence. There was funk and R&B spun by Levi "Who Loves You" Booker who provided the evening's narration over "Stevie's station" on KJLH. Tuning into Stevie Wonder's FM spot on the dial was not just embracing a trend, "though we were wearing shags and Jheri curls," Moore admits. But really the music and the moment was emblematic, a mantra. It was all about who we *could* be. "There I'd be, [driving from] LA to Compton, in my yellow-and-black Karmann Ghia, [my] radio blasting 'Good Times.'" They'd earned those easy, open-ended days: "During the week we were up at school. Then at our jobs, Lockheed or Northrop. We were on our way to something. You didn't think it would end."

Those were the years before crack and gangs and murder stats headlined international news, when a sort of straight-back dignity seemed to escort you out of any sort of mess. "It was a beautiful time," says Moore. "To be twenty-one. A black man with a legitimate job, taking that long way home on a clear, bright night, cruising Crenshaw. But it didn't stick. We were the last generation. But man, it was a beautiful time."

Modern Languages

When I think about landscape, what's been razed and built over, I realize that though it all seems to have happened in an instant, it didn't. The transformation is traceable.

By the eighties, radio allegiance was something that categorized you—or branded you. In my new school across town, we'd begun to see chaos over something as "simple" as radio: Fist-fights. Customized suitcase-sized boom boxes tipped over, innards flowing. But while many of my friends were sliding into punk or new wave (via KROQ's Rodney on the Roq) or hip-hop or "the new rap game" (via Greg Mack and Russ Parr at KDAY), led by a posse of DJs at the right end of the band, I kept edging further and further left, until I stumbled upon something: the churning flow of African Highlife, the sun and melancholy of Bahia. Art song and tango.

Tom Schnabel was the host of these leisurely morning excursions on KCRW and ran his show, *Morning Becomes Eclectic,* as a sort of graduate seminar in listening across lines.

How we think about radio now has been radically reformed by podcasts, web-only streaming on demand, and what has been altered is that in-the-moment connection over space, the very thing that made you feel part of a larger conversation. As a listener, I know what that now means and what I've lost, but what of the DJs who built all those intricately constructed atmospheres? As it so happens, my talk with Schnabel occurs both the very week of the final sign-off of his on-air show at KCRW and on the very day that he has put the finishing touches on his first weekly show for the web. We spend some time trying to resurrect that vanished Los Angeles, both the easy drives across town and the vivid landscape of the city's idiosyncratic airwaves. It's all still there, afloat in his head. He's memorized (and can recite) the theme songs and fill-music over which the DJs back-announced their "sets," stretching across decades. He remembers frequencies and their various reincarnations. "Was it *simply* the music that you tuned in for," I ask, "or the host, or did it matter?"

"Oh yes, it mattered. You *bet* it mattered." For the listener, he explains, "radio was about searching for something good." It's what you hadn't heard yet, what you couldn't possibly know. "That's gestalt. It just doesn't happen now."

At the edge of something new, Schnabel considers the difference: a show on the web, packaged into a podcast, versus broadcasting in real time from a terrestrial station, interacting with callers in-the-moment. It's all still new, full of possibility. But what is certain is that it alters his understanding of connectedness and immediacy.

This shift in the transmission is like a signal you lose as you make your way to the next destination. As you press forward, you shed what you know. But as long as there are hosts—guides—still rooted in a tradition and creating atmospheres that connect listeners, why can't a "station" continue to become a meeting place, a hub, a virtual city, a spot on the map?

....

Within us we carry memorized maps, ways through which we navigate a city that is both present and past, locations that are still with us and those that have passed beyond us. Some of those stations we tuned to—stations that nudged past velvet ropes, over the zigzag of abandoned railroad tracks, and ignored the "No trespassing" signs—forced us to create shortcuts and workarounds to understand and embrace what we'd heard. In doing so, they broadened our sense of community and consequently ourselves.

Our maps are collective but they are also deeply personal. Those radio addresses tell us a bit about our paths, our sense of possibility. They are the places where we sometimes felt most like ourselves; they were the places in the city where we were never alone.

If I think about it, those stations that physically housed some of my most sacred, life-altering sounds weren't necessarily rooted where the broadcasts actually took place. What on earth did Chuck Niles ("Bebop Charlie") have to do with the glass-and-steel high-rises of Wilshire Boulevard? These DJs and hosts created worlds. While they may have referenced places we frequented, they also urged us to cross boundaries, both physical and those of perception. And through it, they ultimately allowed us to find a place that certainly wouldn't have been on any physical map—some sweet, essential spot, a brand-new territory that we didn't know lived inside of us.

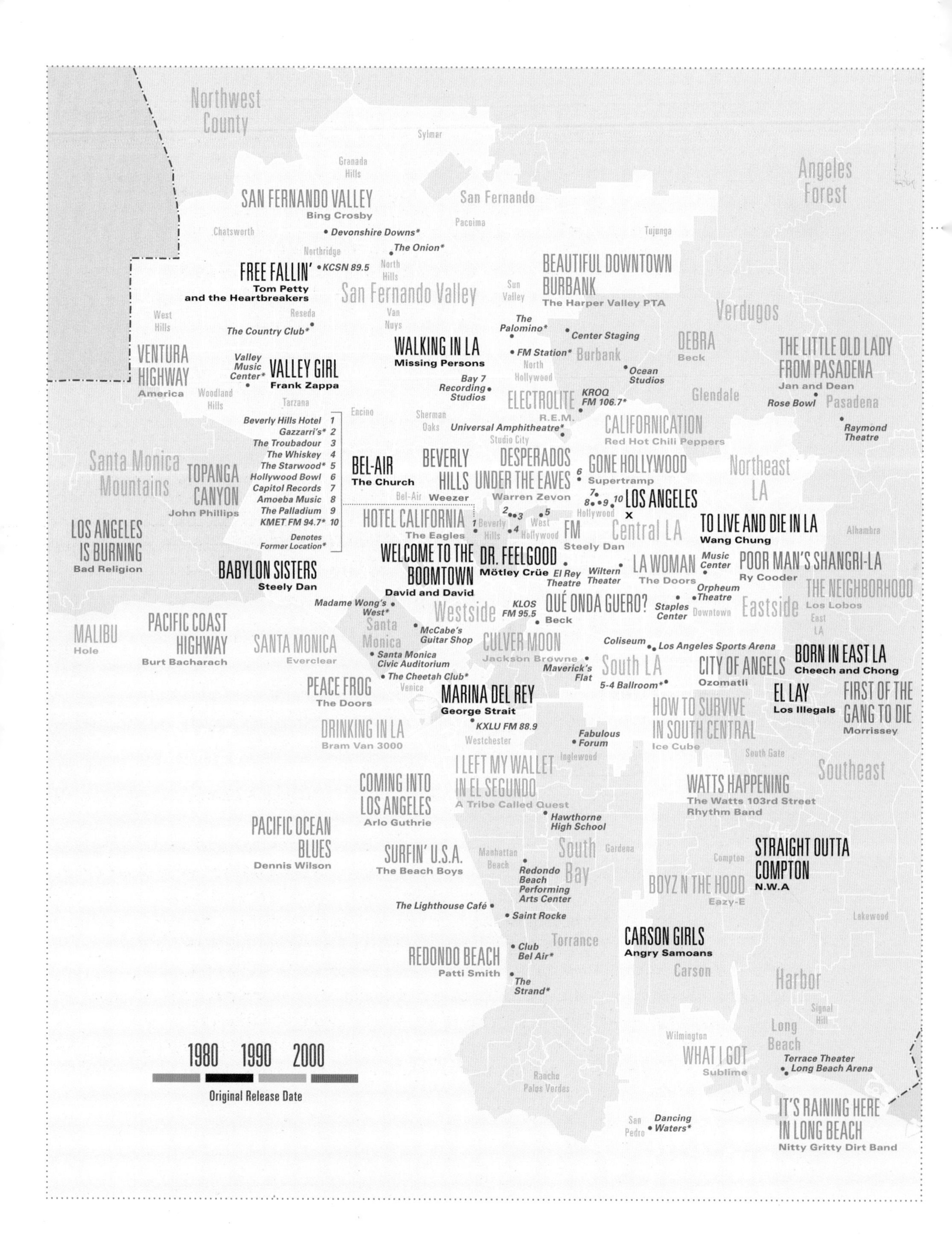
Northwest County
Sylmar
Granada Hills
San Fernando
Angeles Forest
SAN FERNANDO VALLEY
Bing Crosby
Chatsworth
Pacoima
Tujunga
Devonshire Downs*
Northridge
The Onion*
FREE FALLIN'
Tom Petty and the Heartbreakers
KCSN 89.5
North Hills
BEAUTIFUL DOWNTOWN BURBANK
The Harper Valley PTA
San Fernando Valley
Sun Valley
Verdugos
West Hills
Reseda
Van Nuys
The Country Club*
The Palomino*
Center Staging
DEBRA
Beck
THE LITTLE OLD LADY FROM PASADENA
Jan and Dean
WALKING IN LA
Missing Persons
FM Station*
Burbank
VENTURA HIGHWAY
America
Valley Music Center*
VALLEY GIRL
Frank Zappa
North Hollywood
Ocean Studios
Woodland Hills
Tarzana
Bay 7 Recording Studios
ELECTROLITE
R.E.M.
KROQ FM 106.7*
Glendale
Rose Bowl
Pasadena
Encino
Sherman Oaks
Universal Amphitheatre*
Studio City
CALIFORNICATION
Red Hot Chili Peppers
Raymond Theatre
Beverly Hills Hotel 1
Gazzarri's* 2
The Troubadour 3
The Whiskey 4
The Starwood* 5
Hollywood Bowl 6
Capitol Records 7
Amoeba Music 8
The Palladium 9
KMET FM 94.7* 10
Denotes Former Location*
Santa Monica Mountains
TOPANGA CANYON
John Phillips
BEL-AIR
The Church
BEVERLY HILLS
Weezer
Bel-Air
DESPERADOS UNDER THE EAVES
Warren Zevon
GONE HOLLYWOOD
Supertramp
Northeast LA
LOS ANGELES
X
Hollywood
LOS ANGELES IS BURNING
Bad Religion
HOTEL CALIFORNIA
The Eagles
Beverly Hills
West Hollywood
FM
Steely Dan
Central LA
TO LIVE AND DIE IN LA
Wang Chung
Alhambra
BABYLON SISTERS
Steely Dan
WELCOME TO THE BOOMTOWN
David and David
DR. FEELGOOD
Mötley Crüe
El Rey Theatre
Wiltern Theater
LA WOMAN
The Doors
Music Center
POOR MAN'S SHANGRI-LA
Ry Cooder
THE NEIGHBORHOOD
Los Lobos
Orpheum Theatre
Madame Wong's West*
KLOS FM 95.5
QUÉ ONDA GUERO?
Beck
Westside
Staples Center
Downtown
Eastside
East LA
MALIBU
Hole
PACIFIC COAST HIGHWAY
Burt Bacharach
SANTA MONICA
Everclear
Santa Monica
McCabe's Guitar Shop
CULVER MOON
Jackson Browne
Coliseum
Los Angeles Sports Arena
BORN IN EAST LA
Cheech and Chong
Santa Monica Civic Auditorium
Maverick's Flat
South LA
CITY OF ANGELS
Ozomatli
The Cheetah Club*
Venice
5-4 Ballroom*
PEACE FROG
The Doors
MARINA DEL REY
George Strait
EL LAY
Los Illegals
FIRST OF THE GANG TO DIE
Morrissey
HOW TO SURVIVE IN SOUTH CENTRAL
Ice Cube
DRINKING IN LA
Bram Van 3000
KXLU FM 88.9
Westchester
Fabulous Forum
Inglewood
South Gate
I LEFT MY WALLET IN EL SEGUNDO
A Tribe Called Quest
Southeast
COMING INTO LOS ANGELES
Arlo Guthrie
WATTS HAPPENING
The Watts 103rd Street Rhythm Band
Hawthorne High School
PACIFIC OCEAN BLUES
Dennis Wilson
SURFIN' U.S.A.
The Beach Boys
Manhattan Beach
South Bay
Gardena
Compton
STRAIGHT OUTTA COMPTON
N.W.A
Redondo Beach Performing Arts Center
BOYZ N THE HOOD
Eazy-E
The Lighthouse Café
Saint Rocke
Lakewood
Torrance
CARSON GIRLS
Angry Samoans
REDONDO BEACH
Patti Smith
Club Bel Air*
Carson
Harbor
The Strand*
Signal Hill
Long Beach
Wilmington
WHAT I GOT
Sublime
Terrace Theater
Long Beach Arena
1980 1990 2000
Original Release Date
Rancho Palos Verdes
San Pedro
Dancing Waters*
IT'S RAINING HERE IN LONG BEACH
Nitty Gritty Dirt Band

Maps of cities usually include streets, freeways, neighborhoods, parks, and other landmarks. But what if the city—like Los Angeles in the dreams of essayist Josh Kun—is made of songs? Listen, figuratively, to Southern California mapped as a conurbation of songs that mirror the accents, attitudes, and cultural styles of the people of the region. Only a tiny fraction of the songs written about LA are here, more than enough to get you from Patti Smith's "Redondo Beach" to Bing Crosby's "San Fernando Valley" without getting lost.

Los Angeles Is Singing

Josh Kun

The song still remains which names the land over which it sings.
—Martin Heidegger, "What Are Poets For?"

singing asphalt songs in the midst of seagulls
—Kamau Daáood, "Los Angeles"

Sometimes when I'm driving, I dream that the city is made of songs. It usually happens on the 110 freeway, heading north out of downtown and into the Arroyo Seco watershed of Northeast LA where I live. The material landscape around me dissolves into layers of invisible, acoustic sediment: echoes, frequencies, vibrations, voices, but more than anything, fully formed songs. The entire built environment—every freeway, every tunnel, every off-ramp and shoulder, every stone and brick and slab of cement, every building—melts into an acoustic fantasia, as if urban planners, architects, and Caltrans had only sound to work with. The landscape opens up into a centuries-long songbook of local odes and regional hymns and three-minute GPS pop songs that come to life at full volume: a Santa Monica overpass that blasts The Ronettes' "I Wish I Never Saw the Sunshine," the Sixth Street Bridge shimmying to Rene Bloch's "Mambo Chicano," the entire 405 nothing but the gurgling, beeping wash of Flying Lotus's "Orbit 405."

In "Diamonds on My Windshield," his 1973 song about driving the I-5 and the 101 north from San Diego up to Los Angeles, Tom Waits coos "late nights and this freeway flying it always makes me sing," but when I'm under this spell, when I'm freeway flying, it's the freeway that's singing. That's the Los Angeles I dream about, a melodic climatology of wailing blues and twangy surf rock and 808 bass booms and shimmering brassy banda, a living graveyard of compacted sound and song, a musical marine layer, glorious in its gloom.

In my dream, you don't drive to the beach but to "Surf City," not down Rodeo but "Down Rodeo," not to Beverly Hills but "Beverly Hills" or "Beverly Kills" and to find Anthony Keidis under the bridge at MacArthur Park, you take "MacArthur Park" until you hit "Under the Bridge." If you want to visit the Whiskey A Go Go, head for "Sunset Blvd" (past all of the "Sunset People" and the "Sunset Grill") and the "Sunset Strip" until you arrive at "Maybe the People Would Be the Times or Between Clark and Hilldale," and if it's Hollywood Boulevard you're looking for, try the intersection of "Heartattack and Vine" or where "Hollywood Swinging" crosses "Hooray for Hollywood" (bearing right off of "Hollywood (Africa)" but making sure to avoid the tempting dead end of "Celluloid Heroes"). *The Thomas Guide* is no longer a glove-box tome, but a bottomless box set of recordings. You can go anywhere that's been sung about: "Leimert Park," "La Brea," "Ventura Boulevard," "Vine St," "Summit Ridge Drive," "Boyle Heights," "Laurel Canyon Boulevard," "El Cerrito Place," "Coldwater Canyon," "Studio City," "Century City," "Bunker Hill," "Garden Grove," "Echo Park," "Pershing Square," "Santa Monica," "Malibu," "Fountain and Franklin," "Campo de Encino," and "Pico and Sepulveda." You can have "Memories of El Monte" or meet a "Little Old Lady from Pasadena," you can visit "64 Bars on Wilshire" and then have a "Central Avenue Breakdown." You can do the "Central Avenue Boogie" or the "Slauson Shuffle," or you can grab some Pioneer Chicken on Alvarado with "Carmelita" and then a coffee at the Hollywood Hawaiian hotel in "Desperados Under the Eaves."

Is it the place that creates the music, or the music that creates the place?

When I was growing up, my physical Los Angeles geography was fairly hemmed in, a Westside grid of Culver City to the south, the beach to the west, Westwood to the north, and West Hollywood to the east, emotionally centered around the facades of the 20th Century

Fox back lot and the water that danced along the Avenue of the Stars of Century City. In my family, East LA was anything east of La Brea. Yet my musical geography was immense. Living inside songs, I was in Inglewood and Watts, Topanga and the San Fernando Valley, Hollywood and the East LA east of the LA River. Through the music of the Minutemen, I spent days and nights in San Pedro long before I ever visited. San Onofre and Compton were part of my urban atlas only because songs had put them there.

Songs can orient us to where we are, ground us in a sense of home, but they can also help us imagine where we want to go and reimagine just what home can mean. They are locators, but they are also bridges, sparks, launch pads. Their disorientations can lead to radical awakenings: We just might not be who we thought we were. It's one of the more common musician origin stories: "I was born *here,* but when I heard that song, I wanted to go *there.*" In the space of a song, we can try on new identities, sing through voices not our own, and come to realize that we are not the center of the world. Songs are handshakes and encounters, dances with strangers, and if we truly get lost in them, they become passports, luggage, and moving trucks.

The critic Sophie Arkette has proposed a useful model for how music can alter our experience of a city. We are given the reductionist city, she says, the one designed for us by city planners, zoning ordinances, development grids, and infrastructural systems, but we live in the phenomenological city, the corporeal, sensual, and psychological one we plan ourselves with the music we listen to and make. Our bodies become the architects of the urban. "Space does not have a priori character," she writes. "It is defined and moulded by the subjectivity and social consciousness of those who experience it and inhabit it."

There is the official space of Koreatown, for example, and then there is the Koreatown as mapped by rapper Dumbfoundead, whose "K-Town Story" starts in a bar on Western and moves through karaoke haunts and cafés in order to put "Koreatown right on the map." Or there is Inglewood, the 9.1-square-mile city—official coordinates 33°55'27" north and 118°20'46" west—that is remapped by Mexican American singer and rapper Becky G in her "Becky from the Block" according to her own personal landmarks: Oak Street Elementary, the Inglewood cemetery, Kelso Ranch market, Randy's Donuts, The Forum, the 405 freeway, and the parking lot of In-N-Out Burger on Century Boulevard. In the song's video, the camera follows her walking through city, her personalized cartography given shape and substance by the music. It's a slightly different Inglewood from the one we meet in Mack 10's "Inglewood Swangin'." He also mentions The Forum, but adds the library and the courthouse, charts Manchester, Century, and

Market Street, and mentions "señoritas and Inglewood familias" because "as far as race goes we probably even these days, about 50 percent black and the rest is eses." To echo George Simmel's 1903 prophecy, there is the metropolis with its ruthless economic bottom lines, and then there are the mental lives of its inhabitants, which need to be protected and nurtured, precisely because they can so creatively revolt against the rules of the grid.

Music has addresses of its own.

Arguably the most famous urban ecological take on Los Angeles as a built environment belongs to Reyner Banham's landmark 1971 *Los Angeles: The Architecture of Four Ecologies*. Those four ecologies, which have become part of local critical parlance, were missing music entirely. Banham drove through the city with his eyes glued to the windshield and the rearview mirror, but he never bothered to turn on the car radio. If he had, he would have quickly found that his ecologies all had their own musical alter egos. Their soundscapes shape and define them as much as any building code, design aesthetic, or parade of regional quirks. So, for the sake of Sonic Los Angeles, here goes a little Reyner remix. The first four are his; the last three are some suggested bonus cuts.

Surfurbia: Perhaps the easiest Banham ecology to imagine musically, a mythic endless summer, sunshine and sand, playlist of The Beach Boys, Jan & Dean, Frankie & Annette, and Dick Dale. Musical surfurbia stretches back at least to early booster tunes like 1896's "California Beside the Sunset Sea" advertising coastal paradise at tourist beach hotels, and up through 1980s hip-hop pioneer Arabian Prince sampling breaking waves and seagulls over electro-beats on "Let's Hit the Beach," declaring "the beach is where you go when you want to be free." But it also includes plenty of the "Pacific Coast Blues" Dinah Washington sang about, plenty of noir mixed in with sandy fantasies. We remember The Beach Boys' "Good Vibrations," not the "poison" and "ecological aftermath" of their "Don't Go Near the Water." We remember Brian Wilson posing in Pendletons with a longboard but forget he was afraid of the ocean and was happier "In My Room." His brother Dennis looked out at the Pacific and saw only "the flagship of death" (slaughtered otters, not carefree surfers). There are the dystopic Venice bohemias of The Doors—"blood stains the roofs and the palm trees of Venice, blood in my love in the terrible summer, bloody red sun of fantastic LA"—and the coastal hallucinations of Jane's Addiction's "Ocean Size." "Wish I was ocean size," Perry Farrell howled over a smoggy scream of guitars, "I want to be as deep as the ocean." The iconic California girls of *Gidget* and *Baywatch* were invented creatures of the musically infused surf, and in 1970 Randy Newman introduced us to one of them, Lucinda, whose summer came to an early end—she gets buried alive in the sand in her graduation gown, steamrolled by "the beach-cleaning man."

....

Foothills: The spread of residential foothill communities Banham surveyed covered an incredible amount of terrain, from Boyle Heights to Los Feliz to Silver Lake to Beverly Hills to Topanga. This "alternative kind of hill country," with its precarious developments, mountain-cropped homes, and mazes of snaky roads, is responsible for a large part of LA geography and not surprisingly responsible for a large part of the city's music as well. "Let's go to my place in the canyon where we can be alone," begins Dory Previn's "Coldwater Canyon," and that promise of a bucolic urban life ("shades of Camelot," Jackie DeShannon sang in "Laurel Canyon") runs through so much of the foothills songbook. Compared to "dark and dirty" New York City, the musical hills of LA—the muse of James Taylor, Carole King, Joni Mitchell, and countless others—are full of quiet mornings and light-soaked afternoons, nature developed into a domestic Eden where, as the Mamas & the Papas put it, they could escape the streets and the cops and "the world on fire" and be "safe in my garden." Yet that safety was always illusive. The hills also burn, the hills also slide, their promised peace always haunted by riots, murder, and death (cue "For What It's Worth" and "Riot on Sunset Strip"). "What is up the canyon," Van Dyke Parks sang, "will eventually come down." It was looking out of his living-room window on "Blue Jay Way" in the hills above Sunset that George Harrison sparked a hazy, psychedelic cloud of organs, violins, and vocal distortion and issued a classic musical statement from the hills: "There's a fog upon LA and my friends have lost their way. We'll be over soon they said, now they've lost themselves instead." The songs of the foothills give us a few of the found, but mostly the lost, the burned out, and the pissed. "I hear that Laurel Canyon is full of famous stars," Neil Young warbled, in character as a Charles Manson–inspired cult leader who turned the foothills into a headquarters of hate and blood, "But I hate them worse than lepers and I'll kill them in their cars."

....

The Plains of Id: The Foothills met the Flatlands in 1965 when Frank Zappa watched the Watts Riots erupt on his TV set in Echo Park, and he reacted with an ecology-crossing blast of protest. "I'm not black," he sang, "but there's a whole lots of times I wish I could say I'm not white." Watts was the center of the expansive spread of flatlands that Banham claimed were "the heartlands of the city's Id," but his gloss on the impulsiveness and "crude urban lusts" of communities from the San Fernando Valley in the north to Torrance in the south missed the cultural, political, and ethnic complexities that the ecology's music makes far more audible. LA's flatlands are also ego terrain—working-class neighborhoods where reality is faced head-on in struggle and survival. It was the flatlands, after all, that gave birth to the music of Black Los Angeles, starring the strip of Central Avenue as the beating heart of angel city blues, jazz, and gospel. Black *music* flourished in South Los Angeles because black *people* flourished in South Los Angeles, the geographic outcome of decades-long restrictive covenants and racially discriminatory zoning laws. There's never been anything flat about the music of the flatlands: Johnny Otis's "Watts Breakaway," Lionel Hampton's "Central Ave. Breakdown," Horace Tapscott's "The Dark Tree," Doris Akers's "Lead Me, Guide Me," N.W.A's "Straight Outta Compton," Kendrick Lamar's "Swimming Pools (Drank)" are just a few of the area's more influential soundmarks. The flatlands, of course, were where LA hip-hop was born, the bass-boomed and rhyme-built terrain of Egyptian Lover dreaming of "Egypt, Egypt," of LAPD battle rams and "6 in the Mornin'" police raids, "Dopeman" economics and "Colors" gang wars, the Compton Swap Meet where Wan Joon Kim sold DJ Quik's first CDs and the Good Life health food store that doubled as an after-hours cipher laboratory. The area's shifting racial demographics—from white to black to immigrant brown—continue to influence the city's current musical atlas. The flatlands—from Compton to Long Beach—are now where Mexican banda and norteño music thrives, the biggest home for the modern corrido on either side of the US–Mexico border. Or as Jenni Rivera, the self-anointed "Mariposa de Barrio" (butterfly of the barrio) liked to put it: "Ayyyy! Y ahí te va Long Beach, playa larga baby!"

Autopia: If I could just get off of this "LA Freeway" so I could just get on the "Ventura Highway," because "only a nobody walks in LA" Missing Persons were wrong, of course; LA is full of walking and bus-riding somebodies (Shorty Rogers's "Westwood Walk" was one early testament), but there's no denying that the city grew up with the automobile and was raised on the freeway, no denying it's a city where cars—and the psychological, economic, and cultural worlds that go along with them—rule. Their dominance has helped shape how music in LA is produced (bass, for example, lots and lots of bass, how else to dominate a street as you roll down it with your windows cracked?) and how music is listened to, in the auditory cocoon of a front seat. We listen in private, in public; we share our sounds only if we want to. We manage temporalities with the flick of a track advance, the forward-moving time of a song helping us forget just how slow time passes sitting in traffic. Entire genres of LA music have been born of car culture (guitar-revved hot-rod instrumentals and the hot-rod scene; R&B oldies and the lowrider scene) and cars have played starring roles in music culture (a '64 Chevy Impala staring down an El Camino kicked off *Boyz n the Hood*). There have been countless make- and model-specific autopia odes—"Ol' '55," "Little Deuce Coupe," and of course "Low Rider"—and on The Duals' hot-rod classic "Stick Shift," we hear a car start up before the music does. If you listen to The Doors' "LA Woman" it's a heavy-handed study in how to read a city as a woman; if you watch the video it's a driver's-seat valentine to the built environment. "Drive through your suburbs and into your blues," Jim Morrison sang, but he ends up parked at the beach at sunset.

Downtown: Save for a couple of Bunker Hill tunes (courtesy of Michael Penn and the Red Hot Chili Peppers), downtown LA has kept a low profile in the city's pop output. But there would be no "LA music" without it. It's a musical ur-ecology of sorts. The history of LA music—the commodity that helped grow the city—starts here. Downtown *was* the city's music industry at the turn of the twentieth century, home to the city's first theaters, concert halls, music stores, hotel ballrooms, and publishing houses. If you wanted to listen to music in public, buy some sheet music, pick up the latest cylinder recording, or finally get a piano for your living room, you came downtown. In 1913, the musical director of The Orpheum, Abraham F. Frankenstein, teamed up with downtown department store owner Francis B. Silverwood to pen "I Love You, California," the state's official song. Downtown also housed an ecology with an ecology: the city's early Mexican music industry, a web of movie theaters and vaudeville houses like Teatro Novel, Teatro Hidalgo, and the Million Dollar, not to mention the Old Mexico Disneyland of Olvera Street, where Spanish-language entertainment shaped on both sides of the border was always available for locals and tourists alike.

Arroyolandia: The history of LA music as representative of a deep regional and often mythic Southern California culture most likely starts here, out in the arroyo at El Alisal. The home of journalist, librarian, publisher, collector, and sound recordist Charles Fletcher Lummis, El Alisal was where Lummis threw his "Noises" parties, entertaining guests like John Muir and Mary Austin with music and stories from what Lummis promoted as "Old California": Native American, Mexican, and Spanish California filtered through the romance of Mission life. He turned El Alisal into the city's first recording studio, preserving over five hundred songs by Native American and Mexican artists on cylinder recordings in the early 1900s. Some of the very first recordings ever made in Los Angeles were, in Lummis's own words, "songs of the soil, and songs of poets and of troubadours in this far, lone, beautiful, happy land; and songs that came over from Mother Spain and up from Stepmother Mexico." Lummis's mini-industry of musical boosterism was part of a larger sonically tinged Mission mania that included the first Fiesta pageant, various iterations of Ramona songs, and a series of Mission pop songs that included "Where the Mission Bells Are

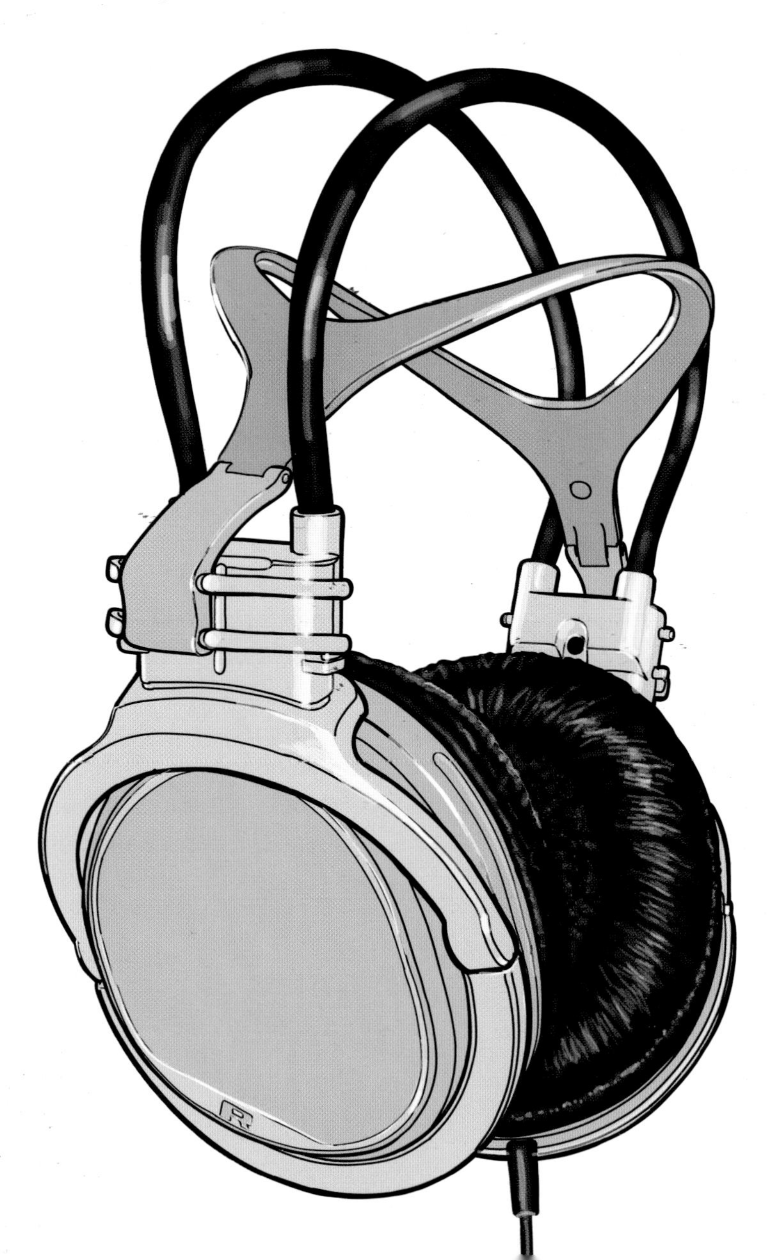

Chiming (Down by the Sea)" and "The Bells of San Gabriel's." Ramona's mother, novelist Helen Hunt Jackson, heard what Lummis heard. The original songs of the city, she wrote in an 1883 essay, are Spanish and Mexican, songs that haunt LA as echoes of a lost world.

Eastside: In February of 1965, the Shrine Auditorium hosted a night of music pinned to a geographically specific musical ecology, the "West Coast East Side Revue." Featuring bands from across East Los Angeles such as The Atlantics, The Sisters, The Premiers, and Cannibal & The Headhunters, the concert celebrated what had quickly become known as "the Eastside sound," a distinctly Mexican American blend of R&B, doo-wop, and rock and roll that was brewed in garages and high-school auditoriums throughout the "Land of 1000 Dances" that lies across the Sixth Street bridge from downtown. The Eastside sound was always linked to pride of barrio place, of being from neighborhoods that were long-standing foundations of Mexican American and Chicano community, identity, and politics. Trojan Records put out thirteen volumes of *East Side Story* albums in 1970, each with a different photograph of Chicano Eastside life on its cover. Thee Midniters' debut album included both their instrumental ode to East LA's main drag "Whittier Boulevard" and a shot of the band posing in front of the street's Golden Gate Theater (a later eighties Eastside tribute chose the nearby Paramount Ballroom). What made it an Eastside tune was less the music itself—it was essentially a reworking of the Rolling Stones song "2120 Michigan Avenue"—more that it was made on the Eastside, played on the Eastside, and named after the Eastside street that spawned it. The music was the place, and the place was the music, just as it is now, but instead of R&B, it's son jarocho up and down Cesar Chavez and punk and banda blasting through backyard party nights.

Of course, musical ecologies only get us so far. They are not soundproof, but sound porous. Their songs bleed across neighborhood (and national) borderlines, travel across bridges, and change hands among friends and band mates. They shift according to population flows, immigration patterns, demographic transitions, and economic booms and busts. They mark temporary territories but never determine influence and exchange.

Take the musical geography of Ritchie Valens's classic LA reimagining of the jarocho traditional from Veracruz, "La Bamba." Often associated with the Eastside sound, "La Bamba" was actually the suburban product of Pacoima in the San Fernando Valley, where Valens's parents moved from Long Beach where they met working at a munitions factory during World War II. The song was then workshopped in a Silver Lake basement and recorded at Gold Star Studios in Hollywood. It's just one example of how music constitutes its own version of what Kazys Varnelis has called LA's "networked ecologies," with each song as a node in larger circuit of influence, economy, and exchange that stretches across the city map.

....

What will the future city sound like? What new musical maps will unfold? What new musical ecologies will change the way we hear?

In 1928, the Los Angeles Department of Playground and Recreation published *Los Angeles is Singing!*, an "official song book" compiled by Glenn M. Tindall, the city's Supervisor of Musical Activities (there was such a thing). Consisting of lyrics to over one hundred songs, the songbook was organized by genres, many of which may not have lasted far beyond 1928. There were "nonsense" songs and "patriotic" songs, "pep" songs and "college" songs, "sea" songs and "smile" songs, a few "California" songs, but only two songs billed as "Los Angeles" songs.

The songbook was to be just the starting point of a new urban culture of song, in which Angelenos would sing together from one end of the city to the other, from playground to playground, swimming pool to swimming pool (a list of exact addresses was included). "Its plans for the future," wrote a Playground and Recreation official, "include the stipulation of music everywhere in the city, the organization of bands, orchestras, ukulele clubs, choruses, and above all informal 'community sings' where neighbors may meet and speak with each other in the universal language of the soul, which is music."

The future LA songbook will need to be a mix of standards and new hits, the playlists we already cherish and the playlists that have yet to be assembled. There will be K-pop sung in Mixtec on Sixth Street, Cambodian punk covers of "Hotel California" in Long Beach, and instrumental Indian chiptunes that sample vintage Rodney Bingenheimer KROQ broadcasts in Fullerton. The new "I Love LA" will be something like Kendrick Lamar's "Sing About Me, I'm Dying of Thirst," which is more of a city prayer than a song: "When the lights shut off and it's my turn to settle down, promise that you will sing about me, promise that you will sing about me."

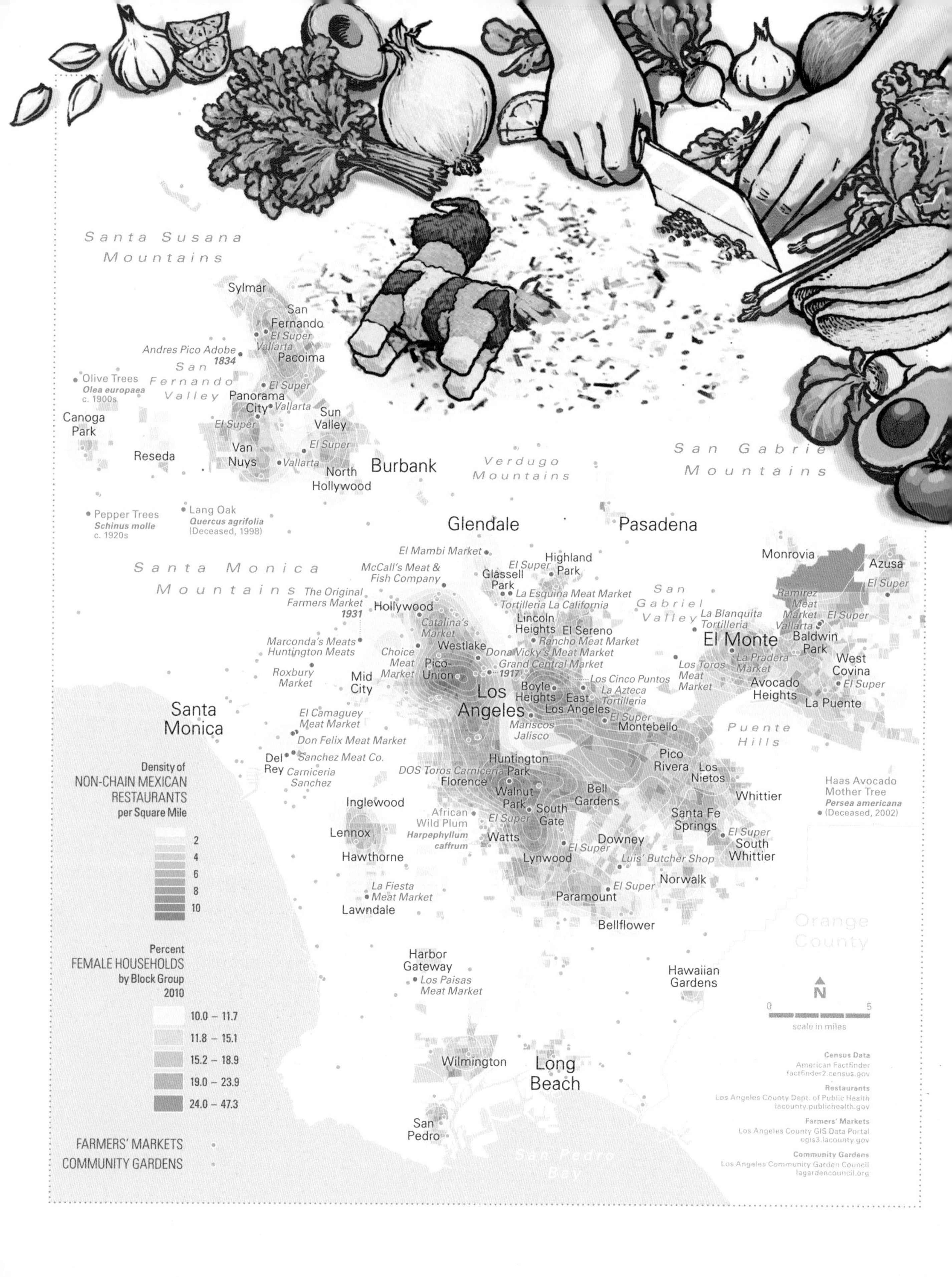

Santa Susana Mountains
Sylmar
San Fernando
El Super Vallarta
Andres Pico Adobe 1834
Pacoima
San Fernando Valley
Olive Trees
Olea europaea
c. 1900s
El Super
Panorama City
Vallarta
Canoga Park
El Super
Sun Valley
El Super
Reseda
Van Nuys
Vallarta
Burbank
North Hollywood
Verdugo Mountains
San Gabriel Mountains
Pepper Trees
Schinus molle
c. 1920s
Lang Oak
Quercus agrifolia
(Deceased, 1998)
Glendale
Pasadena
El Mambi Market
Highland Park
Monrovia
Azusa
Santa Monica Mountains
McCall's Meat & Fish Company
El Super
Glassell Park
La Esquina Meat Market
Tortilleria La California
El Super
The Original Farmers Market 1931
Hollywood
San Gabriel Valley
Ramirez Meat Market
Vallarta
El Super
La Blanquita Tortilleria
Catalina's Market
Lincoln Heights
El Sereno
El Monte
Baldwin Park
Marconda's Meats
Huntington Meats
Westlake
Rancho Meat Market
Dona Vicky's Meat Market
Grand Central Market 1917
Choice Meat Market
Pico-Union
Los Toros Meat Market
La Pradera Market
West Covina
Roxbury Market
Mid City
Los Angeles
Boyle Heights
Los Cinco Puntos
La Azteca Tortilleria
East Los Angeles
Avocado Heights
El Super
La Puente
Santa Monica
El Camaguey Meat Market
Mariscos Jalisco
El Super
Montebello
Don Felix Meat Market
Puente Hills
Del Rey
Sanchez Meat Co.
Carniceria Sanchez
Huntington Park
Pico Rivera
DOS Toros Carniceria
Florence
Los Nietos
Density of
NON-CHAIN MEXICAN RESTAURANTS
per Square Mile
2
4
6
8
10
Walnut Park
Bell Gardens
Whittier
Haas Avocado Mother Tree
Persea americana
(Deceased, 2002)
Inglewood
African Wild Plum
Harpephyllum caffrum
El Super
South Gate
Santa Fe Springs
Lennox
Watts
Downey
El Super
South Whittier
El Super
Hawthorne
Lynwood
Luis' Butcher Shop
Norwalk
La Fiesta Meat Market
El Super
Paramount
Lawndale
Bellflower
Orange County
Percent
FEMALE HOUSEHOLDS
by Block Group
2010
10.0 – 11.7
11.8 – 15.1
15.2 – 18.9
19.0 – 23.9
24.0 – 47.3
Harbor Gateway
Los Paisas Meat Market
Hawaiian Gardens
N
0
5
scale in miles
Census Data
American Factfinder
factfinder2.census.gov
Wilmington
Long Beach
Restaurants
Los Angeles County Dept. of Public Health
lacounty.publichealth.gov
San Pedro
Farmers' Markets
Los Angeles County GIS Data Portal
egis3.lacounty.gov
FARMERS' MARKETS
COMMUNITY GARDENS
Community Gardens
Los Angeles Community Garden Council
lagardencouncil.org
San Pedro Bay

Thousands of small businesses, from donut shops to nail salons, are tucked in mini-malls and private homes throughout LA. Essayist Michael Jaime-Becerra paints a moving portrait of Maria, a widow with a successful taco catering business who is part of two larger trends: the steady rises of taquero enterprises and of women-owned businesses (nationally, one in three of these women-owned businesses are minority-owned). This map suggests a density of women like Maria: Female-headed households significantly overlap with concentrations of non-chain Mexican restaurants. Entrepreneurs like Maria are supported by a vast network of noncorporate food sources in the greater LA area, such as community gardens, farmers' markets, and specialty markets and restaurant suppliers, some of which are mapped here.

Speakeasy Tacos

Michael Jaime-Becerra

Your family makes it all by hand. The meat. Beans and rice, nopales, and potato salad. A large platter of freshly cut fruit. Garnishes of finely minced white onions and cilantro and two kinds of salsa, red and green. One spiced enough to thrill the palate. One for those that prefer to be set aflame, because it is better to make your clients sweat and suffer than to overhear veiled insults about the salsa being tasty, but not hot.

Including your mother, Maria, there are four of you. You may be Miriam, the oldest child, now in your twenties. Your high-school years would have been spent either making tacos or keeping an eye on your brothers, but now you have a chair in an upscale hair salon and you plan on owning your own shop one day. Or you are Samuel, just old enough to buy beer, but already showing the talent and sensibility of a chef on the way to greatness. You were hired at Pollo Loco to wipe down tables and your years of making tacos vaulted you to unofficial Grill Master in a week. Now the goal is to be a nurse. To have solid, stable, official work. Or you are Eli, the youngest. The one who gets to go to college, to study United States history and try out accounting because it seems like it would be interesting and useful.

For three hours of catered taco service at a Saturday party, the preparation begins the Wednesday before. While you're cutting hair or tending to convalescents or studying, your mother is beating other taqueros to the best produce when local markets post their weekly specials. With the meat, she insists that the beef for her carne asada be shredded by the wholesale butchers' knives because it is damaged when they do it with the machine. Purchased in El Monte, it's the best any of you have ever found, the contents of the ten-pound bags tender and raw, blood pooling at the corners. Her pork adobada and her chicken come from a second wholesaler in Azusa. He's from Jalisco as well. Not the same pueblo as your family, but close enough that his seasoning is correct and trustworthy, the chicken tinged the yellow of saffron, the chunks of pork a deep orange that will become the color of charred brick as you tend to it in the pan. When beef tongue is requested, your mother will poach it in a broth of onion and garlic. In the morning, one of you will peel the rough outer layer, then dice the rich inner meat into tiny, succulent cubes to later be simmered in their own fat.

The prep work continues on Friday. In South El Monte, your mother picks lemons from her cousin's tree, and that night, instead of going out, you watch *Qué bonito amor* together, peeling and chopping into the early hours of Saturday. After a few hours' rest, you start again. Your hands become pruned because they're constantly wet—from bloody meat, from rinsing radishes, and dozens of white onions releasing musky milk. You wash and rewash the same knife and cutting board. You work the knife until it seems the top of the blade is slicing your index finger. A quick double-check to make sure you're holding the blade with the sharp side down.

Sweating constantly and eating as you go. No stopping for breakfast or lunch because time is passing and you're expected to serve a hundred hungry people in a few hours. Sampling along the way, carne asada scooped from the pan, salsa spooned out of the blender jar, pineapple plucked from the cutting board. Eat something now, your mother reminds you. There won't be time to eat later.

The stove is on the entire time, the same four gas burners as any household stove, but on this one, only two still work. Three of the four knobs are gone, a remaining white plastic stem melted like a used birthday candle. The large pans atop it are blackened and a little misshapen from countless hours of simmering meat. The pots' plastic handles are cracked or missing.

Stirring, keeping things in motion because whatever isn't moving is absorbing heat immediately and might soon burn. In the minute it takes to transfer rice from the pot to the chafing dish, the chafing dish will get hot enough to scorch your hand, pain then pulsing under cool water.

A rookie mistake. For the next two weeks, your fingerprints will have the smooth, warped texture of Silly Putty.

Maria has made airplane parts in one El Monte factory and has assembled trophies in another. To clean offices in downtown Los Angeles high-rises, she had to learn how to drive, doing so in a car so questionable that the steering wheel popped off during the test drive. Thereafter, she'd stick to the first lane of the 10 freeway until she reached the Alameda exit. Before that, she sold popsicles at the Edward's Drive-In swap meet in Arcadia, her first job in the US, one that made her cry at night from the shame of being recognized by others from home. Remembering her as a proud, willful young woman, they asked, "¿Que haces aquí? ¿Por qué haces esto?"

What are you doing here?

Why are you doing this?

Thirty-some years later and she is still willful, still proud, though these aspects of her personality are now applied to the things that matter most: her three children and her taco business.

The business became "The Business" nearly a decade ago in the emergency room at Queen of the Valley Hospital, on the evening when her husband died. Prior to this, Maria and her husband would sometimes make tacos on the weekends in the backyards of relatives and family friends. It had been extra money, supplementary to his work as a gardener and her time in the factories. Miriam was seventeen then. Samuel was thirteen. Eli, twelve. In the plain white room, where the doctor said he had done everything he could, that the heart attack was just too much, the moment was a whirlwind of shock, grief, and panic about what to do next.

There was also the understanding that God had to take him. Miriam remembers a sense of peace accompanying this thought. Responsibility settling in. Certainty that they would eventually be fine.

Tacos then become the means to survive. How the mortgage gets paid. How the utilities stay on. Literally putting food on their table. Without any licenses, permits, or written contracts. No Yelp reviews and no requests to friend them on Facebook. Just business cards with two phone numbers, one for Spanish-speaking clients and one for those that only know English. Those who have this card have probably been at a party Maria's family catered, because this is the main way they're distributed. But word of mouth is fluid, and with Maria's food, the word is good. Her tacos are the sort that are remembered. *She* is remembered.

When she is not working the business, she is searching out cardboard and scrap metal, and on trash nights, she goes through a regular route of recycling bins. She keeps busy not just for the extra income, but because when she stops moving, her body is wracked with mysterious pain. Her hands now shake so uncontrollably that she has trouble serving tacos. Some regular clients have promised her a cure from Mexico, medicine purportedly blessed by the Pope, and when she falls asleep, her children witness her exhaustion and wonder about Parkinson's. Despite all this, Maria will still say that the taco business is greatest job she's ever had. It allows her to meet people from all walks of life, to be at a different party every week. But the very best part about the business is that has kept her children with her. It has ensured that they remain together.

For one event, it's relentless heat all the way to Lancaster. In their father's truck, named "Guapa" by its original owners, now dented and scratched, flaking blue paint, something always needing to be fixed. Now the temperature gauge is creeping up. The event is at a retirement home, and when they arrive, radiator steam gushes from the hood.

The business grows to the point that they are often booked for two parties on the same day, with half the calls coming from clients in increasingly higher tax brackets. While Guapa isn't out of place on the eastern side of Los Angeles, she might not seem presentable to an NBC producer or a trust-fund kid or a family that spent thirty-thousand dollars to celebrate their daughter turning sixteen.

Miriam stretches her credit to its limit on a new truck, a V-8 engine to haul all the equipment and an extra cab to fit the family. Still at the Toyota dealership, the negotiations over, the loan papers signed in the sales manager's office. Since she's given him some business, why not return the favor? Two weeks later, she's back, the grill set up beside the service bays. Tacos for fifty: car techs, salesmen, the girls who answer the phones.

The business is torn between two different philosophies:

Maria accommodates her clients as fully as possible. If she's told that there are still people coming at the end of her three contracted hours, she'll wait for the latecomers at no extra charge. Fifteen minutes. Thirty minutes. An hour. The extra time doesn't matter because it lets her become part of the party. She'll gather everyone around the cake to sing "Las mañanitas" or "Happy Birthday." If there's dancing to be done, she'll get it started. Pour her a shot of Patrón and she'll cheer loudest during the toast. Her spirit is infectious, and it is genuine, for these are not just clients to her. Maria considers those who book her for recurring annual or semiannual parties as family. These clients often call her "Tía Maria" and their children are encouraged to say hello and hug her as if she were a blood relative. Sometimes these hugs seem awkward, the child's embrace tentative and reluctant. Sometimes the hugs are real because Maria is kindly remembered from the last time as "la señora de los tacos."

Besides the extra time, these are the people who also get a tray of potato salad and an overloaded fruit platter they didn't specify in their order. They might also get an added portion of lengua or fifteen pounds of carne asada instead of ten, the extra meat packed in one of the family's clear Tupperware containers that Samuel and Eli are reminded and reminded and reminded not to forget.

Maria sees these extras both as gifts to her regular clients for their loyalty and as investments in the business's future. She believes a potential new client will recall being poolside or before an inflatable jumper, in their hand an empty Styrofoam plate smeared with the last swirls of orange grease and salsa, their mouth pleasantly smoldering. Their appetite called for more and their body didn't have room for another bite. This person won't know that their satisfaction is the same satisfaction Maria and her children get from having seen their food enjoyed.

Maria's children know that each of those extras cuts into the profit margin. At $4.99 per pound, the two beef tongues for an extra chafing dish of lengua cost nearly fifty dollars, and that's without the additional garlic, onions, and seasonings to prepare them, the cooking time, and the time needed for peeling and cubing them the following morning. It all might be used for something else. Like a new stove or a professional-grade onion cutter. At the end of the night, Maria's boys can wait another ten or twenty minutes if the party hosts were generally respectful

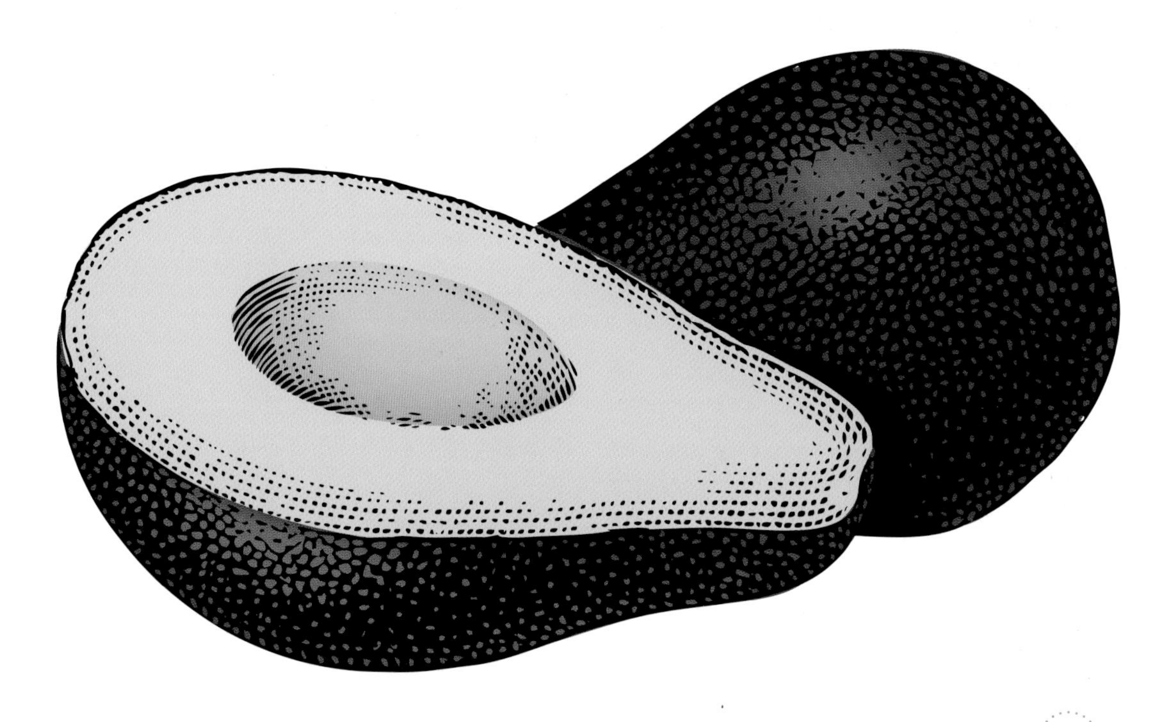

and paid what they owe. But, unlike their mother, Samuel and Eli believe that when the three hours are up, the three hours are up. Part of this is the fact that it is Saturday night. They both have girlfriends waiting for them and their phones buzz with text messages.

But their thinking is also rooted in confidence. Samuel and Eli have been doing this work, weekend after weekend, since they were in junior high. Eli knows that if you're calling him, you've probably had their tacos and you know they are very, very good. If you try to talk down the price he quotes you, he will feel mildly insulted because he knows eight dollars per person is more or less what other people charge. He'll work with you, removing extras until he hits a number you like. But if you live outside a ten-mile radius, he'll also charge you a fifty-dollar transportation fee to cover the cost of extra gas.

You are up in Silver Lake, up a narrow street, both sides lined with cars. Just enough room for the truck to approach the two-story glass-wall experiment attached to the hillside. Up concrete steps, a geometric hike past ripening grapefruit and kumquats, to the patio, the lighter of the two grill pans, a seventy-pound slab of stainless steel, hoisted by your brother. The grill stand is next, a two-person task guided by someone on the other end, you backing up and being careful not to scratch the silver Jaguar parked at the base of the steps, lifting, angling your way. Next is a second, smaller and circular grill for today's requested vegetarian preparation of grilled mushrooms, multicolored bell peppers, and onions. Up with the propane tanks and a cooler the size of a coffin for anything perishable.

Most times the event is a birthday party, and today is no different. Today a father turns eighty, the milestone used to reunite three generations. T-shirts for the occasion sported by family from all over California. Nashville also represented. Munich, too. Talk of how cousins are related. Grandmothers the children never got to meet. The mandatory trip to Disneyland.

A quick connection to the propane tank under the grill stand, followed by three flicks from a long-stemmed lighter, and then the grill begins radiating unceasing heat at four-hundred degrees. There are four different kinds of tacos this afternoon. Rice and beans in the chafing trays beside the grill pan, a separate table with the potato salad, nopales, and fruit. The two kinds of salsa and a tray of freshly roasted jalapeños. The line moves quickly, forty-some curious and hungry people. Orders for one of each taco, absolutely to beans and rice because this is better than anything they've had in Tennessee, because there's absolutely no Mexican food in Germany. The men ask if the jalapeños are hot, then goad one another to try them. You suggest that two be taken in case they're not lucky with the first one.

Your family has worked parties at this home for nearly a decade. These clients, a husband and wife, know your family. They ask how your mother's doing. They knew your father. When they found out that he'd died, they took up a tip collection that amounted to over five hundred dollars. As the years went by, their friends began to hire you. Their friends' friends too. Each of them in parts of LA you'd never been to before. And so this husband and wife have become two of the business's most important clients, meaning that with them you adhere to your mother's philosophy of giving out extras for free. After a full shift at the hair salon the day before, your sister worked until three, peeling, blanching, and chopping the nopales, nopales that go untouched—partly because the tacos rule the evening and partly because this clientele doesn't really have the appetite or appreciation for a salad of minced cactus paddles.

The grill is cleared to make way for a slide show, and you remove the other equipment and supplies with the same sort of hurry you had when carrying them up. There is plenty of remaining food—food for days, as the host notes with resignation. People did come back for seconds, a few for thirds, and still the meat is piled high in the chafing dishes. Emptied, packaged up, and set next to the other side dishes with the inescapable sense that much of it will eventually be in trash. Even as you prepared it, you knew this would happen. When you were younger, the squandered expense, the wasted labor and time bothered you. Maybe it still does. Your mother's way of doing things makes you want to leave the business to focus on your hairdressing clients. Or move out of the house. Or dream of teaching high-school students about the Louisiana Purchase. When there was nothing else, tacos allowed your family to live on. Now they hold you back. Each job comes with the deepening sense that either you or the business must change. And until something gives, you must tell yourself that wasted side dishes don't matter because your tacos were loved by those that ate them. You must tell yourself that's what matters most.

A few words on tortillas: The ones that Maria uses are slightly smaller than a compact disc, ordered by the box from a tortilleria in Baldwin Park and picked up the morning of the event. There are at least three other tortillerias minutes from her home, but they've never been considered because as far as Maria's concerned, the Baldwin Park tortillas are perfect. A supple texture that gives slightly to the touch. That doesn't harden easily when heated. The subtle, sweet taste of the corn coming through each bite.

One Christmas Eve is spent doing the usual prep work, all four of them. Christmas morning in an industrial park. A bakery assembly line. Tacos intended as a thank-you for employees packing trays of fancy Danishes and madeleines. Afterwards, a fifty-dollar tip to be split four ways. That night it's decided they'll no longer work holidays.

Next it's nightfall at a horse property at the easternmost edge of the county. A full banda going. White Stetsons and white ostrich-skin belts and white boots that curl upward at the toe. Synchronized trumpets and trombones. A tuba. Dancing makes dancers hungry, and soon the chafing dishes are empty. The host sends someone out and he returns with another twenty-five pounds of carne asada. The tacos keep coming and the banda keeps playing, horses trained to prance in time with the music. Tamborazo a toda madre. Tipped $150 at the end of the night.

....

After three hours over the grill, your face is always sunburned, no matter if you've been outside or indoors. You've sweated enough to have felt embarrassed as you served food to your clients and to also feel thoroughly wrung out. Dehydrated. Now that the gear has cooled off and has been loaded onto the truck, everything about you also seems coated with the unique oily sheen that comes from adobada and asada smoke.

The ride home is quiet. Relief that cash is in your pocket and that looming bills will be paid, that this job is over. Curving along dark freeway lanes, all roads leading back to El Monte, the occasional rattles of shifting equipment in the truck bed reminding you that there is still more to be done once you get home.

You swing the cooler through the front door and collapse onto the couch. The answering machine blinks, the house quiet because your mother is still out at the other event booked for today. Everything in the back of your truck must be washed and cleaned, but if this evening is the first of a weekend with back-to-back events, the washing and cleaning must happen tonight instead of tomorrow. This maintenance will be the last thing you want to do. If you wait until tomorrow, your mother will be up before you, with degreaser and a pumice stone, scouring blackened oil off the spots where the grill pan gets hottest. You can already hear her complaining that you always use too much oil when you cook.

The chaffing dishes and the utensils are waiting for you too, as are the pans and pots from the morning's prep work. And because they'll be the first things you'll need tomorrow morning, you begin by washing them. You can hear your mother saying, "Cada quien tiene que traer su tortilla a la casa." And you can sense the answering machine's light pulsing behind you. The empty weekend spaces on the calendar will taunt you until you play the message.

It will be a woman looking for tacos. She will be someone you don't already know and she will start in English, her voice unsure of itself because there is purposely no identifying greeting on the answering machine. She will switch to Spanish, and it will be clear from how poorly she speaks it, her pronunciation wooden and stilted, that this was the language of her parents or her grandparents, that it is no longer her own. She will sound out her phone number in the protracted manner of someone recollecting numerals for an exam.

She may be from someplace that you've never heard of before except for traffic updates and weather reports. She will say that she is a friend of Vijay. Or that she knows Adriana. Or that she was at the party for someone named Douglas. She will be expecting fifty people, but from the way she will describe the event, you can tell that it will more likely be twenty. Or a hundred. She will hope that you can work with her budget and you can already sense that she's the kind that probably won't tip.

In a few years, there may not be a business to receive this call. The business depends on your mother's health. And it depends on what you decide to do with your life. These ideas press intense guilt upon you, and yet the business no longer existing may also be its best possible outcome. If that day comes, it will be because you've each achieved something with your individual lives, something greater than what tacos can currently offer it. And you will have used skills passed down from your mother and honed in front of the grill: resourcefulness, tenacity, and the ability to be fearless in front of strangers.

But on this evening you will write down the woman's phone number and her name. You will do this with the same pen that you use to book appointments for your hairdressing clients, or that you used to fill out the paperwork for a position as a certified nursing assistant, or that you have in history class when you're taking notes on the Great Depression.

It will be too late to call the woman back tonight, but tomorrow morning, early, she will definitely hear from you.

Acknowledgments

LAtitudes: An Angeleno's Atlas is the result of an ambitious multiyear collaboration between independent publisher Heyday and some of LA's best writers and thinkers to discover, explore, and chart this ill-understood city, ensnared in its own mythology. We wanted to tease out stories that live in the shadows of the stereotypes, to divulge deep linkages and undercurrents of truth about the city and its vast urban cultures.

Rebecca Solnit's extraordinary atlas of San Francisco, *Infinite City,* planted the seed for this book. We were enamored with the intelligence and intimacy with which she explored San Francisco. She covered underserved and deeply relevant topics with a fresh but learned eye, pairing her (and other contributors') essays with innovative, thought-provoking maps; the overall effect was one of surprising insight into an iconic city. Indeed, it was Rebecca who first suggested that we create a Los Angeles literary atlas, one that was worthy of a city with this breadth of experience. So we convened dozens of writers, journalists, poets, as well as artists, cultural leaders, curators, and educators throughout Los Angeles, sharing many pastrami sandwiches, fish tacos, and donburi with people who not only seemed to know everyone in LA, but could also describe the city's neighborhoods by their smells and sounds. They were crucial in helping us to develop a compelling, LA-appropriate template.

In 2012, we approached local philanthropists at the Durfee Foundation with a proposal to create a book that would allow readers to conceptually experience the city through great writing on a broad, inclusive array of subjects and imaginative cartography. Our goal was lofty: to transform readers' attitudes about LA. To our infinite delight and gratitude, Durfee agreed to support the project.

Rather than select writers with whom we were familiar, Heyday sent out an open call inviting the general public to send proposals for essays to be newly written, confident that a rich variety of writers would produce the most exciting results and that restriction to new content would ensure timeliness and expand conversations rather than regurgitate them. We received nearly 150 proposals from across the country that explored aspects of LA that had been lost, underappreciated, crowded out by stereotypes, or were just softly sung under one's breath. We strove to include as many different kinds of essays as possible—personal, critical, humorous, biographical—and to cover as much geographical ground within Los Angeles County as possible. We chose nineteen writers whose proposed topics had the right balance of curiosity, substance, and surprise. Early in the project, we assembled all of our authors and our cartographer, a team of illustrious advisers, and the Heyday production team to allow everyone to introduce their topics, their visions for the project, and to spend the day in rich conversation.

The range of ideas presented in this collection is awesome. Take a look at the (admittedly reductive) subject list: geography, architecture, infrastructure, history, industry, racial injustice, utopias, iconography, cultural influences, urban nature, transportation, immigration, music, radio, and food. A spirit of investigation underlies each essay and map in this book, triggering alternative examinations of identity, value, and possibility. Some of the authors in this collection, writing out of passion and conviction, make no bones about their position as social critics as they challenge readers to conceive a future for the city by considering its myriad past.

From the beginning, this book has fostered a collegial spirit, and interaction and diversity was an essential factor in shaping it. We thank Rebecca Solnit for encouraging us to build this atlas of Los Angeles. Claire Peeps and Carrie Avery at the Durfee Foundation recognized the need for this book and provided major support. In the very beginning of this project, there was a "gathering of the beards" (each participant wore a clip-on beard in playful solidarity with Heyday's famously bearded publisher, Malcolm Margolin)—friends who brought tremendous enthusiasm and creativity, a specific Los Angeles vocabulary, noteworthy words of caution, and invaluable Rolodexes. These original "beards" were Ken Brecher, president of the Library Foundation of Los Angeles; Louise Steinman, literary curator for the Los Angeles Public Library's ALOUD series; William Deverell, author, history professor at USC, and director of the Huntington-USC Institute on California and the West; and David Kipen, writer and purveyor of Libros Schmibros Lending Library, in addition to Claire Peeps and Malcolm Margolin. Additionally, Lia Tjandra, Karen Mack, Gregory Rodriguez, Mark Allen, David Eng, Wendy Cheng, Juan Devis, Felicia Kelley, Tonya Jones, Jonathan Spaulding, Lewis MacAdams, Jon Christensen, Tisa Bryant, Sesshu Foster, Sojin Kim, Judy Harper, Stephanie Pincetl, Steven Wong, Rick Noguchi, Sharon Sekhon, and Billy Mark played key roles in the earliest phases of the project. D. J. Waldie deserves a special shout-out for helping us evaluate the proposals we received.

The atlas would not have been possible without the patient attention and great knowledge of the librarians and archivists who helm some of Los Angeles's wonderful archives. We are indebted to Marva Felchlin, director of the libraries and archives of the Autry National Center; Liza Posas, head librarian of the Braun Research Library and coordinator for LA as Subject; at UCLA: Susan Anderson, former curator, and Jennifer

Osorio, bibliographer, of Collecting Los Angeles; Tom Hyry, director of special collections, Genie Guerard, manuscripts librarian; Teresa Barnett, director of the Center for Oral History Research; Charlotte Brown, university archivist, Russell Johnson, curator/librarian of History & Special Collections for the Sciences, and Peggy Alexander, curator, Performing Arts at the Charles E. Young Research Library; at the USC Doheny Memorial Library: Dace Taube, head of the Regional History Collection; Michael Holland at the Los Angeles City Archives; Wim de Wit, Christopher James Alexander, and Marlyn Musicant at the Getty Research Institute; Glen Creason, map librarian at the Los Angeles Public Library, along with his excellent reference staff; and Kris Tacsik, librarian at the CSU Northridge Geography Map Library.

I am also grateful to many people who have provided additional advice and help on our journey: Lorraine Rath, Junnaid Javier, Arvishay Artsy, Lila Higgins, Kat Superfisky, Janet Owen Driggs, Katy Lain, Carren Jao, Rachel Brahinsky, Aaron Paley, Naomi Hirahara, Hector Tobar, Beth Pratt, Sunyoung Lee, Isabel Rojas-Williams and the Mural Conservancy of Los Angeles, Abel Salas, Quetzal Flores, J. Michael Walker, Stacy Lieberman, Ben Fitzsimmons and Robyn Hetrick at the Autry National Center, John Bwarie and Los Angeles Heritage Alliance, LA as Subject, James Rojas, The Center for Land Use Interpretation, the Llano del Rio Collective, Dan Koeppel and the Big Parade for inviting *LAtitudes* authors to do mini-lectures on his astonishing walk route through the city for two years in a row, and the California Studies Association, for inviting me not once, but twice over the years, to give lectures on the development of the book. I would also like to thank Stella Theodoulou, Dean of the College of Social & Behavioral Sciences, and Matthew Terhune, Grants and Contracts Officer at CSU Northridge, for their tremendous support.

I am always humbled by the brilliant team at Heyday, including Diane Lee, Ashley Ingram, Lillian Fleer, Christopher Miya, George Young, Marilee Enge, Mariko Conner, Lindsie Bear, David Isaacson, and Anna Pritt. No writer could wish for a more assured or painstaking managing editor than Gayle Wattawa, or a more gentle, visionary publisher than Malcolm Margolin. Netting renowned playwright Luis Alfaro to bless the book and write the perfect foreword for *LAtitudes* was nothing short of a major triumph. David Deis is our official cartographer and created the maps that grace these pages with a team of researchers from CSU Northridge: Ron Davidson, Aleksandra Ilicheva, Madison Most, and Steven Graves. Leighton Kelly's illustrations enliven the pages, bringing a fresh energy to the maps and essays.

—Patricia Wakida, 2015

Contributor Biographies

WRITERS

Cindi Moar Alvitre is a mother and grandmother and has been an educator and artist activist for over three decades. She is a descendant of the original inhabitants of Los Angeles and Orange Counties and served as the first woman chair of the Gabrieleno/Tongva Tribal Council. In 1985, she and Lorene Sisquoc cofounded Mother Earth Clan, a collective of Indian women devoted to creating a model for cultural and environmental education with a particular focus on traditional art. In the late 1980s, she cofounded Ti'at Society, which shared in the renewal of coastal/island Tongva ancient maritime practices. The Society extended into the public realm when it participated in the World Festival of Sacred Music. Alvitre is currently a Ph.D. candidate at UCLA in the department of world arts and culture; her focus is on traditional medicine, cultural identity, revitalization, and cultural trauma. As a cultural curator, her work extends beyond physical museum exhibitions into ceremonial performitivity, which engages participants into native landscapes and dimensionally refocuses cultural lenses.

Jason Brown is an ambient noisemaker, constellation manipulator, and paranoid historiographer. He is consigliere of Machine Project, a Los Angeles–based nonprofit which encourages heroic experiments of the gracefully overambitious. He is director of Superbunker, a framework for conducting and disseminating critical and creative research. He was a founding member of c-level, a collaborative group which focused on media, protest, and play. He is acting janitor of Betalevel, an underground venue beneath Chinatown. He is an instructional technologist at Pomona College.

Lynell George is a native Angeleno who has lived and worked in more than a half dozen far-flung neighborhoods across the basin. She has been here long enough to remember when you could get just about anywhere in greater LA in a half hour by car, windows rolled down, radio turned up full blast. All of those bits and pieces of the city were up for sampling and consequently helped to define who you were. Part of the reason George became a writer was to better fix LA's elusive sense of the place on the page. Her first efforts were short pieces of fiction, but later she was drawn to writing true stories—scene pieces, family histories. She has worked as a feature writer for *LA Weekly,* where she reported on identity politics and social issues and on her watch spun together an hour-to-hour narrative of the early days of the 1992 unrest. Later, as a staff writer for the *Los Angeles Times,* George continued to write about the city through the prism of social justice, while also covering literature, music, and visual art rooted in place. Her essays and reportage about LA have appeared in many collections, news outlets, websites, and her book, *No Crystal Stair: African-Americans in the City of Angels,* a portrait-in-motion of Black LA in the late twentieth century.

Wendy Gilmartin is a fourth-generation Angeleno with a family lineage of building in Southern California. She is an architect, critic, and journalist living and working in Los Angeles. She's helped realize notable public and private design projects in the region including Grand Park in downtown Los Angeles, Elephant Gallery in Glassell Park, and an artists' retirement community at the edge of the Salton Sea. A product of the California public-school system, Gilmartin was born in Arcadia and has lived in Venice, Pasadena, West Hollywood, Hancock Park, Highland Park, Park La Brea, and Century City, as well as Paris, France, and Houston, Texas. In 2011, at the request of her editor at *LA Weekly,* Gilmartin launched a series of articles about LA's ugliest buildings on the publication's website. Her intention with the *Fugly Buildings* blog has been to extract a more meaningful understanding of the city and its physical manifestations, while seeking to draw new audiences into that conversation.

Steven M. Graves was born into a large working-class family in a run-down factory town in Ohio. He moved to Los Angeles in 2003 to teach geography at CSU Northridge and escape the grey skies of his fatherland. His long-running love affair with postwar American landscapes, gas stations, diners, and other elements of car culture led him to study with landscape geographer John Jakle at the University of Illinois. Much of Graves's research has focused on the landscapes of subprime lending, but occasionally he has written about pop music, television, and crime. At home in the vast stretches of 1950s suburbia where he can live largely free from the annoyances of pretension, Graves thinks he'll do as Bing Crosby suggested in 1943, "settle down and never more roam—and make the San Fernando Valley my home."

Anthea M. Hartig is a public historian and the executive director of the California Historical Society. Previously, she worked at the National Trust for Historic Preservation, where she was Western office director, serving the six continental far-western states along with Hawai'i, Alaska, and the Pacific Island territories of Guam and Micronesia. Hartig has taught history and cultural studies at La Sierra University in Riverside and graduate courses in historic preservation at UC Riverside, from where she holds a Ph.D. and master's degree. She was the tenth in her family to earn her bachelor's degree at UCLA. Hartig's interest in the relevance of California's stories and places has come to define her professional and advocational life. She served as a municipal preservation planner for over a decade, and owned a cultural resources consulting firm. She has served on many local, statewide, and national history-related nonprofit foundations' boards of directors, including the California Preservation Foundation, and is currently on the board of the Sam and Alfreda Maloof Foundation for Arts and Culture. Under Governor Gray Davis, she served as chairperson of the State Historical Resources Commission. Anthea writes whenever possible, and has published in both academic and professional journals and books. Anthea lives with her husband, two sons, and their big dog in San Mateo.

Jen Hofer is a Los Angeles–based poet, translator, social justice interpreter, teacher, knitter, bookmaker, public letter writer, urban cyclist, and cofounder of the language justice and literary activism collaborative Antena, antenaantena.org. Her latest books include *Denotative Skies* (DIY/DIT, 2013), *En las maravillas/In Wonder* (Libros Antena/Antena Books, 2012), *Front Page News* (LRL Textile Editions, 2013), *we do not see what we do not see* (DIY/DIT, 2013), and *Ivory Black,* a translation of *Negro marfil* by Myriam Moscona (Les Figues Press, 2011). Her other books are available from numerous small presses, including Action Books, Atelos, Dusie Books, Insert Press, Kenning Editions, Litmus Press, Palm Press, Subpress, and Ugly Duckling Presse. She teaches poetics, translation, and bookmaking at CalArts and Otis College of Art and Design.

Charles Hood grew up in East Los Angeles but now lives on the other side of the mountains, on the edge of the Mojave Desert. He is a research fellow at the Center for Art + Environment and his books include *Río de Dios,* a survey of the Los Angeles River, and *South x South,* a book based on an arts residency in Antarctica. A reformed birder, Hood says, "I stopped listing birds when I got to 5,000 species. Now, though, as I drive around LA, I inventory all the kinds of trees I pass. It's a wonder I don't crash."

Michael Jaime-Becerra is a native of El Monte, California, a working-class suburb of Los Angeles. He is also the author of *Every Night Is Ladies' Night,* a collection of interrelated stories, and *This Time Tomorrow,* a novel. He has written for the *Los Angeles Times, Zócalo Public Square,* and KCRW, and he teaches creative writing at UC Riverside.

Dan Koeppel has lived, worked, and walked in Los Angeles since he arrived here in the early 1990s. Originally from Brooklyn, New York, he's a classic transplant, with more civic pride in his adopted hometown than the one he actually came from. Koeppel is the creator of The Big Parade, an annual two-day walk that covers many of LA's historic landmarks, pathways, and public stairways. His writing has been selected three times for Houghton Mifflin Harcourt's Best American series, including, most recently, his story of Briton Robert Garside's attempt to circumnavigate the globe on foot, which appeared in *The Best American Sportswriting of 2013*. His most recent book, *Banana: The Fate of the Fruit that Changed the World,* will be published in a revised edition in 2015. His website is www.dankoeppel.com and his Twitter username is @soulbarn.

Josh Kun was born and raised in Los Angeles and is now a professor in the Annenberg School for Communication and Journalism at USC. His books include *Audiotopia: Music, Race, and America; Black and Brown Los Angeles: Beyond Conflict and Coalition* (coedited with Laura Pulido); and most recently *Songs in the Key of Los Angeles,* his collaboration with the Los Angeles Public Library and the Library Foundation of Los Angeles. In 2012, he curated the Pacific Standard Time exhibition *Trouble in Paradise: Music and Los Angeles 1945–1975* at the Grammy Museum. He is still looking for the first song ever recorded in Los Angeles.

Nathan Masters is a writer specializing in Los Angeles history. His regular blog posts for Gizmodo, KCET, and *Los Angeles Magazine* tell often-surprising stories about Southern California's past while providing visibility for the archival collections of LA as Subject. He also contributes freelance stories to *Los Angeles Magazine* and other publications. Masters works in USC's historic Doheny Memorial Library, where he serves as manager of academic events and programming for the USC Libraries, the host institution for LA as Subject. In addition to his writing duties, he manages the libraries' social media presence and as part of an amazing communications team helps develop original programming. Born and raised in suburban Orange County, California, Masters now lives in downtown Los Angeles with his cat, Marengo.

Laura Pulido is a professor in the department of American studies and ethnicity at USC where she studies race, political activism, and Los Angeles. Her books include *Black, Brown, Yellow, and Left: Radical Activism in Los Angeles; A People's Guide to Los Angeles* (with Laura Barraclough and Wendy Cheng); and *Black and Brown in Los Angeles: Beyond Conflict and Coalition* (coedited with Josh Kun).

Luis J. Rodriguez was born on the US-Mexico border almost sixty years ago. In Los Angeles since age two, Rodriguez has lived in the gaps, between and outside borders, often at the periphery of culture, especially now when the center is hollow and the real heartbeat is at the margins. He has fifteen books of poetry, fiction, children's literature, and nonfiction, including the oft-banned memoir *Always Running: La Vida Loca: Gang Days in L.A.* He is founder/editor of Tia Chucha Press, a leading cross-cultural small publisher, and cofounder of Tia Chucha's Centro Cultural & Bookstore, both in the San Fernando Valley. Despite forays into Chicago, the Bay Area, and the Inland Empire, Luis has lived in the LA area most of his life. In 2014, he was appointed Los Angeles Poet Laureate by Mayor Eric Garcetti.

Josh Sides is a writer, editor, and history professor living in Los Angeles. He is the author of the books *L.A. City Limits: African American Los Angeles from the Great Depression to the Present* (University of California Press, 2006) and *Erotic City: Sexual Revolutions and the Making of San Francisco* (Oxford University Press, 2009), and numerous articles. Sides is the Whitsett Professor of California History at CSU Northridge, and the editor of *California History.*

Sylvia Sukop writes about art, faith, community, and other good causes. A first-generation American raised in rural Pennsylvania, her second hometowns include Boston, New York, and Los Angeles, along with three tiny villages in Germany, Hungary, and Greece. Photography has been an integral part of her journey as a visual artist and storyteller. Founder of the teen photography project Boulevard Without Borders, documenting the diverse communities along LA's Pico Boulevard, she was awarded PEN Center USA's Emerging Voices Fellowship in 2009 and a Fulbright Fellowship to Germany in 1995–96. A contributing writer to *Flaunt* magazine, the *Huffington Post,* and the Society for Photographic Education's journal *Exposure,* she is currently working on her first book.

David L. Ulin is the author, most recently, of the novella *Labyrinth.* His other books include *The Lost Art of Reading: Why Books Matter in a Distracted Time* and the Library of America's *Writing Los Angeles: A Literary Anthology,* which won a California Book Award. Born and raised in Manhattan, he has lived in Southern California since 1991. He is book critic, and former book editor, of the *Los Angeles Times.*

Teddy Varno teaches history and government at the Oakwood School in North Hollywood, California. He holds a doctorate from UC Berkeley, where he studied the history of evolutionary biology and genetics. A relative newcomer to Los Angeles, Varno lives just south of the Griffith Observatory on land that was once a part of Rancho Los Feliz. He is currently researching the history of chicken breeding.

Andrew O. Wilcox is a Southern California native living within an infrastructure at its efficient limits. He is a landscape architect and an associate professor of landscape architecture at California State Polytechnic University, Pomona, where he has wandered the Los Angeles landscape considering and confronting the nature clichés and feral actualities of the built environment. As a result he values the actual nature of the city more than the idealized. Wilcox understands that LA's fertile future lies in the seemingly unorganized wild. He lives in Northeast LA with his family.

Rosten Woo moved to Los Angeles in 2009. He collaborates with grassroots organizations, nonprofits, researchers, artists, and designers to make work about place and politics. He is particularly interested in the ways that representations of places are used to make and support decisions about them. His work has been exhibited at the Cooper-Hewitt Design Triennial, the Venice Architecture Biennale, Netherlands Architecture Institute, the Storefront for Art and Architecture, and various piers, public housing developments, shopping malls, and parks in New York and Los Angeles. He is cofounder and former executive director of the New York–based nonprofit, the Center for Urban Pedagogy. His recent writing includes the books *Street Value,* about Fulton Mall in Brooklyn, NY, and *Willowbrook is...*about the unincorporated part of LA County between Watts and Compton. His website is wehavenoart.net.

CARTOGRAPHER

David Deis is a cartographer and graphic designer from Los Angeles. He currently serves as the staff cartographer in the Department of Geography at CSU Northridge.

MAP RESEARCHERS

Ron Davidson is an associate professor of geography at CSU Northridge. He received his Ph.D. from UCLA in 2003. His research interests include urban/social geography and public space.

Aleksandra Ilicheva is a geographer and writer from Los Angeles. She holds degrees in environmental studies and geography from UCLA and CSU Northridge. Her interests are urban geography and ecology, animal welfare, conservation, and science studies.

Madison Most is a graduate student at CSU Northridge, currently pursuing a master's degree in geography with an emphasis on geographic information science. She holds a bachelor's degree in environmental studies from UC Santa Cruz. Madison's areas of interest include human-wildlife interactions, biogeography, and conservation issues in developing nations.

ILLUSTRATOR

Leighton Kelly does what he wants while living the dream one day at a time.

FOREWORD

Luis Alfaro is a critically acclaimed writer/performer who has been working in theater, performance, poetry, and journalism since 1982. A Chicano born and raised in the Pico-Union district of downtown Los Angeles, Alfaro is the recipient of a John D. and Catherine T. MacArthur Foundation fellowship and is currently a Mellon Fellow at the Oregon Shakespeare Festival. His plays and performances have been seen throughout the United States, Canada, England, France, and Romania. He teaches at USC.

INTRODUCTION

Glen Creason has been the map librarian for the Los Angeles Public Library for the past twenty-five years and a reference librarian in the history department since 1979. He was a co-curator of the landmark map exhibit *Los Angeles Unfolded* in 2009, and in October of 2010 he published the book *Los Angeles in Maps* for Rizzoli International. Creason has written about local history, maps, and popular culture for publications including the *Los Angeles Downtown News, Mercator's World, The Public Historian, The International Map Collectors' Society Journal,* the *Los Angeles Times,* and *Edible Ojai & Ventura County.* He blogs weekly about maps for *Los Angeles Magazine* and is a contributor on research topics for *The Huffington Post.* For twenty-one years, he has written regularly on entertainment and food for *Los Cerritos Community Newspaper.* Creason is a native Angeleno and UCLA grad, born and raised in South Gate and now living in Glassell Park. Besides maps, he likes native gardening, cats, baseball, and his only daughter, Katya.

EDITOR

Patricia Wakida is a writer, artist, and community historian. She is the coeditor of *Only What We Could Carry: The Japanese American Internment Experience, Highway 99: A Literary Journey through California's Central Valley,* and *Unfinished Message: Selected Works of Toshio Mori.* Most recently, she was the associate curator of history at the Japanese American National Museum in Los Angeles.

Photograph Captions and Credits

Page 13 Aerial photograph of Los Angeles taken from a hot-air balloon at 9,000 feet by Edwin H. Husher, 1887. Courtesy of Los Angeles Public Library.

Page 16 Aerial view of Los Angeles's Harbor Freeway, with pollution and smog visible. © Keith Tarrier, courtesy of Shutterstock.

Page 49 "Not a Cornfield," by Lauren Bon, Los Angeles State Historic Park. © 2009 by Eric Lowenbach.

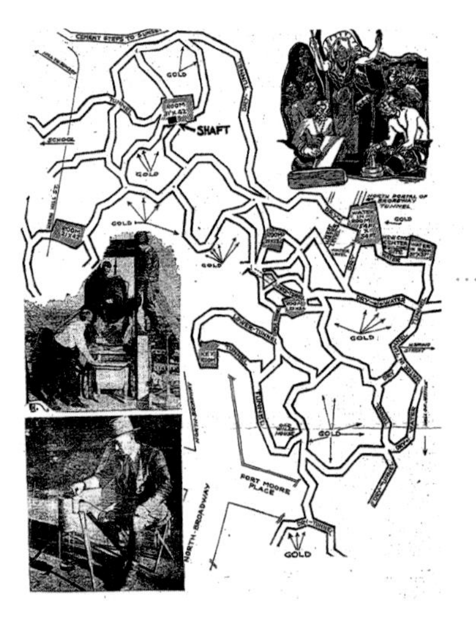

Page 74 George Warren Shufelt's map of underground tunnels below Fort Moore Hill, which he presumed were once inhabited by the ancient "Lizard People." January 29, 1934. Courtesy of the *Los Angeles Times*.

Page 79 Battle of Los Angeles, February 26, 1942. Courtesy of the *Los Angeles Times*.

Page 81 Fort Moore Pioneer Memorial, by Henry Kreis & Albert Stewart, 1957. © 2008 by Michael Locke.

Page 102 Horace Dobbins, creator of the California Cycleway, showing off in 1900 what would be the Cycleway's downfall: an automobile. Courtesy of Pasadena Museum of History.

Page 105 The Great California Cycleway in 1900. Courtesy of Pasadena Museum of History.

Page 126 Bonnie S. Kaplan and Sylvia Sukop celebrate marriage equality in West Hollywood. © 2013 by Kat Salerno.

About Heyday

Heyday is an independent, nonprofit publisher and unique cultural institution. We promote widespread awareness and celebration of California's many cultures, landscapes, and boundary-breaking ideas. Through our well-crafted books, public events, and innovative outreach programs we are building a vibrant community of readers, writers, and thinkers.

Thank You

It takes the collective effort of many to create a thriving literary culture. We are thankful to all the thoughtful people we have the privilege to engage with. Cheers to our writers, artists, editors, storytellers, designers, printers, bookstores, critics, cultural organizations, readers, and book lovers everywhere!

We are especially grateful for the generous funding we've received for our publications and programs during the past year from foundations and hundreds of individual donors. Major supporters include:

Alliance for California Traditional Arts; Anonymous (6); Arkay Foundation; Judith and Phillip Auth; Judy Avery; Carol Baird and Alan Harper; Paul Bancroft III; Bancroft Library; Richard and Rickie Ann Baum; BayTree Fund; S. D. Bechtel, Jr. Foundation; Jean and Fred Berensmeier; Berkeley Civic Arts Program and Civic Arts Commission; Joan Berman; Nancy Bertelsen; Barbara Boucke; Beatrice Bowles, in memory of Susan S. Lake; John Briscoe; David Brower Center; Lewis and Sheana Butler; Helen Cagampang; California Historical Society; California Indian Heritage Center Foundation; California State Parks Foundation; Joanne Campbell; The Campbell Foundation; James and Margaret Chapin; Graham Chisholm; The Christensen Fund; Jon Christensen; Cynthia Clarke; Community Futures Collective; Compton Foundation; Creative Work Fund; Lawrence Crooks; Lauren B. Dachs; Nik Dehejia; Topher Delaney; Chris Desser and Kirk Marckwald; Lokelani Devone; Frances Dinkelspiel and Gary Wayne; Doune Fund; The Durfee Foundation; Megan Fletcher and J.K. Dineen; Michael Eaton and Charity Kenyon; Richard and Gretchen Evans; Flow Fund Circle; Friends of the Roseville Library; Furthur Foundation; The Wallace Alexander Gerbode Foundation;

Patrick Golden; Nicola W. Gordon; Wanda Lee Graves and Stephen Duscha; The Walter and Elise Haas Fund; Coke and James Hallowell; Theresa Harlan and Ken Tiger; Cindy Heitzman; Carla Hills; Sandra and Charles Hobson; Nettie Hoge; Donna Ewald Huggins; JiJi Foundation; Claudia Jurmain; Kalliopeia Foundation; Marty and Pamela Krasney; Robert and Karen Kustel; Guy Lampard and Suzanne Badenhoop; Thomas Lockard and Alix Marduel; Thomas J. Long Foundation; Bryce Lundberg; Sam and Alfreda Maloof Foundation for Arts & Crafts; Michael McCone; Giles W. and Elise G. Mead Foundation; Moore Family Foundation; Michael J. Moratto, in memory of Major J. Moratto; Stewart R. Mott Foundation; The MSB Charitable Fund; Karen and Thomas Mulvaney; Richard Nagler; National Wildlife Federation; Native Arts and Cultures Foundation; Humboldt Area Foundation, Native Cultures Fund; The Nature Conservancy; Nightingale Family Foundation; Steven Nightingale and Lucy Blake; Northern California Water Association; Ohlone-Costanoan Esselen Nation; Panta Rhea Foundation; David Plant; Jean Pokorny; Steven Rasmussen and Felicia Woytak; Restore Hetch Hetchy; Robin Ridder; Spreck and Isabella Rosekrans; Alan Rosenus; The San Francisco Foundation; Santa Barbara Museum of Natural History; Thomas and Sheila Schwartzburg; Sierra College; Stephen M. Silberstein Foundation; Ernest and June Siva, in honor of the Dorothy Ramon Learning Center; William Somerville; Carla Soracco; Martha Stanley; John and Beverly Stauffer Foundation; Radha Stern, in honor of Malcolm Margolin and Diane Lee; Roselyne Chroman Swig; TomKat Charitable Trust; Tides Foundation; Sonia Torres; Michael and Shirley Traynor; The Roger J. and Madeleine Traynor Foundation; Lisa Van Cleef and Mark Gunson; Patricia Wakida; John Wiley & Sons, Inc.; Peter Booth Wiley and Valerie Barth; Bobby Winston; Dean Witter Foundation; Yocha Dehe Wintun Nation; and Yosemite Conservancy.

Board of Directors

Getting Involved